NIGHT WALKS
A Bedside Companion

NIGHT WALKS
A Bedside Companion

compiled by
JOYCE CAROL OATES

The Ontario Review Press
Princeton, New Jersey

Copyright © 1982 by The Ontario Review Press
All rights reserved. Printed in the U.S.A.

Library of Congress Cataloging in Publication Data
Main entry under title:

Nightwalks: a bedside companion.

1. American literature. 2. English literature. 3. Night — Literary collections.
4. Sleep — Literary collections. 5. Insomnia — Literary collections.
I. Oates, Joyce Carol, 1938-
PS509.N54N5   1982   808.8'033   82-12582
ISBN 0-86538-022-8

Book design: Larry Zirlin

Distributed by Persea Books, Inc.
225 Lafayette St.
New York, NY 10012

Elizabeth Bishop: "Insomnia" from *Elizabeth Bishop: The Complete Poems*. Copy-
right © 1951, 1969 by Elizabeth Bishop. Copyright renewed © 1979 by Eliza-
beth Bishop. Reprinted by permission of Farrar, Straus and Giroux, Inc.
Robert Bly: "Six Winter Privacy Poems" (pp. 3-4) from *Sleepers Joining Hands* by
Robert Bly. Copyright © 1970 by Robert Bly. Reprinted by permission of
Harper & Row, Publishers, Inc.
Paul Bowles: "The Eye" from *Midnight Mass* by Paul Bowles. Copyright © 1981 by
Paul Bowles. Reprinted by permission of the author and Black Sparrow Press.
Brock Brower: "Storm Still" by Brock Brower. Copyright © 1967. Reprinted by
permission of Candida Donadio & Associates, Inc.
Hortense Calisher: "The Scream on Fifty-seventh Street" by Hortense Calisher.
Copyright © 1962. Reprinted by permission of Candida Donadio & As-
sociates, Inc.
Lewis Carroll: "Pillow Problems" from *Lewis Carroll's Bedside Book*, edited by
Edgar Cuthwellis. Copyright © 1979 by Vicorama Ltd. Reprinted by permis-
sion of Houghton Mifflin Company.
Emily Dickinson: poems #410 and #419 from *The Complete Poems of Emily Dickinson*,
edited by Thomas H. Johnson. Copyright 1935 by Martha Dickinson Bianchi;
© renewed 1960 by Mary L. Hampson. Reprinted by permission of Little,
Brown and Company. Reprinted by permission of the publishers and the
Trustees of Amherst College from *The Poems of Emily Dickinson*, edited by
Thomas H. Johnson, Cambridge, Mass.; The Belknap Press of Harvard University Press. Copyright 1951, © 1955, 1979 by the President and the Fellows
of Harvard College.

*—for those who love best to read
between Dusk and Dawn—*

Contents

Joyce Carol Oates
Preface

THERE IS A NOCTURNAL PERSONALITY, a nocturnal spirit, distinct from that of daylight and available only in solitude: hence the secret pride of the insomniac who, for all his anguish, for all his very real discomfort, knows himself set apart from others — if only as a consequence of his addiction to sleepless nights. Some of us are naturally — temperamentally and psychologically — inclined to insomnia (my own intermittent bouts began at approximately the age of fourteen); some of us experience random, but no less amazing, insomniac flights. Unable to sleep, one suddenly grasps the profound meaning of *being awake*: a revelation that shades subtly into horror, or into instruction. Sartre imagines Hell as a region in which one's eyelids have vanished — perpetual consciousness. Yet this wakefulness is also a region of profound revelations, of images that seem to pierce the very soul — as the testimonies of the men and women collected in this volume suggest. We experience Night but are also Night.

This collection of fiction, poetry, and essays, originally dreamt into being for the "comfort" of the chronic insomniac, has evolved into a more spacious and generous assemblage. Only the exigencies of space prevented my including any number of other works, including excerpts from novels, for it turns out that there is a remarkably vast literature relevant to this theme. (Then again, what is not relevant? The very phenomenon of literature itself — the intimate sharing of consciousness by way of print — seems to require solitude, a kind of "nocturnal" concentration.) The absence, too, of certain familiar and "obvious" choices (Poe's "The Fall of the House of Usher," Macbeth's elegiac rhapsodizing on sleep) is deliberate.

Though emphasis has been placed upon imaginative literature, *Night Walks* contains a number of pieces that address themselves directly to the phenomena of sleeplessness, the nocturnal "self," and the perennially fascinating experience of dreams. Emerson's little-known essay on "Demonology" ("dreams, omens, coincidences, luck, sortilege, magic, and other experiences which shun rather than court inquiry") is as provocative as anything he ever wrote; Jung's meditative thoughts on dreams are unfailingly perceptive; Robert Burton's melancholic excesses of language and speculation constitute a triumph of the serio-comic style. The volume as a whole has been arranged with an eye, or an ear, for certain subtle modulations of theme, vision, texture, voice: it seemed necessary for me to begin with Dickens and his "night fancies," and to end with those extraordinary late poems of the dying D. H. Lawrence. Though *Night Walks* has been assembled like a loose, lyric prose-poem of a novel, in which divers voices both harmonize and contend, it can, like any anthology, be read at random — for its preoccupations are, as Whitman says, those themes "thou lovest best": Night, Sleep, Death, and the Stars.

I am particularly indebted to Robert Phillips and Raymond J. Smith for their excellent advice regarding the selection of many of these titles.

NIGHT WALKS
A Bedside Companion

Charles Dickens
Night Walks

SOME YEARS AGO, a temporary inability to sleep, referable to a distressing impression, caused me to walk about the streets all night, for a series of several nights. The disorder might have taken a long time to conquer, if it had been faintly experimented on in bed; but, it was soon defeated by the brisk treatment of getting up directly after lying down, and going out, and coming home tired at sunrise.

In the course of those nights, I finished my education in a fair amateur experience of houselessness. My principal object being to get through the night, the pursuit of it brought me into sympathetic relations with people who have no other object every night in the year.

The month was March, and the weather damp, cloudy, and cold. The sun not rising before half-past five, the night perspective looked sufficiently long at half-past twelve: which was about my time for confronting it.

The restlessness of a great city, and the way in which it tumbles and tosses before it can get to sleep, formed one of the first entertainments offered to the contemplation of us houseless people. It lasted about two hours. We lost a great deal of companionship when the late public-houses turned their lamps out, and when the potmen thrust the last brawling drunkards into the street; but stray vehicles and stray people were left us, after that. If we were very lucky, a policeman's rattle sprang and a fray turned up; but, in general, surprisingly little of this diversion was provided. Except in the Haymarket, which is the worst kept part of London, and about Kent-street in the Borough, and along a portion of the line of the Old Kent-road, the peace was seldom violently broken. But, it was always the case that London, as if in imitation of individual citizens belonging to it, had expiring fits and starts of restlessness. After all seemed quiet, if one cab rattled by, half-a-dozen would surely follow; and Houselessness even observed that intoxicated people appeared to be magnetically attracted towards each other; so that we knew when we saw one drunken object staggering against the shutters of a shop, that another drunken object would stagger up before five mintues were out, to fraternise or fight with it. When we made a divergence from the regular species of drunkard, the thin-armed, puff-faced, leaden-lipped gin-drinker, and encountered a rarer specimen of a more decent appearance, fifty to one but that specimen was dressed in soiled mourning. As the street experience in the night, so the street experience in the day; the common folk who come unexpectedly into a little property, come unexpectedly into a deal of liquor.

At length these flickering sparks would die away, worn out — the last veritable sparks of waking life trailed from some late pieman or hot-potato man — and London would sink to rest. And then the yearning of the houseless mind would be for any sign of company, any lighted place, any movement, anything suggestive of any one being up — nay, even so much as awake, for the houseless eye looked out for lights in windows.

Walking the streets under the pattering rain, Houselessness would walk and walk and walk, seeing nothing but the interminable tangle of streets, save at a corner, here and there, two policemen in conversation, or the sergeant or inspector looking after his men. Now and then in the night — but rarely — Houselessness would become aware of a furtive head peering out of a doorway a few yards before him, and, coming up with the head, would find a man standing bolt upright to keep within the doorway's shadow, and evidently intent upon no particular service to society. Under a kind of fascination, and in a ghostly silence suitable to the time, Houselessness and this gentlemen would eye one another from head to foot, and so, without exchange of speech, part, mutually suspicious. Drip, drip, drip, from ledge and coping, splash from pipes and water-spouts, and by-and-by the houseless shadow would fall upon the stones that pave the way to Waterloo-bridge; it being in the house-less mind to have a halfpenny worth of excuse for saying "Good night" to the toll-keeper, and catching a glimpse of his fire. A good fire and a good great-coat and a good woollen neck-shawl, were comfortable things to see in conjunction with the toll-keeper; also his brisk wakefulness was excellent company when he rattled the change of half-pence down upon that metal table of his, like a man who defied the night, with all its sorrowful thoughts, and didn't care for the coming of dawn. There was need of encourage-ment on the threshold of the bridge, for the bridge was dreary. The chopped-up murdered man had not been lowered with a rope over the parapet when those nights were; he was alive, and slept then quietly enough most likely, and undisturbed by any dream of where he was to come. But the river had an awful look, the buildings on the banks were muffled in black shrouds, and the reflected lights seemed to originate deep in the water, as if the spectres of suicides were holding them to show where they went down. The wild moon and clouds were as restless as an evil con-science in a tumbled bed, and the very shadow of the immensity of London seemed to lie oppressively upon the river.

Between the bridge and the two great theatres, there was but the distance of a few hundred paces, so the theatres came next. Grim and black within, at night, those great dry Wells, and lonesome to imagine, with the rows of faces faded out, the lights extinguished, and the seats all empty. One would think that nothing in them knew itself at such a time but Yorick's skull. In one of my night walks, as the church steeples were shaking the March winds and rain with strokes of Four, I passed the outer boundary of one of these great deserts, and entered it. With a dim lantern in my hand, I groped my well-known way to the stage and looked over the orchestra — which was like a great grave dug for a time of pestilence — into the void beyond. A dismal cavern of an immense aspect, with the chandelier gone dead like everything else, and nothing visible through mist and fog and space, but tiers of winding-sheets. The ground at my feet where, when last there, I had seen the peasantry of Naples dancing among the vines, reckless of the burning mountain which threatened to overwhelm them, was now in possession of a strong serpent of engine-hose, watchfully lying in wait for the serpent Fire, and ready to fly at it if it showed its forked tongue. A ghost of a watchman, carrying a faint corpse candle, haunted the distant upper gallery and flitted away. Retiring within the proscenium, and holding my light above my head towards the rolled-up curtain — green no more, but black as ebony — my sight lost itself in a gloomy vault, showing faint indications in it of a shipwreck of canvas and cordage. Methought I felt much as a diver might, at the bottom of the sea.

In those small hours when there was no movement in the streets, it afforded matter for reflection to take Newgate in the way, and, touching its rough stone, to think of the prisoners in their sleep, and then to glance in at the lodge over the spiked wicket, and see the fire and light of the watching turnkeys, on the white wall. Not an inappropriate time either, to linger by that wicked little Debtors' Door — shutting tighter than any other door one ever saw — which has been Death's Door to so many. In the days of the uttering of forged one-pound notes by people tempted up from the country, how many hundreds of wretched creatures of both sexes — many quite innocent — swung out of a pitiless and inconsistent world, with the tower of yonder Christian church of Saint Sepulchre monstrously before their eyes! Is there any haunting of the Bank Parlour, by the remorseful souls of old directors, in the nights of these later days, I wonder, or is it as quiet as this degenerate Aceldama of an Old Bailey?

To walk on to the Bank, lamenting the good old times and bemoaning the present evil period, would be an easy next step, so I would take it, and would make my houseless circuit of the Bank, and give a thought to the treasure within; likewise to the guard of soldiers passing the night there, and nodding over the fire. Next, I went to Billingsgate, in some hope of market-people, but it proving as yet too early, crossed London-bridge and got down by the waterside on the Surrey shore among the buildings of the great brewery. There was plenty going on at the brewery; and the reek, and the smell of grains, and the rattling of the plump dray horses at their mangers, were capital company. Quite refreshed by having mingled with this good society, I made a new start with a new heart, setting the old King's Bench prison before me for my next object, and resolving, when I should come to the wall, to think of poor Horace Kinch, and the Dry Rot in men.

A very curious disease the Dry Rot in men, and difficult to detect the beginning of. It had carried Horace Kinch inside the wall of the old King's Bench prison, and it had carried him out with his feet foremost. He was a likely man to look at, in the prime of life, well to do, as clever as he needed to be, and popular among many friends. He was suitably married, and had healthy and pretty children. But, like some fair-looking houses or fair-looking ships, he took the Dry Rot. The first strong external revelation of the Dry Rot in men, is a tendency to lurk and lounge; to be at street-corners without intelligible reason; to be going anywhere when met; to be about many places rather than at any; to do nothing tangible, but to have an intention of performing a variety of intangible duties tomorrow or the day after. When this manifestation of the disease is observed, the observer will usually connect it with a vague impression once formed or received, that the patient was living a little too hard. He will scarcely have had leisure to turn it over in his mind and form the terrible suspicion "Dry Rot," when he will notice a change for the worse in the patient's appearance: a certain slovenliness and deterioration, which is not poverty, nor dirt, nor intoxication, nor ill-health, but simply Dry Rot. To

this, succeeds a smell as of strong waters, in the morning; to
that, a looseness respecting money; to that, a stronger smell
as of strong waters, at all times; to that, a looseness respecting everything; to that, a trembling of the limbs,
somnolency, misery, and crumbling to pieces. As it is in
wood, so it is in men. Dry Rot advances at a compound
usury quite incalculable. A plank is found infected with it,
and the whole structure is devoted. Thus it had been with
the unhappy Horace Kinch, lately buried by a small subscription. Those who knew him had not nigh done saying,
"So well off, so comfortably established, with such hope
before him — and yet, it is feared, with a slight touch of Dry
Rot!" when lo! the man was all Dry Rot and dust.

From the dead wall associated on those houseless nights
with this too common story, I chose next to wander by
Bethlehem Hospital; partly, because it lay on my road round
to Westminster; partly, because I had a night fancy in my
head which could be best pursued within sight of its walls
and dome. And the fancy was this: Are not the sane and the
insane equal at night as the sane lie a dreaming? Are not all of
us outside this hospital, who dream, more or less in the condition of those inside it, every night of our lives? Are we not
nightly persuaded, as they daily are, that we associate
preposterously with kings and queens, emperors and em-
presses, and notabilities of all sorts? Do we not nightly
jumble events and personages and times and places, as
these do daily? Are we not sometimes troubled by our own
sleeping inconsistencies, and do we not vexedly try to account for them or excuse them, just as these do sometimes in
respect of their waking delusions? Said an afflicted man to
me, when I was last in a hospital like this, "Sir, I can frequently fly." I was half ashamed to reflect that so could
I — by night. Said a woman to me on the same occasion,
"Queen Victoria frequently comes to dine with me, and her
Majesty and I dine off peaches and macaroni in our night-
gowns, and his Royal Highness the Prince Consort does us
the honour to make a third on horseback in a Field-Marshal's
uniform." Could I refrain from reddening with consciousness when I remembered the amazing royal parties I

myself had given (at night), the unaccountable viands I had put on table, and my extraordinary manner of conducting myself on those distinguished occasions? I wonder that the great master who knew everything, when he called Sleep the death of each day's life, did not call Dreams the insanity of each day's sanity.

By this time I had left the Hospital behind me, and was again setting towards the river; and in a short breathing space I was on Westminster-bridge, regaling my houseless eyes with the external walls of the British Parliament — the perfection of a stupendous institution, I know, and the admiration of all surrounding nations and succeeding ages, I do not doubt, but perhaps a little the better now and then for being pricked up to its work. Turning off into Old Palace-yard, the Courts of Law kept me company for a quarter of an hour; hinting in low whispers what numbers of people they were keeping awake, and how intensely wretched and horrible they were rendering the small hours to unfortunate suitors. Westminster Abbey was fine gloomy society for another quarter of an hour; suggesting a wonderful procession of its dead among the dark arches and pillars, each century more amazed by the century following it than by all the centuries going before. And indeed in those houseless night walks — which even included cemeteries where watchmen went round among the graves at stated times, and moved the tell-tale handle of an index which recorded that they had touched it at such an hour — it was a solemn consideration what enormous hosts of dead belong to one old great city, and how, if they were raised while the living slept, there would not be the space of a pin's point in all the streets and ways for the living to come out into. Not only that, but the vast armies of dead would overflow the hills and valleys beyond the city, and would stretch away all round it, God knows how far.

When a church clock strikes, on houseless ears in the dead of night, it may be at first mistaken for company and hailed as such. But, as the spreading circles of vibration, which you may perceive at such a time with great clearness, go opening out, for ever and ever afterwards widening perhaps (as the philosopher has suggested) in eternal space, the mistake is rectified and the sense of loneliness is profounder. Once — it was after leaving the Abbey and turning my face north — I came to the great steps of St. Martin's church as the clock was striking Three. Suddenly, a thing that in a moment more I should have trodden upon without seeing, rose up at my feet with a cry of loneliness and houselessness, struck out of it by the bell, the like of which I never heard. We then stood face to face looking at one another, frightened by one another. The creature was like a beetle-browed hair-lipped youth of twenty, and it had a loose bundle of rags on, which it held together with one of its hands. It shivered from head to foot, and its teeth chattered, and as it stared at me — persecutor, devil, ghost, whatever it thought me — it made with its whining mouth as if it were snapping at me, like a worried dog. Intending to give this ugly object money, I put out my hand to stay it — for it recoiled as it whined and snapped — and laid my hand upon its shoulder. Instantly, it twisted out of its garment, like the young man in the New Testament, and left me standing alone with its rags in my hands.

Covent-garden Market, when it was market morning, was wonderful company. The great waggons of cabbages, with growers' men and boys lying asleep under them, and with sharp dogs from market-garden neighbourhoods looking after the whole, were as good as a party. But one of the worst night sights I know in London, is to be found in the children who prowl about this place; who sleep in the baskets, fight for the offal, dart at any object they think they can lay their thieving hands on, dive under the carts and barrows, dodge the constables, and are perpetually making a blunt pattering on the pavement of the Piazza with the rain of their naked feet. A painful and unnatural result comes of the comparison one is forced to institute between the growth of corruption as displayed in the so much improved and cared for fruits of the earth, and the growth of corruption as displayed in these all uncared for (except inasmuch as ever-hunted) savages.

There was early coffee to be got about Covent-garden

Market, and that was more company — warm company, too, which was better. Toast of a very substantial quality, was likewise procurable; though the towzled-headed man who made it, in an inner chamber within the coffee-room, hadn't got his coat on yet, and was so heavy with sleep that in every interval of toast and coffee he went off anew behind the partition into complicated cross-roads of choke and snore, and lost his way directly. Into one of these establishments (among the earliest) near Bow-street, there came one morning as I sat over my houseless cup, pondering where to go next, a man in a high and long snuff-coloured coat, and shoes, and, to the best of my belief, nothing else but a hat, who took out of his hat a large cold meat pudding; a meat pudding so large that it was a very tight fit, and brought the lining of the hat out with it. This mysterious man was known by his pudding, for on his entering, the man of sleep brought him a pint of hot tea, a small loaf, and a large knife and fork and plate. Left to himself in his box, he stood the pudding on the bare table, and, instead of cutting it, stabbed it, overhand, with the knife, like a mortal enemy; then took the knife out, wiped it on his sleeve, tore the pudding asunder with his fingers, and ate it all up. The remembrance of this man with the pudding remains with me as the remembrance of the most spectral person my houselessness encountered. Twice only was I in that establishment, and twice I saw him stalk in (as I should say, just out of bed, and presently going back to bed), take out his pudding, stab his pudding, wipe the dagger, and eat his pudding all up. He was a man whose figure promised cadaverousness, but who had an excessively red face, though shaped like a horse's. On the second occasion of my seeing him, he said huskily to the man of sleep "Am I red to-night?" "You are," he uncompromisingly answered. "My mother," said the spectre, "was a red-faced woman that liked drink, and I looked at her hard when she laid in her coffin, and I took the complexion." Somehow, the pudding seemed an unwholesome pudding after that, and I put myself in its way no more.

When there was no market, or when I wanted variety, a railway terminus with the morning mails coming in, was remunerative company. But like most of the company to be had in this world, it lasted only a very short time. The station lamps would burst out ablaze, the porters would emerge from places of concealment, the cabs and trucks would rattle to their places (the post-office carts were already in theirs), and, finally, the bell would strike up, and the train would come banging in. But there were few passengers and little luggage, and everything scuttled away with the greatest expedition. The locomotive post-offices, with their great nets — as if they had been dragging the country for bodies — would fly open as to their doors, and would disgorge a smell of lamp, an exhausted clerk, a guard in a red coat, and their bags of letters; the engine would blow and heave and perspire, like an engine wiping its forehead and saying what a run it had had; and within ten minutes the lamps were out, and I was houseless and alone again.

But now, there were driven cattle on the high road near, wanting (as cattle always do) to turn into the midst of stone walls, and squeeze themselves through six inches' width of iron railing, and getting their heads down (also as cattle always do) for tossing-purchase at quite imaginary dogs, and giving themselves and every devoted creature associated with them a most extraordinary amount of unnecessary trouble. Now, too, the conscious gas began to grow pale with the knowledge that daylight was coming, and straggling work-people were already in the streets, and, as waking life had become extinguished with the last pieman's sparks, so it began to be rekindled with the fires of the first street-corner breakfast-sellers. And so by faster and faster degrees, until the last degrees were very fast, the day came, and I was tired and could sleep. And it is not, as I used to think, going home at such times, the least wonderful thing in London, that in the real desert region of the night, the houseless wanderer is alone there. I knew well enough where to find Vice and Misfortune of all kinds, if I had chosen; but they were put out of sight, and my houselessness had many miles upon miles of streets in which it could, and did, have its own solitary way.

W. S. Merwin
At Night

THOSE WHO WORK at night are one body, and sometimes they are aware of their larger self. There are watchmen, helmsmen, surgeons, purveyors, thieves, bakers, mothers, beginners, and all the others. Together they are alive under the presence of the spaces of night, and it seems as though their veins might go on growing out of them into the dark sky, like a tree. They hear a fire differently. There are those who work at night, alone. Only alone. When they work it becomes night, and they become alone, they alone are awake. All places become the same. The worker may be one of the fingers of night, one of the ears of night, one of the veins of night. Even one of the eyes of night, as the eyes are the eyes of day. He or she may be the mind of night, in which all those others are, and their days with them. You forget so much of yourself most of the time, they all say to me so that I can almost hear them. So much of yourself you know nothing about, and never will know anything about, they say. So much of you makes you uncomfortable. Some of yourself you are clearly ashamed of, they say. Well, you know. Anyway, what is wrong with working at night? You have the bell-frogs. You have the owls in the walnut trees. You have the sound of a well. You have the sleepers, with their dreams moving all around you. There are even dreams of you working at night, sometimes. You dream of it yourself. Do you really work in the dreams alone? Do dreams help you to work at night? Do anyone's dreams have any effect? Growing alone into the night all around you.

John R. Reed
City Cemetery

Night steals in. The gates are closed upon
the dead. Along the glaucous aisles white monuments
like blind eyes stare as one lone bird's late warble
wakes a possum playing dead. The wild creatures'
lairs are here from which they range
like vandals through the neighborhoods nearby.

A raccoon wobbles home to ditch his take
beside a grave, his robber's mask highlighting eyes
that blink quick as a Nikon. In their trench's throat
gorged mice tremble as the owl's hushing
wing threatens on the air.
Earthworms in their cells are minting earth.

Flotsam of the evening's theft is strewn
like swindler's grift across the tended sod dappled
by a lean, dalmation shade. Dry leaves
rustle on the gravel walks like the shuffle
of a thief as he hustles
from his nightwork dead-tired to his home.

Reflections on Jack the Ripper

At the age's fag end
foggy London felt terror's tug
in the soft midsection of Whitechapel.
Outside the soiled pubs
screams tore the air
and bellies spilled their fillings
on the quaint and cracking cobblestones.

Who cared for saucy grisettes
who died their unbecoming deaths
perhaps because a maddened peer
had ruined his cock by tapping
too often in their tubs?

The flaneur who lounged through drawing rooms
and moodily peered through the velvet drapes
shot his seed in dingy shacks
then found himself in a pocket of flesh
stitched up with pain overcast by pain.

The body's a waterfall of blood
and salmon leap from marrow to brain:
the first failed spring foretells
a desert's spreading reign.
What must the dandy's terror have been
when his rod of Jesse turned dead sea fruit
and the grapy clusters collapsed into ash
cast in the rotten valleys they spoiled?

A pulsing throat spilled out an atonement.
The white skin draped along the stones.
Bracelets from the fallen arms
rolled off in the stone-deaf night.
And in his carriage, sopping
a chill dew from his face,
some gent in his Edwardian cloak
felt the feast whose burrowing
would work its way along his spine
and slowly turn his brain to paste.

Richard Wilbur
Walking to Sleep

As a queen sits down, knowing that a chair will be
    there,
Or a general raises his hand and is given the field-glasses,
Step off assuredly into the blank of your mind.
Something will come to you. Although at first
You nod through nothing like a fogbound prow,
Gravel will breed in the margins of your gaze,
Perhaps with tussocks or a dusty flower,
And, humped like dolphins playing in the bow-wave,
Hills will suggest themselves. All such suggestions
Are yours to take or leave, but hear this warning:
Let them not be too velvet green, the fields
Which the deft needle of your eye appoints,
Nor the old farm past which you make your way
Too shady-linteled, too instinct with home.
It is precisely from Potemkin barns
With their fresh-painted hex signs on the gables,
Their sparkling gloom within, their stanchion-rattle
And sweet breath of silage, that there comes
The trotting cat whose head is but a skull.
Try to remember this: what you project
Is what you will perceive; what you perceive
With any passion, be it love or terror,

May take on whims and powers of its own.
Therefore a numb and grudging circumspection
Will serve you best, unless you overdo it,
Watching your step too narrowly, refusing
To specify a world, shrinking your purview
To a tight vision of your inching shoes —
Which may, as soon you come to think, be crossing
An unseen gorge upon a rotten trestle.
What you must manage is to bring to mind
A landscape not worth looking at, some bleak
Champaign at dead November's end, its grass
As dry as lichen, and its lichens grey,
Such glumly simple country that a glance
Of flat indifference from time to time
Will stabilize it. Lifeless thus, and leafless,
The view should set at rest all thoughts of ambush.
Nevertheless, permit no roadside thickets
Which, as you pass, might shake with worse than wind;
Revoke all trees and other cover; blast
The upstart boulder which a flicking shape
Has stepped behind; above all, put a stop
To the known stranger up ahead, whose face
Half turns to mark you with a creased expression.
Here let me interject that steady trudging
Can make you drowsy, so that without transition,
As when an old film jumps in the projector,
You will be wading a dun hallway, rounding
A newel post, and starting up the stairs.
Should that occur, adjust to circumstances
And carry on, taking these few precautions:
Detach some portion of your thought to guard
The outside of the building; as you wind
From room to room, leave nothing at your back,
But slough all memories at every threshold;
Nor must you dream of opening any door
Until you have foreseen what lies beyond it.

Regardless of its seeming size, or what
May first impress you as its style or function,
The abrupt structure which involves you now
Will improvise like vapor. Groping down
The gritty cellar steps and past the fuse-box,
Brushing through sheeted lawn-chairs, you emerge
In some cathedral's pillared crypt, and thence,
Your brow alight with carbide, pick your way
To the main shaft through drifts and rubbly tunnels.
Promptly the hoist, ascending toward the pit-head,
Rolls downward past your gaze a dinted rock-face
Peppered with hacks and drill-holes, which acquire
Insensibly the look of hieroglyphics.
Whether to surface now within the vast
Stone tent where Cheops lay secure, or take
The proffered shed of corrugated iron
Which gives at once upon a vacant barracks,
Is up to you. Need I, at this point, tell you
What to avoid? Avoid the pleasant room
Where someone, smiling to herself, has placed
A bowl of yellow freesias. Do not let
The thought of her in yellow, lithe and sleek
As lemonwood, mislead you where the curtains,
Romping like spinnakers which taste the wind,
Bellying out and lifting till the sill
Has shipped a drench of sunlight, then subsiding,
Both warm and cool the love-bed. Your concern
Is not to be detained by dread, or by
Such dear acceptances as would entail it,
But to pursue an ever-dimming course
Of pure transition, treading as in water
Past crumbling tufa, down cloacal halls
Of boarded-up hotels, through attics full
Of glassy taxidermy, moping on
Like a drugged fire-inspector. What you hope for
Is that at some point of the pointless journey,

Indoors or out, and when you least expect it,
Right in the middle of your stride, like that,
So neatly that you never feel a thing,
The kind assassin Sleep will draw a bead
And blow your brains out.
                              What, are you still awake?
Then you must risk another tack and footing.
Forget what I have said. Open your eyes
To the good blackness not of your room alone
But of the sky you trust is over it,
Whose stars, though foundering in the time to come,
Bequeath us constantly a jetsam beauty.
Now with your knuckles rub your eyelids, seeing
The phosphenes caper like St. Elmo's fire,
And let your head heel over on the pillow
Like a flung skiff on wild Gennesaret.
Let all things storm your thought with the moiled flocking
Of startled rookeries, or flak in air,
Or blossom-fall, and out of that come striding
In the strong dream by which you have been chosen.
Are you upon the roads again? If so,
Be led past honeyed meadows which might tempt
A wolf to graze, and groves which are not you
But answer to your suppler self, that nature
Able to bear the thrush's quirky glee
In stands of chuted light, yet praise as well,
All leaves aside, the barren bark of winter.
When, as you may, you find yourself approaching
A crossroads and its laden gallows tree,
Do not with hooded eyes allow the shadow
Of a man moored in air to bruise your forehead,
But lift your gaze and stare your brother down,
Though the swart crows have pecked his sockets hollow.
As for what turn your travels then will take,
I cannot guess. Long errantry perhaps
Will arm you to be gentle, or the claws

Of nightmare flap you pathless God knows where,
As the crow flies, to meet your dearest horror.
Still, if you are in luck, you may be granted,
As, inland, one can sometimes smell the sea,
A moment's perfect carelessness, in which
To stumble a few steps and sink to sleep
In the same clearing where, in the old story,
A holy man discovered Vishnu sleeping,
Wrapped in his maya, dreaming by a pool
On whose calm face all images whatever
Lay clear, unfathomed, taken as they came.

Hortense Calisher
The Scream on Fifty-seventh Street

WHEN THE SCREAM CAME, from downstairs in the street five flights below her bedroom window, Mrs. Hazlitt, who in her month's tenancy of the flat had become the lightest of sleepers, stumbled up, groped her way past the empty second twin bed that stood nearer the window, and looked out. There was nothing to be seen of course — the apartment house she was in, though smartly kept up to the standards of the neighborhood, dated from the era of front fire escapes, and the sound, if it had come at all, had come from directly beneath them. From other half-insomniac nights she knew that the hour must be somewhere between three and four in the morning. The "all-night" doorman who guarded the huge façade of the apartment house opposite had retired, per custom, to some region behind its canopy; the one down the block at the corner of First, who blew his taxi-whistle so incessantly that she had for some nights mistaken it for a traffic policeman's, had been quiet for a long time. Even the white-shaded lamp that burned all day and most of the night on the floor of the little gray townhouse sandwiched between the tall buildings across the way — an invalid's light perhaps — had been quenched. At this hour the wide expanse of the avenue, Fifty-seventh Street at its easternmost end, looked calm, reassuring and amazingly silent for one of the main arteries of the city. The crosstown bus service had long since ceased; the truck traffic over on

First made only an occasional dim rumble. If she went into the next room, where there was a French window opening like a double door, and leaned out, absurd idea, in her nightgown, she would see, far down to the right, the lamps of a portion of the Queensboro bridge, quietly necklaced on the night. In the blur beneath them, out of range but comfortable to imagine, the beautiful cul-de-sac of Sutton Square must be musing, Edwardian in the starlight, its one antique bow-front jutting over the river shimmering below. And in the façades opposite her, lights were still spotted here and there, as was always the case, even in the small hours, in New York. Other consciousnesses were awake, a vigil of anonymous neighbors whom she would never know, that still gave one the hive-sense of never being utterly alone.

All was silent. No, she must have dreamed it, reinterpreted in her doze some routine sound, perhaps the siren of the police car that often keened through this street but never stopped, no doubt on its way to the more tumultuous West Side. Until the death of her husband, companion of twenty years, eight months ago, her ability to sleep had always been healthy and immediate; since then it had gradually, not unnaturally deteriorated, but this was the worst; she had never done this before. For she could still hear very clearly the character of the sound, or rather its lack of one — a long, oddly sustained note, then a shorter one, both perfectly even, not discernible as a man's or a woman's, and without — yes, without the color of any emotion — surely the sound that one heard in dreams. Never a woman of small midnight fears in either city or country, as a girl she had done settlement work on some of this city's blackest streets, as a mining engineer's wife had nestled peacefully within the shrieking velvet of an Andes night. Not to give herself special marks for this, it was still all the more reason why what she had heard, or thought she had heard, must have been hallucinatory. A harsh word, but she must be stern with herself at the very beginnings of any such, of what could presage the sort of disintegrated widowhood, full of the mouse-fears and softening self-indulgences of the manless, that she could not, would not abide. Scarcely a second or two could have elapsed between that long — yes, that was it, soulless — cry, and her arrival at the window. And look, down there on the street and upward, everything remained motionless. Not a soul, in answer, had erupted from a doorway. All the fanlights of the lobbies shone serenely. Up above, no one leaned, not a window had flapped wide. After twenty years of living outside of the city, she could still flatter herself that she knew New York down to the ground — she had been born here, and raised. Secretly mourning it, missing it through all the happiest suburban years, she had kept up with it like a scholar, building a red-book of it for herself even through all its savage, incontinent rebuilding. She still knew all its neighborhoods. She knew. And this was one in which such a sound would be policed at once, such a cry serviced at once, if only by doormen running. No, the fault, the disturbance must be hers.

Reaching into the pretty, built-in wardrobe on her right — the flat, with so many features that made it more like a house, fireplace, high ceilings, had attracted her from the first for this reason — she took out a warm dressing gown and sat down on the bed to put on her slippers. The window was wide open and she meant to leave it that way; country living had made unbearable the steam heat of her youth. There was no point to winter otherwise, and she — she and Sam — had always been ones to enjoy the weather as it came. Perhaps she had been unwise to give up the dog, excuse for walks early and late, outlet for talking aloud — the city was full of them. Unwise too, in the self-denuding impulse of loss, to have made herself that solitary in readiness for a city where she would have to remake friends, and no longer had kin. And charming as this flat was, wooed as she increasingly was by the delicately winning personality of its unknown, absent owner, Mrs. Berry, by her bric-a-brac, her cookbooks, even by her widowhood, almost as recent as Mrs. Hazlitt's own — perhaps it would be best to do something about getting the empty second twin bed removed from this room. No doubt Mrs. Berry, fled to London, possibly even residing in the rooms of yet a third woman in search of recommended change, would understand. Mrs. Hazlitt stretched her arms, able to smile at this imagined procession of women inhabiting each other's rooms, fallen one against the other like a pack of playing cards. How could she have forgotten what anyone who had reached middle age through the normal amount of trouble should know, that the very horizontal position itself of sleep, when one could not, laid one open to every attack from within, on a couch with no psychiatrist to listen but oneself. The best way to meet the horrors was on two feet, vertical. What she meant to do now was to fix herself a sensible hot drink, not coffee, reminiscent of shared midnight snacks, not even tea, but a nursery drink, cocoa. In a lifetime, she thought, there are probably two eras of the sleep that is utterly sound: the nursery sleep (if one had the lucky kind of childhood I did) and the sleep next or near the heart and body of the one permanently loved and loving, if one has been lucky enough for that too. I must learn from within, as well as without, that both are over. She stood up, tying her sash more firmly. And at that moment the scream came again.

She listened, rigid. It came exactly as remembered, one shrilled long note, then the shorter second, like a cut-off Amen to the first and of the same timbre, dreadful in its cool, a madness expended almost with calm, near the edge of joy. No wonder she had thought of the siren; this had the same note of terror controlled. One could not tell whether it sped toward a victim or from one. As before, it seemed to come from directly below.

Shaking, she leaned out, could see nothing because of the high sill, ran into the next room, opened the French window and all but stood on the fire escape. As she did so, the sound, certainly human, had just ceased; at the same moment a cab, going slowly down the middle of the avenue, its toplight up, veered directly toward her, as if the driver too had heard, poised there beneath her with its nose pointed toward the curb, then veered sharply back to the center of the street, gathered speed, and drove on. Immediately behind it another cab, toplight off, slowed up, performed exactly the same orbit, then it too, with a hasty squeal of brakes, made for the center street and sped away. In the confusion of noises she thought she heard the grind of a window-sash coming down, then a slam — perhaps the downstairs door of the adjoining set of flats, or of this one. Dropping to her knees, she leaned both palms on the floor-level lintel of the window and peered down through the iron slats of her fire escape and the successive ones below. Crouched that way, she could see straight back to the building line. To the left, a streetlamp cast a pale, even glow on an empty sidewalk and the free space of curb either side of a hydrant; to the right, the shadows were obscure, but motionless. She saw nothing to conjure into a half-expected human bundle lying still, heard no footfall staggering or slipping away. Not more than a minute or two could have elapsed since she had heard the cry. Tilting her head up at the façade opposite, she saw that their simple pattern of lit windows seemed the same. While she stared, one of the squares blotted out, then another, both on floors not too high to have heard. Would no one, having heard, attend? Would she?

Standing up, her hand on the hasp of the French window, she felt herself still shaking, not with fear, but with the effort to keep herself from in some way heeding that cry. Again she told herself that she had been born here, knew the city's ways, had not the *auslander's* incredulity about some of them. These ways had hardened since her day, people had warned her, to an indifference beyond that of any civilized city; there were no "good" neighborhoods now, none of any kind really, except the half-hostile enclosure that each family must build for itself. She had discounted this, knowing unsentimentally what city life was; even in the tender version of it that was her childhood there had been noises, human ones, that the most responsible people, the kindest, had shrugged away, saying, "Nothing, dear. Something outside." What she had not taken into account was her own twenty years of living elsewhere, where such a cry in the night would be succored at once if only for gossip's sake, if only because one gave up privacy — anonymity — forever, when one went to live in a house on a road. If only, she thought, holding herself rigid to stop her trembling, because it would be the cry of someone one knew. Nevertheless, it took all her strength not to rush downstairs, to hang on to the handle, while in her mind's eye she ran out of her apartment door, remembering to take the key, pressed the elevator button and waited, went down at the car's deliberate pace. After that there would be the inner, buzzer door to open, then at last the door to the outside. No, it would take too long, and it was already too late for the phone; by the time police could come or she could find the number of the superintendent in his back basement — and when either answered — what would she say? She looked at the fire escape. Not counting hers, there must be three others between herself and the street. Whether there was a ladder extending from the lowest one she could not remember; possibly one hung by one's hands and dropped to the ground. Years ago there had been more of them, even the better houses had had them in their rear areaways, but she had never in her life seen one used. And this one fronted direct on the avenue. It was this that brought her to her senses — the vision of herself in her blue robe creeping down the front of a building on Fifty-seventh Street, hanging by her hands until she dropped to the ground. She shut the long window quickly, leaning her weight against it to help the slightly swollen frame into place, and turned the handle counterclockwise, shooting the long vertical bolt. The bolt fell into place with a thump she had never noticed before but already seemed familiar. Probably, she thought, sighing, it was the kind of sound — old hardware on old wood — that more often went with a house.

In the kitchen, over her cocoa, she shook herself with a reminiscent tremble, in the way one did after a narrow escape. It was a gesture made more often to a companion, an auditor. Easy enough to make the larger gestures involved in cutting down one's life to the pattern of the single: the selling of a house, the arranging of income or new occupation. Even the abnegation of sex had a drama that lent one strength, made one hold up one's head as one saw oneself traveling a clear, melancholy line. It was the small gestures for which there was no possible sublimation, the sudden phrase, posture — to no auditor, the constant clueing of identity in another's — its cessation. "Dear me," she would have said — they would have come to town for the winter months as they had often planned, and he would have just returned from an overnight business trip — "what do you supposed I'd have done, Sam, if I'd gone all the way, in my housecoat, really found myself outside? Funny how the distinction between outdoors and in breaks down in the country. I'd forgotten how absolute it is here — with so many barriers between." Of course, she thought, that's the simple reason why here, in the city, the sense of responsibility has to weaken. Who could maintain it, through a door, an elevator, a door and a door, toward everyone, anyone, who screamed? Perhaps that was the real reason she had come here, she thought, washing the cup under the faucet. Where the walls are sound-proofed there are no more "people next door" with their ready "casserole" pity, at worst with the harbored glow of their own family life peering from their averted eyelids like the lamplight from under their eaves. Perhaps she had known all along that the best way to learn how to live alone was to come to the place where people really were.

She set the cup out for the morning and added a plate and a spoon. It was wiser not to let herself deteriorate to the utterly casual; besides, the sight of them always gave her a certain pleasure, like a greeting, if only from herself of the night before. Tomorrow she had a meeting, of one of the two hospital boards on which, luckily for now, she had served for years. There was plenty more of that kind of useful occupation available and no one would care a hoot whether what once she had done for conscience' sake she now did for her own. The meeting was not scheduled until two. Before that she would manage to inquire very discreetly, careful not to appear either eccentric or too friendly, both of which made city people uneasy, as to whether anyone else in the building had heard what she had. This too she would do for discipline's sake. There was no longer any doubt that the sound had been real.

The next morning at eight-thirty, dressed to go out except for her coat, she waited just inside her door for one or the other of the tenants on her floor to emerge. Her heart pounded at the very queerness of what she was doing, but she overruled it; if she did feel somewhat too interested, too much as if she were embarking on a chase, then let her get it out of her system at once, and have done. How to do so was precisely what she had considered while dressing. The problem was not to make too many inquiries, too earnest ones, and not to seem to be making any personal overture, from which people would naturally withdraw. One did not make inconvenient, hothouse friendships in the place one lived in, here. Therefore she had decided to limit her approaches to three — the first to the girl who lived in the adjacent apartment, who could usually be encountered at this hour and was the only tenant she knew for sure lived in the front of the building — back tenants were less likely to have heard. For the rest, she must trust to luck. And whatever the outcome, she would not let herself pursue the matter beyond today.

She opened the door a crack and listened. Still too early. Actually the place, being small — six floors of four or five flats each — had a more intimate feeling than most. According to the super's wife, Mrs. Stump, with whom she had had a chat or two in the hall, many of the tenants, clinging to ceiling rents in what had become a fancier district, had been here for years, a few for the thirty since the place had been built. This would account for so many middle-aged and elderly, seemingly either single or the remnants of families — besides various quiet, well-mannered women who, like herself, did not work, she had noticed at times two men who were obviously father and son, two others who, from their ages and nameplate, noticed at mail-time, might be brothers, and a mother with the only child in the place — a subdued little girl of about eight. As soon as a tenant of long standing vacated or died, Mrs. Stump had added, the larger units were converted to smaller, and this would account for the substratum of slightly showier or younger occupants:

two modish blondes, a couple of homburged "decorator" types — all more in keeping with the newly sub-theatrical, antique-shop character of the neighborhood — as well as for the "career girl" on her floor. Mrs. Berry, who from evidences in the flat should be something past forty like herself, belonged to the first group, having been here, with her husband of course until recently, since just after the war. A pity that she, Mrs. Berry, who from her books, her one charming letter, her own situation, might have been just the person to understand, even share Mrs. Hazlitt's reaction to the event of last night, was not here. But this was nonsense; if she were, then she, Mrs. Hazlitt, would not be. She thought again of the chain of women, sighed, and immediately chid herself for this new habit of sighing, as well as for this alarming mound of gratuitous information she seemed to have acquired, in less than a month, about people with whom she was in no way concerned. At that moment she heard the door next hers creak open. Quickly she put on her coat, opened her door and bent to pick up the morning paper. The girl coming out stepped back, dropping one of a pile of boxes she was carrying. Mrs. Hazlitt returned it to her, pressed the button for the elevator, and when it came, held the door. It was the girl she had seen twice before; for the first time they had a nice exchange of smiles.

"Whoops, I'm late," said the girl, craning to look at her watch.

"Me too," said Mrs. Hazlitt, as the cage slid slowly down. She drew breath. "Overslept, once I did get to sleep. Rather a noisy night outside — did you hear all that fuss, must have been around three or four?" She waited hopefully for the answer: Why yes indeed, what on earth was it, did you?

"Uh-uh," said the girl, shaking her head serenely. " 'Fraid the three of us sleep like a log, that's the trouble. My roommates are still at it, lucky stiffs." She checked her watch again, was first out of the elevator, nodded her thanks when Mrs. Hazlitt hurried to hold the buzzer door for her because of the boxes, managed the outer door herself, and departed.

Mrs. Hazlitt walked briskly around the corner to the bakery, came back with her bag of two brioches, and reentered. Imagine, there are three of them, she thought, and I never knew. Well, I envy them their log. The inner door, usually locked, was propped open. Mrs. Stump was on her knees just behind it, washing the marble floor, as she did every day. It was certainly a tidy house, not luxurious but up to a firmly well-bred standard, just the sort a woman like Mrs. Berry would have, that she herself, when the sublease was over, would like to find. Nodding to Mrs. Stump, she went past her to the row of brass mail slots, pretending to search her own although she knew it was too early, weighing whether she ought to risk wasting one of her three chances on her.

"Mail don't come till ten," said Mrs. Stump from behind her.

"Yes, I know," said Mrs. Hazlitt, recalling suddenly that they had had this exchange before. "But I forgot to check yesterday."

"Yesterday vass holiday."

"Oh, so it was." Guiltily Mrs. Hazlitt entered the elevator and faced the door, relieved when it closed. The truth was that she had known yesterday was a holiday and had checked the mail anyway. The truth was that she often did this even on Sundays here, often even more than once. It made an errand in the long expanse of a day when she either flinched from the daily walk that was too dreary to do alone on Sunday, or had not provided herself with a ticket to something. One had to tidy one's hair, spruce a bit for the possible regard of someone in the hall, and when she did see someone, although of course they never spoke, she always returned feeling refreshed, reaffirmed.

Upstairs again, she felt that way now; her day had begun in the eyes of others, as a day should. She made a few phone calls to laundry and bank, and felt even better. Curious how, when one lived alone, one began to feel that only one's own consciousness held up the world, and at the very same time that only an incursion into the world, or a recognition from it, made one continue to exist at all. There was another phone call she might make, to a friend up in the country, who had broken an ankle, but she would save that for a time when she needed it more. This was yet another discipline — not to become a phone bore. The era when she herself had been a victim of such, had often thought of the phone as a nuisance, now seemed as distant as China. She looked at the clock — time enough to make another pot of coffee. With it she ate a brioche slowly, then with the pleasant sense of hurry she now had so seldom, another.

At ten sharp she went downstairs again, resolving to take her chance with whoever might be there. As she emerged from the elevator she saw that she was in luck; the owner of a big brown poodle — a tall, well set up man of sixty or so — was bent over his mail slot while the dog stood by. It was the simplest of matters to make an overture to the poodle, who was already politely nosing the palm she offered him, to expose her own love of the breed, remarking on this one's exceptional manners, to skip lightly on from the question of barking to noise in general, to a particular noise.

"Ah well, Coco's had stage training," said his owner, in answer to her compliments. She guessed that his owner might have had the same; he had that fine, bravura face which aging actors of another generation often had, a trifle shallow for its years perhaps but very fine, and he inclined toward her with the same majestic politeness as his dog, looking into her face very intently as she spoke, answering her in the slender, semi-British accent she recalled from matinee idols of her youth. She had to repeat her question on the noise. This time she firmly gave the sound its name — a scream, really rather an unusual scream.

"A scream?" The man straightened. She thought that for a moment he looked dismayed. Then he pursed his lips very judiciously, in almost an acting-out of that kind of response. "Come to think of it, ye-es, I may have heard something." He squared his shoulders. "But no doubt I just turned over. And Coco's a city dog, very blasé fellow. Rather imagine he did too." He tipped his excellent homburg. "Good morning," he added, with sudden reserve, and turned away, giving a flick to the dog's leash that started the animal off with his master behind him.

"Good morning," she called after them, "and thanks for the tip on where to get one like Coco." Coco looked back at her, but his master, back turned, disentangling the leash from the doorknob, did not, and went out without answering.

So I've done it after all, she thought. Too friendly. Especially too friendly since I'm a woman. Her face grew hot at this probable estimate of her — gushy woman chattering over-brightly, lingering in the hall. Bore of a woman who heard things at night, no doubt looked under the bed before she got into it. No, she thought, there was something — when I mentioned the scream. At the aural memory of that latter, still clear, she felt her resolve stiffen. Also — what a dunce she was being — there were the taxis. Taxis, one of them occupied, did not veer, one after the other, on an empty street, without reason. Emboldened, she bent to look at the man's mailbox. The name, Reginald Warwick, certainly fitted her imaginary dossier, but that was not what gave her pause. Apartment 3A. Hers was 5A. He lived in the front, two floors beneath her, where he must have heard.

As she inserted the key in her apartment door, she heard the telephone ringing, fumbled the key and dropped it, then had to open the double lock above. All part of the city picture, she thought resentfully, remembering their four doors, never locked, in the country — utterly foolhardy, never to be dreamed of here. Even if she had, there were Mrs. Berry's possessions to be considered, nothing extraordinary, but rather like the modest crotchety bits of treasure she had inherited or acquired herself — in the matter of bric-a-brac alone there was really quite a kinship between them. The phone was still ringing as she entered. She raced toward it eagerly. It was the secretary of the hospital board, telling her that this afternoon's meeting was put off.

"Oh...oh dear," said Mrs. Hazlitt. "I mean — I'm so sorry to hear about Mrs. Levin. Hope it's nothing serious."

"I really couldn't say," said the secretary. "But we've enough for a quorum the week after." She rang off.

Mrs. Hazlitt put down the phone, alarmed at the sudden sinking of her heart over such a minor reversal. She had looked forward to seeing people of course, but particularly to spending an afternoon in the brightly capable impersonality of the boardroom, among men and women who brought with them a sense of indefinable swathes of well-being extending behind them, of such a superfluity of it, from lives as full as their checkbooks, that they were met in that efficient room to dispense what overflowed. The meeting would have been an antidote to that dark, anarchic version of the city which had been obsessing her; it would have been a reminder that everywhere, on flight after flight of the city's high, brilliant floors, similar groups of the responsible were convening, could always be applied to, were in command. The phone gave a reminiscent tinkle as she pushed it aside, and she waited, but there was no further ring. She looked at her calendar, scribbled with domestic markings — the hairdresser on Tuesday, a fitting for her spring suit, the date when she must appear at the lawyer's for the closing on the sale of the house. Beyond that she had a dinner party with old acquaintances on the following Thursday, tickets with a woman friend for the Philharmonic on Saturday week. Certainly she was not destitute of either company or activity. But the facts were that within the next two weeks, she could look forward to only two occasions when she would be communicating on any terms of intimacy with people who, within limits, knew "who" she was. A default on either would be felt keenly — much more than the collapse of this afternoon's little — prop. Absently she twiddled the dial back and forth. Proportion was what went first "in solitary"; circling one's own small platform in space, the need for speech mute in one's own throat, one developed an abnormal concern over the night cries of others. No, she thought, remembering the board meeting, those high convocations of the responsible, I've promised — Lord knows who, myself, somebody. She stood up and gave herself a smart slap on the buttock. "Come on, Millie," she said, using the nickname her husband always had. "Get on with it." She started to leave the room, then remained in its center, hand at mouth, wondering. Talking aloud to oneself was more common than admitted; almost everyone did. It was merely that she could not decide whether or not she had.

Around eleven o'clock, making up a bundle of lingerie, she went down to the basement where there was a community washing machine, set the machine's cycle, and went back upstairs. Forty minutes later she went through the same routine, shifting the wet clothes to the dryer. At one o'clock she returned for the finished clothes and carried them up. This made six trips in all, but at no time had she met anyone en route; it was Saturday afternoon, perhaps a bad time. At two she went out to do her weekend shopping. The streets were buzzing, the women in the supermarket evidently laying in enough stores for a visitation of giants. Outside the market, a few kids from Third Avenue always waited in hope of tips for carrying, and on impulse, although her load was small, she engaged a boy of about ten. On the way home, promising him extra for waiting, she stopped at the patisserie where she always lingered for the sheer gilt-and-chocolate gaiety of the place, bought her brioches for the morning, and, again on impulse, an éclair for the boy. Going up in the elevator they encountered the mother and small girl, but she had never found any pretext for addressing that glum pair, the mother engaged as usual in a low, toneless tongue-lashing of the child. Divorcée, Mrs. Hazlitt fancied, and no man in the offing, an inconvenient child. In the kitchen, she tipped the boy and offered him the pastry. After an astonished glance, he wolfed it with a practical air, peering at her furtively between bites, and darted off at once, looking askance over his shoulder at her. "See you next Saturday, maybe." Obviously he had been brought up to believe that only witches dispensed free gingerbread. In front of the bathroom mirror, Mrs. Hazlitt, tidying up before her walk, almost ritual now, to Sutton Square, regarded her image, not yet a witch's but certainly a fool's, a country-cookie-jar fool's. "Oh, well, you're company," she said, quite consciously aloud this time, and for some reason this cheered her. Before leaving, she went over face and costume with the laborious attention she always gave them nowadays before going anywhere outside.

Again, when she rode down, she met no one, but she walked with bracing step, making herself take a circuitous route for health's sake, all the way to Bloomingdale's, then on to Park and around again, along the Fifty-eighth Street bridge pass, the dejectedly frivolous shops that lurked near it, before she let herself approach the house with the niche with the little statue of Dante in it, then the Square. Sitting in the Square, the air rapidly blueing now, lapping her like reverie, she wondered whether any of the residents of the windows surrounding her had noticed her almost daily presence, half hoped they had. Before it became too much of a habit, of course, she would stop coming. Meanwhile, if she took off her distance glasses, the scene before her, seen through the tender, Whistlerian blur of myopia — misted gray bridge, blue and green lights of a barge going at its tranced pace downriver — was the very likeness of a corner of the Chelsea embankment, glimpsed throughout a winter of happy teatime windows seven years ago, from a certain angle below Battersea Bridge. Surely it was blameless to remember past happiness if one did so without self-pity, better still, of course, to be able to speak of it to someone in an even, healing voice. Idly she wondered where Mrs. Berry was living in London. The flat in Cheyne Walk would just have suited her. "Just the thing for you," she would have said to her had she known her. "The Sebrings still let it every season. We always meant to go back." Her watch said five and the air was chilling. She walked rapidly home through the evening scurry, the hour of appointments, catching its excitement as she too hurried, half-persuaded of her own appointment, mythical but still possible, with someone as yet unknown. Outside her own building she paused. All day long she had been entering it from the westerly side. Now, approaching from the east, she saw that the fire escape on this side did end in a ladder, about four feet above her. Anyone moderately tall, like herself, would have had an easy drop of it, as she would have done last night. Shaking her head at that crazy image, she looked up at the brilliant hives all around her. Lights were cramming in, crowding on, but she knew too much now about their nighttime progression, their gradual decline to a single indifferent string on that rising, insomniac silence in which she might lie until morning, dreading to hear again what no one else would appear to have heard. Scaring myself to death, she thought (or muttered?), and in the same instant resolved to drop all limits, go down to the basement and interrogate the Stumps, sit on the bench in the lobby and accost anyone who came in, ring doorbells if necessary, until she had confirmation — and not go upstairs until she had. "Excuse me," said someone. She turned. A small, frail, elderly woman, smiling timidly, waited to get past her through the outer door.

"Oh — sorry," said Mrs. Hazlitt. "Why — good evening!" she added with a rush, an enormous rush of relief. "Here — let me," she said more quietly, opening the door with a numb sense of gratitude for having been tugged back from the brink of what she saw now, at the touch of a voice, had been panic. For here was a tenant, unaccountably forgotten, with whom she was almost on speaking terms, a gentle old sort, badly crippled with arthritis, for whom Mrs. Hazlitt had once or twice unlocked the inner door. She did so now.

"Thank you, my dear — my hands are that knobbly." There was the trace of brogue that Mrs. Hazlitt had noticed before. The old woman, her gray hair sparse from the disease but freshly done in the artfully messy arrangements used to conceal the skulls of old ladies, her broadtail coat not new but excellently maintained, gave off the comfortable essence, pleasing as rosewater, of one who had been serenely protected all her life. Unmarried, for she had that strangely deducible aura about her even before one noted the lack of ring, she had also a certain simpleness, now almost bygone, of those household women who had never gone to business — Mrs. Hazlitt had put her down as perhaps the relict sister of a contractor, or of a school superintendent of the days when the system had been Irish from top to bottom, at the top, of Irish of just this class. The old lady fumbled now with the minute key to her mailbox.

"May I?"

"Ah, if you would now. Couldn't manage it when I came down. The fingers don't seem to warm up until evening. It's 2B."

Mrs. Hazlitt, inserting the key, barely noticed the name — Finan. 2B would be a front apartment also, in the line adjacent to the A's.

"And you would be the lady in Mrs. Berry's. Such a nicely spoken woman, she was."

"Oh yes, isn't she," said Mrs. Hazlitt. "I mean... I just came through the agent. But when you live in a person's house — do you know her?"

"Just to speak. Half as long as me, they'd lived here. Fifteen years." The old lady took the one letter Mrs. Hazlitt passed her, the yellow-fronted rent bill whose duplicate she herself had received this morning. "Ah well, we're always sure of this one, aren't we?" Nodding her thanks, she shuffled toward the elevator on built-up shoes shaped like hods. "Still, it's a nice, quiet building, and lucky we are to be in it these days."

There was such a rickety bravery about her, of neat habits long overborne by the imprecisions of age, of dowager hat set slightly askew by fingers unable to deal with a key yet living alone, that Mrs. Hazlit, reluctant to shake the poor, tottery dear further, had to remind herself of the moment before their encounter.

"Last night?" The old blue eyes looked blank, then brightened. "Ah no, I must have taken one of my Seconals. Otherwise I'd have heard it surely. 'Auntie,' my niece always says — 'what if there should be a fire, and you there sleeping away?' Do what she says, I do sometimes, only to hear every pin drop till morning." She shook her head, entering the elevator. "Going up?"

"N-no," said Mrs. Hazlitt. "I — have to wait here for a minute." She sat down on the bench, the token bench that she had never seen anybody sitting on, and watched the car door close on the little figure still shaking its head, borne upward like a fairy godmother, willing but unable to oblige. The car's hum stopped, then its light glowed on again.

Someone else was coming down. No, this is the nadir, Mrs. Hazlitt thought. Whether I heard it or not, I'm obviously no longer myself. Sleeping pills for me too, though I've never — and no more nonsense. And no more questioning, no matter who.

The car door opened. "Wssht!" said Miss Finan, scuttling out again. "I've just remembered. Not last night, but two weeks ago. And once before that. A scream, you said?"

Mrs. Hazlitt stood up. Almost unable to speak, for the tears that suddenly wrenched her throat, she described it.

"That's it, just what I told my niece on the phone next morning. Like nothing human, and yet it was. I'd taken my Seconal too early, so there I was wide awake again, lying there just thinking, when it came. 'Auntie,' she tried to tell me, 'it was just one of the sirens. Or hoodlums maybe.' " Miss Finan reached up very slowly and settled her hat. "The city's gone down, you know. Not what it was," she said in a reduced voice, casting a glance over her shoulder, as if whatever the city now was loomed behind her. "But I've laid awake on this street too many years, I said, not to know what I hear." She leaned forward. "But — she...they think I'm getting old, you know," she said, in the whisper used to confide the unimaginable. "So...well...when I heard it again I just didn't tell her."

Mrs. Hazlitt grubbed for her handkerchief, found it and blew her nose. Breaking down, she thought — I never knew what a literal phrase it is. For she felt as if all the muscles that usually held her up, knee to ankle, had slipped their knots and were melting her, unless she could stop them, to the floor. "I'm not normally such a nervous woman," she managed to say. "But it was just that no one else seemed to — why, there were people with lights on, but they just seemed to ignore."

The old lady nodded absently. "Well, thank God my hearing's as good as ever. Hmm. Wait till I tell Jennie that!" She began making her painful way back to the car.

Mrs. Hazlitt put out a hand to delay her. "In case it — I mean, in case somebody ought to be notified — do you have any idea what it was?"

"Oh, I don't know. And what could we — ?" Miss Finan shrugged, eager to get along. Still, gossip was tempting. "I did think — " She paused, lowering her voice uneasily. "Like somebody in a fit, it was. We'd a sexton at church taken that way with epilepsy once. And it stopped short like that, just as if somebody'd clapped a hand over its mouth, poor devil. Then the next time I thought — no, more like a signal, like somebody calling. You know the things you'll think at night." She turned, clearly eager to get away.

"But, oughtn't we to inquire?" Mrs. Hazlitt thought of the taxis. "In case it came from this building?"

"This build — " For a moment Miss Finan looked scared, her chin trembling, eyes rounded in the misty, affronted stare that the old gave, not to physical danger, but to a new idea swum too late into their ken. Then she drew herself up, all five feet of her bowed backbone. "Not from here it wouldn't. Across from that big place, maybe. Lots of riffraff there, not used to their money. Or from Third Avenue, maybe. There's always been tenements there." She looked at Mrs. Hazlitt with an obtuse patronage that reminded her of an old nurse who had first instructed her on the social order, blandly mixing up all first causes — disease, money, poverty, snobbery — with a firm illogic that had still seemed somehow in possession — far more firmly so than her own good-hearted parents — of the crude facts. "New to the city, are you," she said, more kindly. "It takes a while."

This time they rode up together. "Now you remember," Miss Finan said, on leaving. "You've two locks on your door, one downstairs. Get a telephone put in by your bed. Snug as a bug in a rug you are then. Nothing to get at you but what's there already. That's what I always tell myself when I'm wakeful. Nothing to get at you then but the Old Nick."

The door closed on her. Watching her go, Mrs. Hazlitt envied her the simplicity, even the spinsterhood that had barred her from imagination as it had from experience. Even the narrowing-in of age would have its compensations, tenderly constricting the horizon as it cramped the fingers, adding the best of locks to Miss Finan's snugness, on her way by now to the triumphant phone call to Jennie.

But that was sinful, to wish for that too soon, what's more it was sentimental, in just the way she had vowed to avoid. Mrs. Hazlitt pushed the button for Down. Emerging from the building, she looked back at it from the corner, back at her day of contrived exits and entrances, abortive conversations. People were hurrying in and out now at a great rate. An invisible glass separated her from them; she was no longer in the fold.

Later that night, Mrs. Hazlitt, once more preparing for bed, peered down at the streets through the slats of the Venetian blind. Catching herself in the attitude of peering made her uneasy. Darkening the room behind her, she raised the blind. After dinner in one of the good French restaurants on Third Avenue and a Tati movie afterwards — the French were such competent dispensers of gaiety — she could review her day more as a convalescent does his delirium — "Did I really say — do — that?" And even here she was addressing a vis-a-vis, so deeply was the habit ingrained. But she could see her self-imposed project now for what it was — only a hysterical seeking after conversation, the final breaking point, like the old-fashioned "crisis" in pneumonia, of the long, low fever of loneliness unexpressed. Even the city, gazed at squarely, was really no anarchy, only a huge diffuseness that returned to the eye of the beholder, to the walker in its streets, even to the closed dream of its sleeper, his own mood, dark or light. Dozens of the solitary must be looking down at it with her, most of them with some *modus vivendi*, many of them booking themselves into life with the same painful intentness, the way the middle-aged sometimes set themselves to learning the tango. And a queer booking you gave yourself today, she told herself, the words lilting with Miss Finan's Irish, this being the last exchange of speech she had had. Testing the words aloud, she found her way with accents, always such a delight to Sam, as good as ever. Well, she had heard a scream, had discovered someone else who had heard it. And now to forget it as promised; the day was done. Prowling the room a bit, she took up her robe, draped it over her shoulders, still more providently put it on. "Oh Millie," she said, tossing the dark mirror a look of scorn as she passed it, "you're such a *sensible* woman."

Wear out Mrs. Berry's carpet you will, Millie, she thought, twenty minutes later by the bedroom clock, but the accent, adulterated now by Sam's, had escaped her. Had the scream had an accent? The trouble was that the mind had its own discipline; one could remember, even with a smile, the story of the man promised all the gold in the world if he could but go for two minutes thinking of the word "hippopotamus." She stopped in front of the mirror, seeking her smile, but it too had escaped. "Hippopotamus," she said, to her dark image. The knuckles of one hand rose, somnambulist, as she watched, and pressed against her teeth. She forced the hand, hers, down again. I will say it again, aloud, she thought, and while I am saying it I will be sure to say to myself that I am saying it aloud. She did so. "Hippopotamus." For a long moment she remained there, staring into the mirror. Then she turned and snapped on every light in the room.

Across from her, in another mirror, the full-length one, herself regarded her. She went forward to it, to that image so irritatingly familiar, so constant as life changed it, so necessarily dear. Fair hair, if maintained too late in life, too brightly, always made the most sensible of women look foolish. There was hers, allowed to gray gently, disordered no more than was natural in the boudoir, framing a face still rational, if strained. "Dear me," she said to it. "All you need is somebody to talk to, get it out of your system. Somebody like yourself." As if prodded, she turned and surveyed the room.

Even in the glare of the lights, the naked black projected from the window, the room sent out to her, in half a dozen pleasant little touches, the same sense of its compatible owner that she had had from the beginning. There, flung down, was Mrs. Berry's copy of *The Eustace Diamonds*, a book that she had always meant to read and had been delighted to find here, along with many others of its ilk and still others she herself owned. How many people knew good bisque and how cheaply it might still be collected, or could

let it hobnob so amiably with grandmotherly bits of Tiffany-
ware, even with the chipped Quimper ashtrays that Mrs.
Berry, like Mrs. Hazlitt at the time of her own marriage, must
once have thought the cutest in the world. There were the
white walls, with the silly, strawberry-mouthed Marie
Laurencin just above the Beerbohm, the presence of good
faded colors, the absence of the new or fauve. On the night
table were the scissors, placed, like everything in the house,
where Mrs. Hazlitt would have had them, near them a relic
that winked of her own childhood — and kept on, she would
wager, for the same reason — a magnifying glass exactly like
her father's. Above them, the only floor lamp in the house,
least offensive of its kind, towered above all the table ones,
sign of a struggle between practicality and grace that she
knew well, whose end she could applaud. Everywhere indeed there were the same signs of the struggles toward taste,
the decline of taste into the prejudices of comfort, that went
with a whole milieu and a generation — both hers. And over
there was, even more personally, the second bed.

Mrs. Hazlitt sat down on it. If it were moved, into the
study say, a few things out of storage with it, how sym-
pathetically this flat might be shared. Nonsense, sheer
fantasy to go on like this, to fancy herself embarking on the
pitiable twin-life of leftover women, much less with a
stranger. But was a woman a stranger if you happened to
know that on her twelfth birthday she had received a copy of
Dr. Dolittle, inscribed to Helena Nelson from her loving
father, if you knew the secret, packrat place in the linen
closet where she stuffed the neglected mending, of another,
in a kitchen drawer, full of broken Mexican terrines and
clipped recipes as shamefully grimy as your own cherished
ones, if you knew that on 2/11/58 and on 7/25/57 a Dr. Burke
had prescribed what looked to be sulfa pills, never used, that
must have cured her at the point of purchase, as had embar-
rassingly happened time and again to yourself? If, in short,
you knew almost every endearing thing about her, except
her face?

Mrs. Hazlitt, blinking in the excessive light, looked
sideways. She knew where there was a photograph album,

tumbled once by accident from its shunted place in the bookshelf, and at once honorably replaced. She had seen enough to know that the snapshots, not pasted in separately, would have to be exhumed, one by one, from their packets. No, she told herself, she already knew more than enough of Mrs. Berry from all that had been so trustfully exposed here — enough to know that this was the sort of prying to which Mrs. Berry, like herself, would never stoop. Somehow this clinched it — their understanding. She could see them exchanging notes at some future meeting, Mrs. Berry saying, "Why, do you know — one night, when I was in London — " — herself, the vis-à-vis, nodding, their perfect rapprochement. Then what would be wrong in using, when so handily provided, so graciously awaiting her, such a comforting vis-à-vis, now?

Mrs. Hazlitt found herself standing, the room's glare pressing on her as if she were arraigned in a police line-up, as if, she reminded herself irritably, it were not self-imposed. She forced herself to make a circuit of the room, turning out each lamp with the crisp, no-nonsense flick of the wrist that nurses employed. At the one lamp still burning she hesitated, reluctant to cross over that last shadow-line. Then, with a shrug, she turned it out and sat down in the darkness, in one of the two opposing boudoir chairs. For long minutes she sat there. Once or twice she trembled on the verge of speech, covered it with a swallow. The conventions that guarded the mind in its strict relationship with the tongue were the hardest to flaunt. But this was the century of talk, of the long talk, in which all were healthily urged to confide. Even the children were encouraged toward, praised for, the imaginary companion. Why should the grown person, who for circumstance beyond his control had no other, be denied? As she watched the window, the light in the small gray house was extinguished. Some minutes later the doorman across the way disappeared. Without looking at the luminous dial of the clock, she could feel the silence aging, ripening. At last she bent forward to the opposite chair.

"Helena?" she said.

Her voice, clear-cut, surprised her. There was nothing so strange about it. The walls remained walls. No one could hear her, or cared to, and now, tucking her feet up, she could remember how cozy this could be, with someone opposite. "Helena," she said. "Wait till I tell you what happened while you were away."

She told her everything. At first she stumbled, went back, as if she were rehearsing in front of a mirror. Several times she froze, unsure whether a sentence had been spoken aloud entirely, or had begun, or terminated, unspoken, in the mind. But as she went on, this wavering borderline seemed only to resemble the clued conversation, meshed with silences, between two people who knew each other well. By the time she had finished her account she was almost at ease, settling back into the comfortably shared midnight post-mortem that always restored balance to the world — so nearly could she imagine the face, not unlike her own, in the chair opposite, smiling ruefully at her over the boy and his gingerbread fears, wondering mischievously with her as to in which of the shapes of temptation the Old Nick visited Miss Finan.

"That girl and her *log*!" said Mrs. Hazlitt. "You know how, when they're that young, you want to smash in the smugness. And yet, when you think of all they've got to go through, you feel so maternal. Even if — " Even if, came the nod, imperceptibly — you've never had children, like us.

For a while they were silent. "Warwick!" said Mrs. Hazlitt then. "Years ago there was an actor — Robert Warwick. I was in love with him — at about the age of eight." Then she smiled, bridling slightly, at the dark chair opposite, whose occupant would know her age. "Oh, all right then — twelve. But what is it, do you suppose, always makes old actors look seedy, even when they're not? Daylight maybe. Or all the pretenses." She ruminated. "Why...do you know," she said slowly, "I think I've got it. The way he looked in my face when I was speaking, and the way the dog turned back and he didn't. He was lip-reading. Why, the poor old boy is deaf!" She settled back, dropping her slippers one by one to the floor. "Of course, that's it. And he wouldn't want to admit that he couldn't have heard it. Probably doesn't dare wear an aid. Poor old boy, pretty dreary for him if he is an actor, and I'll bet he is." She sighed, a luxury permitted now.

"Ah, well. Frail reed — Miss Finan. Lucky for me, though, that I stumbled on her." And on you.

A police siren sounded, muffled less and less by distance, approaching. She was at the window in time to see the car's red dome light streak by as it always did, its alarum dying behind it. Nothing else was on the road. "And there were the taxis," she said, looking down. "I don't know why I keep forgetting them. Veering to the side like that, one right after the other, and one had his light out, so it wasn't for a fare. Nothing on the curb either. Then they both shot away, almost as if they'd caught sight of something up here. And wanted no part of it — the way people do in this town. Wish you could've seen them — it was eerie." There was no response from behind her.

She sat down again. Yes, there was a response, for the first time faintly contrary.

"No," she said. "It certainly was *not* the siren. I was up in a flash. I'd have seen it." She found herself clenching the arms of the chair. "Besides," she said, in a quieter voice, "don't you remember? I heard it twice."

There was no answer. Glancing sideways, she saw the string of lights opposite, not quite of last night's pattern. But the silence was the same, opened to its perfect hour like a century plant, multiple-rooted, that came of age very night. The silence was in full bloom, and it had its own sound. Hark hark, no dogs do bark. And there is nobody in the chair.

Never was, never had been. It was sad to be up at this hour and sane. For now is the hour, now is the hour when all good men are asleep. Her hand smoothed the rim of the waste-basket, about the height from the floor of a dog's collar. Get one tomorrow. But how to manage until then, with all this silence speaking?

She made herself stretch out on the bed, close her eyes. "Sam," she said at last, as she had sworn never to do in thought or word, "I'm lonely." Listening vainly, she thought how wise her resolve had been. Too late, now she had tested his loss to the full, knew him for the void he was — far more of a one than Mrs. Berry, who, though unknown, was still somewhere. By using the name of love, when she had been ready to settle for anybody, she had sent him into the void forever. Opening her eyes, adjusted now to the sourceless city light that never ceased trickling on ceiling, lancing from mirrors, she turned her head right to left, left to right on the pillow, in a gesture to the one auditor who remained.

"No," she said, in the dry voice of correction. "I'm not lonely. I'm alone."

Almost at once she raised herself on her elbow, her head cocked. No, she had heard nothing from outside. But in her mind's ear she could hear the sound of the word she had just spoken, its final syllable twanging like a tuning fork, infinitely receding to octaves above itself, infinitely returning. In what seemed scarcely a stride, she was in the next room, at the French window, brought there by that thin, directional vibration which not necessarily even the blind would hear. For she had recognized it. She had identified the accent of the scream.

The long window frame, its swollen wood shoved tight by her the night before, at first would not budge; then, as she put both hands on the hasp and braced her knees, it gave slowly, grinding inward, the heavy man-high bolt thumping down. Both sounds, too, fell into their proper places. That's what I heard before, she thought, the noise of a window opening or closing, exactly like mine. Two lines of them, down the six floors of the building, made twelve possibles. But that was of no importance now. Stepping up on the lintel, she spread the casements wide.

Yes, there was the bridge, one small arc of it, sheering off into the mist, beautiful against the night, as all bridges were. Now that she was outside, past all barriers, she could hear, with her ordinary ear, faint nickings that marred the silence, but these were only the surface scratches on a record that still revolved one low, continuous tone. No dogs do bark. That was the key to it, that her own hand, smoothing a remembered dog-collar, had been trying to give her. There were certain dog whistles, to be bought anywhere — one had hung, with the unused leash, on a hook near a door in the country — which blew a summons so high above the human range that only a dog could hear it. What had summoned her last night would have been that much higher, audible only to those tuned in by necessity — the thin, soaring decibel of those who were no longer in the fold. Alone-oh. Alone-oh. That would have been the shape of it, of silence expelled from the mouth in one long relieving note, cool, irrepressible, the second one clapped short by the hand. No dog would have heard it. No animal but one was ever that alone.

She stepped out onto the fire escape. There must be legions of them, of us, she thought, in the dim alleyways, the high, flashing terraces — each one of them come to the end of his bookings, circling his small platform in space. And who would hear such a person? Not the log-girls, not for years and years. None of any age who, body to body, bed to bed, either in love or in the mutual pluck-pluck of hate — like the little girl and her mother — were still nested down. Reginald Warwick, stoppered in his special quiet, might hear it, turn to his Coco for confirmation which did not come, and persuade himself once again that it was only his affliction. Others lying awake snug as a bug, listening for that Old Nick, death, would hear the thin, sororal signal and not know what they had heard. But an endless assemblage of others all over the city would be waiting for it — all those sitting in the dark void of the one lamp quenched, the one syllable spoken — who would start up, some from sleep, to their windows...or were already there.

A car passed below. Instinctively, she flattened against the casement, but the car traveled on. Last night someone, man or woman, would have been standing in one of the line of niches above and beneath hers — perhaps even a woman in a blue robe like her own. But literal distance or person would not matter; in that audience all would be the same. Looking up, she could see the tired, heated lavender of the midtown sky, behind which lay that real imperial into which some men were already hurling their exquisitely signaling spheres. But this sound would come from breast to breast, at an altitude higher than any of those. She brought her fist to her mouth, in savage pride at having heard it, at belonging to a race some of whom could never adapt to any range less than that. *Some of us,* she thought, *are still responsible.*

Stepping forward, she leaned on the iron railing. At that moment, another car, traveling slowly by, hesitated opposite, its red dome light blinking. Mrs. Hazlitt stood very still. She watched until the police car went on again, inching ahead slowly, as if somebody inside were looking back. The two men inside there would never understand what she was waiting for. Hand clapped to her mouth, she herself had just understood. She was waiting for it — for its company. She was waiting for a second chance — to answer it. She was waiting for the scream to come again.

Robert Penn Warren
Better Than Counting Sheep

For a night when sleep eludes you, I have,
At last, found the formula. Try to summon

All those ever known who are dead now, and soon
It will seem they are there in your room, not chairs enough

For the party, or standing space even, the hall
Chock-full, and faces thrust to the pane to peer.

Then somehow the house, in a wink, isn't there,
But a field full of folk, and some,

Those near, touch your sleeve, so sadly and slow, and all
Want something of you, too timid to ask — and you don't

Know what. Yes, even in distance and dimness, hands
Are out — stretched to glow faintly

Like fox-fire in marshland where deadfall
Rots, though a few trunks unsteadily stand.

Meanwhile, in the grieving susurrus, all wordless,
You sense, at last, what they want. Each,

Male or female, young or age-gnawed, beloved or not —
Each wants to know if you remember a name.

But now you can't answer, not even your mother's name,
    and your heart
Howls with the loneliness of a wolf in

The depth of a snow-throttled forest when the moon, full,
Spills the spruce-shadows African black. Then you are,
    sudddenly,

Alone. And your own name gone, as you plunge in
    ink-shadow or snowdrift.
The shadows are dreams — but of what? And the
    snowdrift, sleep.

Robert Burton
From The Anatomy of Melancholy

Of the Force of Imagination

Wᴴᴀᴛ ɪᴍᴀɢɪɴᴀᴛɪᴏɴ ɪꜱ I have sufficiently declared in my digression of the anatomy of the soul. I will only now point at the wonderful effects and power of it; which, as it is eminent in all, so most especially it rageth in melancholy persons, in keeping the species of objects so long, mistaking, amplifying them by continual and strong meditation, until at length it produceth in some parties real effects, causeth this and many other maladies. And although this phantasy of ours be a subordinate faculty to reason, and should be ruled by it, yet in many men, through inward or outward distemperature, defect of organs, which are unapt, or hindered, or otherwise contaminated, it is likewise unapt, hindered, and hurt. This we see verified in sleepers, which by reason of humours and concourse of vapours troubling the phantasy, imagine many times absurd and prodigious things, and in such as are troubled with *incubus*, or witch-ridden (as we call it); if they lie on their backs, they suppose an old woman rides and sits so hard upon them that they are almost stifled for want of breath; when there is nothing offends but a concourse of bad humours, which trouble the phantasy. This is likewise evident in such as walk in the night in their sleep, and do strange feats: these vapours move the phantasy, the phantasy the appetite, which moving the animal spirits causeth the body to walk up and down as if they were awake. Fracastorius refers all ecstasies to this force of imagination, such as lie whole days together in a trance: as that priest whom Celsus speaks of, that could separate himself from his senses when he list, and lie like a dead man, void of life and sense. Cardan brags of himself that he could do as much, and that when he list. Many times such men, when they come to themselves, tell strange things of heaven and hell, what visions they have seen; as that St. Owen, in Matthew Paris, that went into St. Patrick's Purgatory, and the monk of Evesham in the same author. Those common apparitions in Bede and Gregory, St. Bridget's revelations, Cæsar Vanninus in his Dialogues, etc., reduceth (as I have formerly said), with all these tales of witches' progresses, dancing, riding, transformations, operations, etc., to the force of imagination and the devil's illusions. The like effects almost are to be seen in such as are awake: how many chimeras, antics, golden mountains, and castles in the air do they build unto themselves! I appeal to painters, mechanicians, mathematicians. Some ascribe all vices to a false and corrupt imagination, anger, revenge, lust, ambition, covetousness, which prefers falsehood before that which is right and good, deluding the soul with false shows and suppositions. Bernardus Penottus will have heresy and superstition to proceed from this fountain; as he falsely imagineth, so he believeth; and as he conceiveth of it, so it must be, and it shall be, *contra gentes* [against the world], he will have it so. But most especially in passions and affections it shows strange and evident effects: what will not a fearful man conceive in the dark? what strange forms of bugbears, devils, witches, goblins? Lavater imputes the greatest cause of spectrums, and the like apparitions, to fear, which above all other passions begets the strongest imagination (saith Wierus), and so likewise love, sorrow, joy, etc. Some die suddenly, as she that saw her son come from the battle at Cannæ, etc. Jacob the patriarch, by force of imagination, made speckled lambs, laying speckled rods before his sheep. Persina, that Ethiopian queen in Heliodorus, by seeing the picture of Perseus and Andromeda, instead of a blackamoor, was brought to bed of a fair white child. In imitation of whom, belike, an hard-favoured fellow in Greece, because he and his wife were both deformed, to get a good brood of children, *elegantissimas imagines in thalamo collocavit*, etc., hung the fairest pictures he could buy for money in his chamber, "that his wife, by frequent sight of them, might conceive and bear such children." And if we may believe Bale, one of Pope Nicholas the Third's concubines, by seeing of a bear, was brought to bed of a monster. "If a woman" (saith Lemnius), "at the time of her conception think of another man present or absent, the child will be like him." Great-bellied women, when they long, yield prodigious examples in this kind, as moles, warts, scars, harelips, monsters, especially caused in their children by force of a depraved phantasy in them. *Ipsam speciem quam animo effigiat, fœtui inducit:* she imprints that stamp upon her child which she conceives unto herself. And therefore, Lodovicus Vives gives a special caution to great-bellied women, "that they do not admit such absurd conceits and cogitations, but by all means avoid those horrible objects, heard or seen, or filthy spectacles." Some will laugh, weep, sigh, groan, blush, tremble, sweat, at such things as are suggested unto them by their imagination. Avicenna speaks of one that could cast himself into a palsy when he list; and some can imitate the tunes of birds and beasts, that they can hardly be discerned. Dagobertus' and St. Francis' scars and wounds, like those of Christ's (if at the least any such were), Agrippa supposeth to have happened by force of imagination: that some are turned to wolves, from men to women, and women again to men (which is constantly believed) to the same imagination; or from men to asses, dogs, or any other shapes. Wierus ascribes all those famous transformations to imagination; that in hydrophobia they seem to see the picture of a dog still in their water, that melancholy men and sick men conceive so many phantastical visions, apparitions to themselves, and have such absurd suppositions, as that they are kings, lords, cocks, bears, apes, owls; that they are heavy, light, transparent, great and little, senseless and dead, can be imputed to naught else but to a corrupt, false, and violent imagination. It works not in sick and melancholy

men only, but even most forcibly sometimes in such as are
sound: it makes them suddenly sick, and alters their temper-
ature in an instant. And sometimes a strong conceit or apprehension, as Valesius proves, will take away diseases: in
both kinds it will produce real effects. Men, if they see but
another man tremble, giddy, or sick of some fearful disease,
their apprehension and fear is so strong in this kind that they
will have the same disease. Or if by some soothsayer, wise
man, fortune-teller, or physician they be told they shall have
such a disease, they will so seriously apprehend it that they
will instantly labour of it. A thing familiar in China (saith Ric-
cius the Jesuit): "If it be told them they shall be sick on such a
day, when that day comes they will surely be sick, and will
be so terribly afflicted that sometimes they die upon it." Dr.
Cotta, in his Discovery of Ignorant Practitioners of Physic,
hath two strange stories to this purpose, what fancy is able to
do. The one of a parson's wife in Northamptonshire, *anno*
1607, that, coming to a physician, and told by him that she
was troubled with the sciatica, as he conjectured (a disease
she was free from), the same night after her return, upon his
words, fell into a grievous fit of a sciatica; and such another
example he hath of another goodwife, that was so troubled
with the cramp, after the same manner she came by it, because her physician did but name it. Sometimes death itself
is caused by force of phantasy. I have heard of one that, coming by chance in company of him that was thought to be sick
of the plague (which was not so), fell down suddenly dead.
Another was sick of the plague with conceit. One, seeing his
fellow let blood, falls down in a swoon. Another (saith
Cardan out of Aristotle) fell down dead (which is familiar to
women at any ghastly sight), seeing but a man hanged. A
Jew in France (saith Lodovicus Vives) came by chance over a
dangerous passage or plank that lay over a brook, in the
dark, without harm, the next day, perceiving what danger
he was in, fell down dead. Many will not believe such stories
to be true, but laugh commonly, and deride when they hear
of them; but let these men consider with themselves, as
Peter Byarus illustrates it, if they were set to walk upon a
plank on high, they would be giddy, upon which they dare

securely walk upon the ground. Many (saith Agrippa), "strong-hearted men otherwise, tremble at such sights, dazzle, and are sick if they look but down from a high place, and what moves them but conceit?" As some are so molested by phantasy; so some again, by fancy alone, and a good conceit, are as easily recovered. We see commonly the toothache, gout, falling sickness, biting of a mad dog, and many such maladies cured by spells, words, characters, and charms, and many green wounds by that now so much used *unguentum armarium* [weapon-salve] magnetically cured, which Crollius and Goclenius in a book of late hath defended, Libavius in a just tract as stiffly contradicts, and most men controvert. All the world knows there is no virtue in such charms or cures, but a strong conceit and opinion alone, as Pomponatius holds, "which forceth a motion of the humours, spirits, and blood, which takes away the cause of the malady from the parts affected." The like we may say of our magical effects, superstitious cures, and such as are done by mountebanks and wizards. "As by wicked incredulity many men are hurt" (so saith Wierus of charms, spells, etc.), "we find in our experience, by the same means many are relieved." An empiric oftentimes, and a silly chirurgeon, doth more strange cures than a rational physician. Nymannus gives a reason, because the patient puts his confidence in him, which Avicenna "prefers before art, precepts, and all remedies whatsoever." 'Tis opinion alone (saith Cardan) that makes or mars physicians, and he doth the best cures, according to Hippocrates, in whom most trust. So diversely doth this phantasy of ours affect, turn, and wind, so imperiously command our bodies, which "as another Proteus, or a chameleon, can take all shapes; and is of such force" (as Ficinus adds), that it can work upon others, as well as ourselves. How can otherwise blear eyes in one man cause the like affection in another? Why doth one man's yawning make another yawn? One man's pissing provoke a second many times to do the like? Why doth scraping of trenchers offend a third, or hacking of files? Why doth a carcass bleed when the murderer is brought before it, some weeks after the murder hath been done? Why do witches and old women fascinate and bewitch children? but as Wierus, Paracelsus, Cardan, Mizaldus, Valleriola, Cæsar Vanninus, Campanella, and many philosophers think, the forcible imagination of the one party moves and alters the spirits of the other. Nay more, they can cause and cure not only diseases, maladies, and several infirmities by this means, as Avicenna supposeth, in parties remote, but move bodies from their places, cause thunder, lightning, tempests, which opinion Alkindus, Paracelsus, and some others approve of. So that I may certainly conclude this strong conceit or imagination is *astrum hominis* [a man's guiding star], and the rudder of this our ship, which reason should steer, but, overborne by phantasy, cannot manage, and so suffers itself and this whole vessel of ours to be overruled, and often overturned. . . .

Waking and Terrible Dreams Rectified

As waking that hurts by all means must be avoided, so sleep which so much helps by like ways "must be procured, by nature or art, inward or outward medicines, and be protracted longer than ordinary, if it may be, as being an especial help." [Altomarus, Piso] It moistens and fattens the body, concocts, and helps digestion, as we see in dormice, and those Alpine mice that sleep all winter, which Gesner speaks of, when they are so found sleeping under the snow in the dead of winter, as fat as butter. It expels cares, pacifies the mind, refresheth the weary limbs after long work:

> *Somne quies rerum, placidissime somne deorum,*
> *Pax animi, quem cura fugit, qui corpora duris*
> *Fessa ministeriis mulces reparasque labori.* [Ovid]

> Sleep, rest of things, O pleasing deity,
> Peace of the soul, which cares dost crucify,
> Weary bodies refresh and mollify.

The chiefest thing in all physic, Paracelsus calls it, *omnia arcana gemmarum superans et metallorum* [better than all the secret powers of precious stones and metals]. The fittest time is "two or three hours after supper, whenas the meat is now settled at the bottom of the stomach, and 'tis good to lie on the right side first, because at that site the liver doth rest under the stomach, not molesting any way, but heating him as a fire doth a kettle that is put to it. After the first sleep 'tis not amiss to lie on the left side, that the meat may the better descend" [Crato]; and sometimes again on the belly, but never on the back. Seven or eight hours is a competent time for a melancholy man to rest, as Crato thinks; but as some do, to lie in bed and not sleep, a day, or half a day together, to give assent to pleasing conceits and vain imagination, is many ways pernicious. To procure this sweet moistening sleep, it's best to take away the occasions (if it be possible) that hinder it, and then to use such inward or outward remedies which may cause it. *Constat hodie* (saith Boissardus in his tract *De Magia*) *multos ita fascinari ut noctes integras exigant insomnes, summa inquietudine animorum et corporum*; many cannot sleep for witches and fascinations, which are too familiar in some places; they call it, *dare alicui malam noctem* [giving a person a bad night]. But the ordinary causes are heat and dryness, which must first be removed; a hot and dry brain never sleeps well; grief, fears, cares, expectations, anxieties, great businesses, *in aurem utramque otiose ut dormias* [that you may slumber peacefully on either ear], and all violent perturbations of the mind, must in some sort be qualified, before we can hope for any good repose. He that sleeps in the daytime, or is in suspense, fear, anyway troubled in mind, or goes to bed upon a full stomach, may never hope for quiet rest in the night; *nec enim meritoria somnos admittunt*, as the poet saith [Juvenal]; inns and such-like troublesome places are not for sleep; one calls "Ostler!" another, "Tapster!" one cries and shouts, another sings, whoops, halloos.... Who not accustomed to such noises can sleep amongst them? He that will intend to take his rest must go to bed *animo securo, quieto et libero*, with a secure and composed mind, in a quiet place: *omnia noctis erunt placida composta quiete* [at night all will be hushed in calm tranquillity]: and if that will not serve, or may not be obtained, to seek then such means as are requisite. To lie in clean linen and sweet; before he goes to bed, or in bed, to hear "sweet music," which Ficinus commends, or, as Jobertus, "to read some pleasant author till he be asleep, to have a basin of water still dropping by his bedside," or to lie near that pleasant murmur, *lene sonantis aquæ* [of gently dripping water], some floodgates, arches, falls of water, like London Bridge, or some continuate noise which may benumb the senses; *lenis motus, silentium et tenebra, tum et ipsa voluntas somnos faciunt*: as a gentle noise to some procures sleep, so, which Bernardinus Tilesius well observes, silence, in a dark room, and the will itself, is most available to others. Piso commends frications, Andrew Borde a good draught of strong drink before one goes to bed; I say, a nutmeg and ale, or a good draught of muscadine, with a toast and nutmeg, or a posset of the same, which many use in a morning, but, methinks, for such as have dry brains, are much more proper at night; some prescribe a sup of vinegar as they go to bed, a spoonful, saith Aetius. Piso, "a little after meat, because it rarefies melancholy, and procures an appetite to sleep." Donat. ab Altomar. and Mercurialis approve of it, if the malady proceed from the spleen. Sallust. Salvian., Hercules de Saxonia, Ælianus Montaltus, are altogether against it. Lod. Mercatus in some cases doth allow it. Rhasis seems to deliberate of it; though Simeon commend it (in sauce peradventure), he makes a question of it. As for baths, fomentations, oils, potions, simples or compounds, inwardly taken to this purpose, I shall speak of them elsewhere. If in the midst of the night when they lie awake, which is usual to toss and tumble, and not sleep, Ranzovius would have them, if it be in warm weather, to rise and walk three or four turns (till they be cold) about the chamber and then go to bed again.

Against fearful and troublesome dreams, *incubus* [nightmare], and such inconveniences, wherewith melancholy men are molested, the best remedy is to eat a light supper, and of such meats as are easy of digestion, no hare, venison, beef, etc., not to lie on his back, not to meditate or think in the daytime of any terrible objects, or especially talk of them before he goes to bed. For, as he said in Lucian after such conference, *Hecates somniare mihi videor*, I can think of nothing but hobgoblins: and, as Tully notes, "for the most part our speeches in the daytime cause our phantasy to work upon the like in our sleep," which Ennius writes of Homer: *Et canis in somnis leporis vestigia latrat*: as a dog dreams of a hare, so do men on such subjects they thought on last.

> *Somnia quæ mentes ludunt volitantibus umbris,*
> *Nec delubra deum, nec ab æthere numina mittunt,*
> *Sed sibi quisque facit,* etc.

[The dreams which deceive us with flitting shadows are sent neither from the shrines of the gods nor by the gods themselves, but each of us makes his own.]

For that cause when Ptolemy, King of Egypt, had posed the seventy interpreters in order, and asked the nineteenth man what would make one sleep quietly in the night, he told him, "the best way was to have divine and celestial meditations, and to use honest actions in the daytime." Lod. Vives "wonders how schoolmen could sleep quietly, and were not terrified in the night, or walk in the dark, they had such monstrous questions, and thought of such terrible matters all day long." They had need, amongst the rest, to sacrifice to God Morpheus, whom Philostratus paints in a white and black coat, with a horn and ivory box full of dreams, of the same colors, to signify good and bad. If you will know how to interpret them, read Artemidorus, Sambucus, and Cardan. . . .

Correctors of Accidents to Procure Sleep. Against Fearful Dreams, Redness, etc.

When you have used all good means and helps of alteratives, averters, diminutives, yet there will be still certain accidents to be corrected and amended, as waking, fearful dreams, flushing in the face to some, ruddiness, etc.

Waking, by reason of their continual cares, fears, sorrows,

dry brains, is a symptom that much crucifies melancholy men, and must therefore be speedily helped, and sleep by all means procured, which sometimes is a sufficient remedy of itself without any other physic. Sckenkius, in his Observations, hath an example of a woman that was so cured. The means to procure it are inward or outward. Inwardly taken, are simples, or compounds; simples, as poppy, nymphea, violets, roses, lettuce, mandrake, henbane, nightshade or solanum, saffron, hemp-seed, nutmegs, willows with their seeds, juice, decoctions, distilled waters, etc. Compounds are syrups, or opiates, syrup of poppy, violets, verbasco, which are commonly taken with distilled waters.... *Requies Nicholai, Philonium Romanum, Triphera magna, pilulæ de cynoglossa*, diascordium, *laudanum Paracelsi*, opium, are in use, etc. Country folks commonly make a posset of hempseed, which Fuchsius in his Herbal so much discommends; yet I have seen the good effect, and it may be used where better medicines are not to be had.

Laudanum Paracelsi is prescribed in two or three grains, with a dram of diascordium, which Oswald. Crollius commends. Opium itself is most part used outwardly, to smell to in a ball, though commonly so taken by the Turks to the same quantity for a cordial, and at Goa in the Indies; the dose forty or fifty grains.

Rulandus calls *Requiem Nicholai, ultimum refugium*, the last refuge; but of this and the rest look for peculiar receipts in Victorius Faventinus, Heurnius, Hildesheim, etc. Outwardly used, as oil of nutmegs by extraction or expression with rose water to anoint the temples, oils of poppy, nenuphar, mandrake, purslane, violets, all to the same purpose.

Montan. much commends odoraments of opium, vinegar, and rose water. Laurentius prescribes pomanders and nodules; see the receipts in him; Codronchus, wormwood to smell to.

Unguentum alabastritum, populeum, are used to anoint the temples, nostrils, or, if they be too weak, they mix saffron and opium. Take a grain or two of opium, and dissolve it with three of four drops of rose water in a spoon, and after mingle with it as much *unguentum populeum* as a nut, use it as before: or else take half a dram of opium, *unguentum populeum*, oil of nenuphar, rose water, rose vinegar, of each half an ounce, with as much virgin wax as a nut, anoint your temples with some of it, *ad horam somni* [at bedtime].

Sacks of wormwood, mandrake, henbane, roses made like pillows and laid under the patient's head, are mentioned by Cardan and Mizaldus; "to anoint the soles of the feet with the fat of a dormouse, the teeth with ear-wax of a dog, swine's gall, hare's ears": charms, etc.

Frontlets are well known to every goodwife: rose water and vinegar, with a little woman's milk, and nutmegs grated upon a rose cake applied to both temples.

For an emplaster, take of castorium a dram and a half, of opium half a scruple, mixed both together with a little water of life, make two small plasters thereof, and apply them to the temples.

Rulandus prescribes epithemes and lotions of the head, with the decoction of flowers of nymphea, violet leaves, mandrake roots, henbane, white poppy; Herc. de Saxonia, *stillicidia*, or droppings, etc. Lotions of the feet do much avail of the said herbs: by these means, saith Laurentius, I think you may procure sleep to the most melancholy man in the world. Some use horseleeches behind the ears, and apply opium to the place.

Bayerus sets down some remedies against fearful dreams, and such as walk and talk in their sleep. Baptista Porta, to procure pleasant dreams and quiet rest, would have you take hippoglossa, or the herb horse-tongue, balm, to use them or their distilled waters after supper, etc. Such men must not eat beans, peas, garlic, onions, cabbage, venison, hare, use black wines, or any meat hard of digestion at supper, or lie on their backs, etc.

Rusticus pudor, bashfulness, flushing in the face, high colour, ruddiness, are common grievances, which much torture many melancholy men, when they meet a man, or come in company of their betters, strangers, after a meal, or if they drink a cup of wine or strong drink, they are as red and flect, and sweat, as if they had been at a mayor's feast, *præsertim si metus accesserit* [especially if at the same time they are fearful], it exceeds, they think every man observes, takes notice of it: and fear alone will effect it, suspicion without any other cause. Sckenkius speaks of a waiting-gentlewoman in the Duke of Savoy's court, that was so much offended with it, that she kneeled down to him, and offered Biarus, a physician, all that she had to be cured of it. And 'tis most true, that Antony Lodovicus saith in his book *De Pudore*, "bashfulness either hurts or helps"; such men I am sure it hurts. If it proceed from suspicion or fear, Felix Plater prescribes no other remedy but to reject and contemn it: *Id populus curat scilicet* [of course, people take note of it], as a worthy physician in our town said to a friend of mine in like case, complaining without a cause; suppose one look red, what matter is it? make light of it, who observes it?

If it trouble at or after meals (as Jobertus observes), after a little exercise or stirring, for many are then hot and red in the face, or if they do nothing at all, especially women; he would have them let blood in both arms, first one, then another, two or three days between, if blood abound; to use frictions of the other parts, feet especially, and washing of them, because of that consent which is between the head and the feet. And withal to refrigerate the face, by washing it often with rose, violet, nenuphar, lettuce, lovage waters, and the like: but the best of all is that *lac virginale*, or strained liquor of litharge.... Quercetan commends the water of frogs' spawn for ruddiness in the face. Crato would fain have them use all summer the condite flowers of succory, strawberry water, roses (cupping-glasses are good for the time), and to defecate impure blood with the infusion of senna, savory, balm-water. Hollerius knew one cured alone with the use of succory boiled, and drunk for five months, every morning in the summer. It is good overnight to anoint the face with hare's blood, and in the morning to wash it with strawberry and cowslip water, the juice of distilled lemons, juice of cucumbers, or to use the seeds of melons, or kernels of peaches beaten small, or the roots of arum, and mixed with wheat-bran to bake it in an oven, and to crumble it in strawberry water, or to put fresh cheese-curds to a red face.

If it trouble them at meal-times that flushing, as oft it doth, with sweating or the like, they must avoid all violent passions and actions, as laughing, etc., strong drink, and drink very little, one draught, saith Crato, and that about the midst of their meal; avoid at all times indurate salt, and especially spice and windy meat.

Crato prescribes the condite fruit of wild rose to a nobleman his patient, to be taken before dinner or supper, to the quantity of a chestnut. It is made of sugar, as that of quinces. The decoction of the roots of sow-thistle before meat, by the same author is much approved. To eat of a baked apple some advise, or of a preserved quince, cummin-seed prepared with meat instead of salt, to keep down fumes; not to study or to be intentive after meals. . . .

John Hollander

```
                  On or
               off Either darkness
            unlocked again or feigned
          daylight perhaps graded only by
        stepped intensities fifty watts apart
      In any event no continuities like those
     of flickering no nor even of fading Flick
   Click and there it is suddenly Oh yes I see
   Indeed A mind hung brilliantly upon filaments
   stung by some untongued brightness opening up
   also encloses and the dark unbounded room lit
   by bare bulbs collapses into an unhurting box
   occupied by furniture now avoidable The dot
     of closure menaces the attention which in
        the flutter of eyelids can only tremble
         like a nervous child lying awake lest
         he be aware of the moment a closing
          shutter of sleep claps to But a
          snapped-off dream disperses
             into darkness like gold
               becoming mere motes
               becoming light If
                the eye lies open
                to such dust as
                sunlight brings
                it will never
                burn But that
                creation make
                a visible big
                difference in
                the way minds
                look a shaper
                 will burn
                outwardly
                first and
                thus once
                there was
                 light
```

IDEA
Old Mazda lamp, 50-100-150 W.

John Updike
Vibration

The world vibrates, my sleepless nights
discovered. The air conditioner hummed;
I turned it off. The plumbing
in the next apartment sang;
I moved away, and found a town
whose factories shuddered as they worked
all night. The wires on the poles
outside my windows quivered in an ecstasy
stretched thin between horizons.
I went to where no wires were; and there,
as I lay still, a dragon tremor
seized my darkened body, gnawed
my heart, and murmured, *I am you.*

Tossing and Turning

The spirit has infinite facets, but the body
confiningly few sides.
                              There is the left,
the right, the back, the belly, and tempting
in-betweens, northeasts and northwests,
that tip the heart and soon pinch circulation
in one or another arm.
                              Yet we turn each time
with fresh hope, believing that sleep
will visit us here, descending like an angel
down the angle our flesh's sextant sets,
tilted toward that unreachable star
hung in the night between our eyebrows, whence
dreams and good luck flow.
                              Uncross
your ankles. Unclench your philosophy.
This bed was invented by others; know we go
to sleep less to rest than to participate
in the orthic twists of another world.
This churning is our journey.
                              It ends,
can only end, around a corner
we do not know
                    we are turning.

Brock Brower
Storm Still

IT WAS SOMETIMES WINTRY, probably in 1608, at
Bankside, and he was clearly at the Globe, among the
groundlings, chinned up against the front stage by the
pushing of the farrier's apprentice behind him, and the
garlic-breathed orangegirl on his right. Robert Armin was
playing the Fool. That was why he had come. To see Armin
in his motley, coxcomb, and huge.ass's ears, the bladder
rioting in his lunatic hand. But then Richard Burbage was
also acting that afternoon. He was playing Lear. Brilliantly,
he thought. "Take heed, sirrah; the whip." The steely core of
kingly authority. Lear not yet mad, still regal. He suddenly
wanted to tell somebody, anybody, how fine an actor Burbage was. He turned smiling to the orangegirl. She smiled
back coquettishly. He started to open his mouth to utter
some critical *bon mot*, but closed it quickly around her wild
kiss. Then she was clinging to him like a daughter. "I cannot
heave my heart into my mouth," she cried. "I cannot heave
my heart into my mouth, I cannot heave my heart into my
mouth, I cannot heave my . . . "

Then everything turned on a great dizzy wheel, wrenching
his attention around to the stage again, away from Cordelia,
the orangegirl. He was horrified. Lear *was* whipping the Fool,
beating him mercilessly to the cruel, cheek-cracking tune of
the thunder. The cannonball rolled back and forth behind the
stage, and Armin sang to the beating of the whip.

> He that hath but a tiny little wit,
> With hey, ho, the wind and the rain,
> Must make content with his fortunes fit,
> Though the rain it raineth every day.

The Fool jigged, and the whip cut.

He tried to shout out. The Fool should not be whipped, it wasn't in the play. He started to climb onto the stage. First it grew higher and higher, forcing him down and down as he climbed. Then it collapsed under him. From the three balconies around the octagonal Globe they laughed at him. "But the Fool is *not whipped*," he shouted at them, almost defensively. "Lear must never do such a thing. Never, never, never, never, never." Then they began to disappear, laughing, behind the rising flames. He saw why the stage had collapsed. It was on fire. The great Globe itself was on fire, burning like a wooden bucket. But that was wrong too. The Globe fire was in 1613. "Stop, stop!" he cried at the flames. "Your're too early. Don't burn. Don't whip the Fool. Don't burn. Don't whip the Fool." Then he woke up.

Immediately he felt his old fumbling sense of panic. He'd slipped again in some matter of the play. There was a reference he carelessly hadn't checked all the way back — some date or alternate reading he must look up this very instant, or they were going to catch him out. He knew it was something terribly minor. Some question about the colophon on the Pide Bull Quarto, or a line he'd wrongly attributed to the source play *Leir* or to Holinshed, or even some stupid quibble over the spelling of Cordelia's name. Really that picayune. It didn't affect his main argument in the slightest. But they would crucify him for it, put his whole scholarship in doubt at next spring's meeting, if he didn't find it now and burn it out like a tiny plague spot in his critical acumen.

He knew all this was nonsense, yet he still began shuffling furtively through the papers on his desk to see if he hadn't possibly made a note somewhere, perhaps in the margins of his Spenser. It was one of those involuntary things that had finally become quite voluntary. He needed something to clear his mind when he napped off, and this seemed to do the trick. One of these days, he suspected, he was going to nap off altogether. His mind would simply fail to clear. Last scene of all that ends this strange, eventful history. Second childishness and mere oblivion. But somehow that would be all right too, because, look, he was only here picking over his papers after an insignificant reference. There was nothing really important to get back to. . .

But he was awake enough now to hear the knock. It was hard to tell whether he was hearing it now, actually at the door, or whether memory was echoing it for him. Such distinctions were becoming difficult for him to make at times. Or just not worth making.

"Yes?" he asked peevishly. He wondered if he wheezed at all. Manly voice, turning to childish treble.

His study door opened part way, and a bearded face cocked around at him, its smile still back in the door's shadow. "Busy?"

This was young Nelson's way of asking permission to come in out of the shadows. For a moment he mused on just leaving him there in the shadows. Forever. Perhaps he would eventually fade into the umbra, pulling his bearded smile in after him, and become a complete shadow, instead of the furtive, diffident half shadow he already was. But oh what silliness, he warned himself, and said pleasantly, "No, no, no. Come in, Nelson. Please."

The young instructor bowed out of the doorway, bringing in a towering pile of corrected blue books. On top of them was the marking book, stretched open to the proper page with a rubber band. Nelson seemed to come bearing them almost like a hecatomb, yet at the same time he managed somehow to be putting them aside — to ask about obviously more important work. "How are you coming along with the old fool?"

He meant Lear, of course. Almost certainly, he meant Lear.

Nelson handed him the pile, which was deceptively heavy. He lifted it the little height onto his desk, straining every chest muscle not to puff.

"All right, my boy," he laughed. "I'm having most of my

trouble with the young fool. If I can settle his hash..." He decided he'd better be hospitable. "Can you stay a minute?"

Nelson nodded and slipped over to the other chair by the cold fireplace. On his way he ran his fingers along the books on one shelf. Too lightly, too quickly. Looking for his poems, the older man knew. Feeling for it, actually. An absurdly thin volume, and from the spine, it really was hard to see. A two-dimensional piece of work. If that. It was silly enough to find a scholarly press going in for that sort of publishing, but it was much sillier to have it inspire a beard. An effeminate beard too, he felt, even though it covered those sallow cheeks blackly. A shadow would grow just such a beard. That plushy. His book and his whiskers had both come out far too soon, and that summed up Nelson precisely as far as he was concerned.

Nelson crossed his legs and all his fingers in one nervous motion. "You know," he said, "sometimes I think Shakespeare himself must've been a jester one time or another."

How he hated that kind of remark. Shakespeare was Marlowe, or Bacon, or the Earl of Essex, or the boy who held the horses, and now a Fool. It threw everything out of balance. *The Tragedy of Lear* by Crazy Will.

"Oh?" he said simply.

"Everything he does — well, it has the fool's wit. I was reading an article the other day, sir. You might look at it if you're working on this theme of Folly." He smiled quickly. "I suppose you've got your material down pat as it is, but this man had something really new — I mean, he puts you up against it on a couple of points. Quite up against it."

Nelson had studied a year at Oxford. It had made him an expert at malicious deference. Maddening.

Nelson mentioned where he might find the article. It was in a publication that had not been in existence before his fiftieth birthday. He'd read a few issues, and thought it all nonsense. Then he was flabbergasted to find that he had to suffer a certain amount of condescension for thinking it all nonsense. He kept silent about it nowadays, but he would certainly not read the article.

"Have you been doing anything on *Lear* yourself?" he suddenly thought to ask.

The instructor bowed low before the challenge. "No. Not at all. Nothing on *Lear* itself. I just thought you might like to hear about this man's work. Are those exams all right then?"

"Must be, my boy, if you've done them. You ought to be thanked, of course. It's very pleasant to be left free — "

"Not at all."

Gratitude was the very cup of bitterness sometimes, he thought. But he was too old to be much surprised by the taste. That same taste crept into so many things that were supposed to be ennobling.

"But I'm afraid, sir..."

"You must run along. That it?"

"Yes, I'm afraid."

"Of course. Mustn't keep you. I know better. Thank you again, Nelson. Won't keep you. Must work myself." Sometimes, he calculated, a properly self-effacing old man can lick the pants off any youth for modest demeanor.

Nelson went out, closing the door without a sound, almost as if he didn't want to wake somebody. Maddening.

He leaned back heavily in his chair, lifting the front legs about an inch off the floor, and patted his girth. His Phi Beta Kappa key, comically oversized, topped the hillock like a small tablet of laws. A back leg of the chair suddenly hobbled on its uncertain shank and brought the chair down sharply onto all fours again. The slip shook him for a moment.

So it is all happening to me, he thought. I can't even stay steady in my own chair. I shall simply have to toss up this *Lear* business and seek level ground. Unburthen'd crawl toward death.

That was why he'd asked for young Nelson. Actually asked for him, absurd as that seemed now. So he could gather his thoughts in peace and produce them in final form. Which he hadn't done before, because of the pressure of... now, of course, with young Nelson, he'd be able...able now, with young Nelson.

Calling him Nelson, that was his first blunder. He'd meant

to keep him kindly at a distance by using his last name without the Mister. It would've been just right. Mr. Nelson was too formal, but the last name alone, that set up just the correct balance of friendliness and seniority. Only his name wasn't Thomas R. Nelson. It was R. Nelson Thomas. He must've seen it somewhere on a list as Thomas, R. Nelson, and simply slipped the comma. Bad textual error. Trapped into familiarity. But then he seemed to recall vaguely hearing students call him Mr. Nelson. At least he assumed they were using the Mister. My God, he thought, what has happened to Degree. Take but Degree away and...and you get familiarity, and familiarity breeds contempt. He shook his head ruefully. Could he do no better than that innocuous cliché?

He hauled himself out of his chair, away from these thoughts — away from all thinking, in fact — and stood in front of his long, narrow Queen Anne window. Somebody else would have this window all to himself soon, and he'd be outside it. His study was on the first floor of the Library, and the campus was framed before him, cut into neat, rectangular cards by the panes. He'd be out there somewhere. Mostly bare elms, stark in the winter gloom. A five-o'clock January gloom. He looked at his watch, a little loose on his wrist now. He should be hearing the Library bells, somewhere in the tower above him, ringing a knell in the gloom. Lights were already dotting on in the buildings behind the elms. The wind was coming up, bringing in the snow again.

Yes, of course, there was snow on the ground. How could he stand there and not think of the snow first thing? The white, even stretch of winter over the earth. Fresh and flocculent yesterday. Old and icy today. The hoary, arthritic, fallen snow. A crust.

Tom's a-cold, he mused. Prithee, Nuncle, be contented; 'tis a naughty night to swim in.

Then he noticed somebody running across the campus toward him, struggling hopelessly with the deep, crusted snow that broke under him at every step. Tom's a-cold, he mused again, looking out at the battling figure. Tom's adrift.

Quite suddenly, he felt himself adrift. His eyes watered and wanted to blink, only ever so slowly. He fought to keep his attention on the figure struggling in the snow, and a sensation of steepness, all about him, grew until he felt he was once again climbing onto the stage in the burning Globe to rescue the Fool. Don't whip the Fool. The whip cut, and the Fool jigged, raising the powdery underdown of snow about him like a rich mist.

He had come nearer the window now. He leaped and pirouetted and somersaulted, playing with the snow as if it were a partner. Bells jingled. He ran to an elm tree, even nearer the window, and passionately kicked it. Immediately he was remorseful and threw his arms around the tree. A long kiss on the icy bark. Then he kicked it and laughed. The bells on his cap trembled. He looked about him inquisitively and discovered the window.

He rushed toward it and pressed his nose moistly against a pane of glass, bordered in frost. His face cocked and bobbed on his nose like the ticking moon in an ancient clock. He grinned and brayed through the glass. He shook his bells, and banged the head of the marotte that he carried against the window. And then his own head. The bells rang. The five-o'clock knell rolled through the gloom.

Soberly the old man shook himself, and a certain richness of sensation deserted him. He did blink finally and reassured himself that there was no nose mark on the window pane. Outside, only the gloom. It was the first time in his life he had dozed off still on his feet. Mortifying. He forced himself back to his desk. Work.

I suppose that's really what old age is, he thought. Getting fuzzy about whether you're awake or asleep. When is Lear mad, and when is he sane? He wants to sing like a bird in a cage when he and Cordelia go off to prison. That's mad as much as it is sane. On the heath he wants the storm to strike flat the thick rotundity of the world. That's sane as much as it is mad. What's the difference?

He took the trouble to jot these ideas down in a creaky scrawl, and stuffed the paper in the corner of his blotter.

After supper, he'd come back and reread them. He hadn't yet kept his promise to himself to work after supper, but tonight he would.

But already he knew what he really thought of his jottings. If he'd found them in a freshman paper, he'd have put an encouraging remark in the margin, something like, "An interesting approach, but don't rest on it. Sh. certainly intended L.'s madness and sanity to have a distinction. Same with Ham. What is it?" And in a senior thesis, he'd expect a carefully argued answer.

But *was* there an answer? Could any distinction be made between madness and sanity, wisdom and folly, sleeping and waking? He stared at the clutter of papers, the under-lined books, the closed Quarto interleaved with ragged notecards, the mere inkblots before him. The impulse to plunge his head into his hands and groan helplessly tugged at his dignity like the impish pluck at the king's sleeve by the court imbecile. What were the lines? "O, let me not be mad, not mad, sweet heaven! Come in," he almost moaned. "Come in, come in, come in."

Then he realized he was saying it, and tried to remember hearing a knock. Yes, most certainly. He could distinctly remember hearing a knock. At his door. So things were back in order again, and he must immediately do the next thing. He reached out to open the door. But his hand bumped the knob long before his grasp closed, and the door moved away from him, a good foot, swinging shut.

For a long moment he did not move his hand. He frowned at the knob, trying to remember many more things, and their proper order. Time ran back and forth in his mind, but he still could put nothing between the last two closings of the study door. It was like that discrepancy in exits he'd once discovered in a bad Jacobean quarto, which forced an im-portant extra character on stage and opened up a wholly new interpretation of the entire scene. That had made his reputation. But this shocked him. It suddenly seemed such a wretched business, trying to think things through, and he decided not to think, only listen. He heard the tunnel echo of his own strained silence, and then deep within it, bells, softened by cap and curled toes, jingling almost in a whisper, and then unmistakably, laughter. Inane laughter.

He whirled around in his chair — too quickly for his age — and a small dizziness seized him, so that the riot of color, the grotesquery, the motley patches of things possible over the chimerical fabric, all assailed his sight at once. Then he was at last able to blink again, and the cowl, braided over with a red coxcomb, dipped toward him in a mocking bow, and the bells on the comb's points shifted. Their fleeting tinkle struck at him, and his old, uncompromising body gave way before the onrush of a deep shudder.

The Fool had his motley feet drawn up in the chair. He was grinning much as he had through the window. With great, friendly inanity. Everything in the room seemed instantly to delight him. His head lolled about on his neck, an imbecile motion exaggerated by the huge ass's ears that flopped from his cowl. When he saw something that had any brightness to it, he pointed his marotte's puppet face toward it, and pretended to whisper violently in the marotte's ear.

The old man's first thought was to rush at the coxcomb and beat him from the room. Never in his life had he felt such savagery rise within him, and he sensed it was all about to burst from him with a leaping howl at the Fool's throat.

But the Fool abruptly stopped his meandering and rounded his grin on the old man. The grin was even more imbecile. Stupidly loyal, it seemed. The Fool was waiting. Then suddenly he kicked his motley legs with a great mocking jangle of bells, and teased at the old man with groping fingers, daring him to come ahead. Then one finger only crooking at him blackly, like the dead wick in the lamp of reason.

It would kill me. He saw that one fact, and then began to catch hold altogether. Oblivion was smirking at him through a Fool's grin, but he was not going to let loose from the holds of logic and age and certainty. Not yet.

His first thought — his first self-possessed thought — was whether anybody had heard or seen anything. Whether anybody anywhere in the world had heard or seen anything.

That he had very nearly attacked the Fool — *admitted him* — filled him with terror. Thoughts carried. Even the silence of the mind was suspicious.

Deliberately he turned back to his desk. He picked up the Pide Bull Quarto and set painfully to work on the storm scene. He courted his powers of concentration, and counted upon them to shut out any other presence that might be — that was how he must think of it, *might be* — near him. Gradually they did. The rollings of the bells and the little chuckles merged with the rising storm outside, and together, close to either side of his window, they passed away, out of his ken.

II

He ate his supper in the upper hall of the undergraduate Commons. He frequently did this for the sake of a change from his quiet widower's meal, served up uneventfully by the bad-tempered housekeeper who had outlived his wife's patience with her. But tonight he wanted something else from the dining hall. Something almost tribal.

He listened gratefully to the tumult of undergraduate cutlery. The meal was eaten out of various triangular, oblong, and serpentine depressions in uniform aluminum trays, collected from a cafeteria line, and the din reminded him of nothing so much as the Roman legionaries going into battle, beating their shields. On top of this, there was the babble of at least two hundred youths, all talking at once, none of them yet sure how his voice should really sound. Bedlam, Jericho. Or a thousand twangling instruments.

It all had a strangely reassuring effect on him. The noise and liveliness argued against the Fool. When he got back to work, there would only be frost at his window. In a few days he might be able to talk confidently about hallucination, or tricks of the dozing eye, the dream-fondled ear. He tidied his wrinkled mouth with a napkin, took advantage of his age to leave the tray on the table rather than face the confusing actions of the dishwasher's chute, and left the Commons, mantled in an overcoat.

The walk back to his study followed shoveled canyons

through the old snow. Within the last hour, they had begun to fill up again with a new undergrowth of flakes. A good way to put it, he thought. It stings your face like nettles, it clings to your clothes like burrs, so why shouldn't it be considered some kind of uncontrollable, prickly weed? The false logic of it pleased him. It kept him warm during the rest of the cold, devious walk, barriered him against the increasing storm that whipped at him devilishly. No matter which way he bent his head, it seemed to strike him on his unprotected side.

He reached the Library. Inside, he stamped his boots in the dark corridor — managed to kick one off, but had to stoop over for the other. He walked briskly down the corridor, congratulating himself on his desire to work after supper. Even if it might be false desire. He unlocked his study door and pushed it open, but it moved too lightly ahead of him, and he caught enough glimpse of haste in the Fool to know he'd just skipped back to the fireplace chair in time.

Disappointed, he told himself. Not surprised. Not afraid. Just disappointed.

He sat down at his desk with his back again to the other chair. He would have to do a little work, make a little progress before he could safely turn around. He did not know where the feeling came from, but he was certain that to work well was his only hope against the Fool's inane grin, his seductive, will-o'-the-wisp bells. The stir of the outside world — the noisy community of the dining hall — he realized now was useless.

He decided to give up the Pide Bull Quarto for the evening, in fact, to turn away from *Lear* itself altogether and read *The Tragecall historie of Kinge Leir and his Three Daughters*. Over the years he'd read the source play in patches, little snippets for his lectures, but he'd never sat down to read the whole play through for itself. He suspected it would be dull, wretchedly jangling, and stupid. In only a few pages he was convinced he was right. But he refused to give in to boredom, to let his mind slip out of its set task. The Fool was seated too near him for that.

The verse trotted along like an old dray. He had to stop

reading line by line, and rushed ahead for the sense alone. The play dragged on preposterously. Leir was arrogant, lachrymose, and stupid. Truly stupid.

His patience began to wear. He tried to stifle his irritation, but it grew into a repressed anger. Finally, he yielded to a loss of temper he could hardly understand himself, and flung the book down on his desk. The old fool, he snapped to himself. Yes, precisely. The old fool, because there is no fool worse than Lear without his Fool. And that was Leir.

⁰ Suddenly he had the feeling of tottering on the verge of some immeasurably deep but opulent unknown. It was like that quibble that always touched the unsettled edge of his waking, only he felt he was much nearer the instance this time, that it *was* important after all. Terribly important. They were right to catch him up on it. It was a reference he needed to make. Properly. He had to refer back...and just as he seemed to have it, something frightened him away from the very thought, and his tottering was all nonsense again.

Behind him, the Fool tittered, and in a rage the old man turned on him. Through the waves of his vision, so tired now, he saw the Fool had taken up a new attitude.

He was sitting straight up in the chair, studiously attending upon a large book in his lap. He was turning the pages as fast as he could with the dexterity of one finger, and keeping time to the flipping of the pages by bobbing his cowled head up and down like a mechanical sage. Yes. Certainly. Quite. True. Most. Likely. Yes. Indeed. Why. Of course. He was very soon through the book. Immediately he stuffed it back into its place on the shelf, took down another one right next to it, and began the whole burlesque again.

⁰ Ignore it, he warned himself. But he watched the bobbing head and the passing pages with utter fascination. He was horrified, but somehow the horror did not reach, could not break in upon the rhythm of the mockery itself. The Fool increased his tempo. The pages beat by as if the book had been blown open, and a shifting wind were leafing through it. The Fool began turning pages either way now, in sharp little gusts of mindlessness. It struck him suddenly that the Fool had probably been hunched over a book, clowning an intelligence this way, all the time he'd been reading *Leir*.

He got to his feet, trembling. But the Fool, the moment he rose, stopped turning the pages and slowly, patiently took up his grin again. The horror at last broke through. For the first time, he really looked into the Fool's face. It was like looking not into a mask, but *out* of one. He was not in front of the Fool's face at all. He was *behind* it, staring out of its vacant eyes and teething its ruthless, dumb, ecstatic grin.

Hastily he piled his papers, closed his books. When he took his overcoat from the hook behind the door, he leaned against the door for just a moment, not realizing that a full minute passed before he pushed away from it again. He left the office, locking it behind him. Then he hurried out of the Library, forgetting his boots in the dark corridor. Once outside, he noticed he'd also forgotten the light in his study. Unless it had been turned on again. He went back for his boots, but decided to leave the light. It would go out when it wanted to.

III

The next afternoon his retirement was announced at the faculty meeting. He came in late, and heard the announcement almost as a surprise, having forgotten that it was to be made.

He looked around at his colleagues, who were clapping tenderly and avoiding his eye. Good night, old prince, he mused foolishly, may flights of angels help you up the stairs. He was amazed at himself. For the past few months, he had been planning how to suppress uncontrollable anger at this inevitable insult to dignity, professionally disguised as a tribute. But listening to the mannerly, almost withdrawn applause around him, he wasn't at all angry. There were so many other furies in his bosom now that he was actually relieved. Good, he thought, they haven't caught me out. They don't know. Then he realized exactly what it was they did not know. That he was suddenly unburdened of them. He had begun an existence which simply did not include them among its cares. Even as he stood among them, reaching for their kind hands, he felt he was setting them aside for good and all.

Nelson was among the first to rush up to him. No longer maddening.

"Congratulations," said Nelson. "Forty-three years. That's a long time."

So it is, he thought. Or said. He wasn't sure which. And forty-three on top of twenty-four makes sixty-seven years' presence of mind, and now I've chucked it all. Don't need it. Wish I'd never had it. Wish I'd never been bothered with it.

He looked carefully at Nelson's face to see if he was possibly saying these things too, not just thinking them. But Nelson's face didn't seem to know either.

"Thank you, Nelson," he made sure to say, not think.

"I wanted to mention to you," Nelson went on, "the light was on in your study this morning. I tried to get in to turn it off, but your door was locked, and I couldn't find the janitor."

It occurred to him that Nelson too said all this without thinking. Or at least without thinking of any of the rich and enchanting possibilities. The scene if they had forced the door and found the Fool asleep at his desk, sprawled out in a garish parody of the pedant adoze over his dry books. The great blot of ink on the end of the Fool's nose, making him look like a broken nib. The marotte stuck into the Variorum like a bookmark, grinning over the binding in a frozen mime of the Contents. For all this, no thought. Of course, Nelson did not have *his* knowledge to go on. But somehow that came off as only another very distinct limitation in Nelson himself. He found it easy to fault him for it and set him aside.

Why, there was even snoring. Great hawking at a burbling lip. A grand test. The Fool curled up in exactly his own napping posture, when he opened the door that morning, pretending the noise of entering had troubled his sleep, bestirring himself with a loud carillon from his cap. He'd really almost laughed out loud, but suddenly sensed the open door behind him. He fell back against it, listening hard for any approaching sound outside in the corridor. God's spies, he thought, it's broad daylight. The Fool chuckled, beaming at him over that great noseblot with blank, uncanny eyes, bright with false sleep, and he felt himself pulled another small tug away from the order of things into the clutter of that merry-andrew gaze.

Perhaps he really ought to tip Nelson off. Perhaps it would be better, even now, if he simply leaned over and whispered, "Look, there's a pest of a fellow in my office. Will you run over and tell him I won't be by today?" Only he knew he would be by, and alone, and all he could bring himself to say was, "Thank you again. Stupid of me. Getting a little careless lately. Need to be watched, don't I?"

An older friend in the English department came up to him then and had the good sense not to congratulate him.

"Working on anything now?" he asked simply.

"Yes. *Lear*. Cleaning up, really. Talked about it enough in my lifetime, haven't I? Never make a book. But a little — a little *opusculum* would do, wouldn't it? For 'A poor, infirm, weak, and despised old man'?"

"Utter nonsense," replied his friend, staring at the floor. "You'd better save a little room in the pasture when they put you out there next spring. I'm afraid they won't give me those extra few years of grace they gave you. I'm not that tough."

"Plenty of room." He wondered if Nelson could see how graciously his friend had turned the compliment. Probably not. But then it really made no difference. They were both foolish even to try. Eptly or ineptly, they stayed nothing by it. They were only tarrying here, all three of them.

"What is it you're trying to do with *Lear*?" his friend asked, bringing back the subject.

"Oh, I'm taking up Folly. Much the same way Erasmus does. Though he's quite wrong about her, you know. She isn't a goddess at all. Only a fool."

"I'm not surprised."

"You would be. I've been spending most of my time lately on the Fool. If you stay with him long enough, he becomes a sort of familiar. A goddess is only a conception. The Fool's much more than that." He said all this lightly, edging as near as he dared to his own peccant sense of the matter. The risk was titillating. "I'm really trying to decide just what his existence amounts to."

His friend frowned in a way he quite understood, but Nelson smiled in a way that escaped him. What bit of dried fungi had he managed to fire in that tinderbox this time?

Nelson seemed for a moment to want to hold it all in, but he couldn't resist. "I suppose you might even call him," he said nervously, "the existential fool."

So. That poppycock. When was he going to learn to watch every single word he used in front of this young Holofernes? He felt a wild urge to reach out with grand punctilio and pluck Nelson's velvety beard, but the deepening of his friend's frown kept him off.

"You suppose whatever you wish to suppose, young man," his friend snorted at the instructor, "but remember it's your own tomfoolery." Then he turned back again. "But I must admit I don't quite see what you're driving at either. The Fool's simply a character in the play. His existence is in his role, isn't it?"

And so. More poppycock. This was harder, riskier. "Of course," he agreed affably, "but I'm wondering if that role isn't just a bit wider than you think it is. The Fool is a character in all of sixteenth, seventeenth century life. He has a role even *off* the stage. We find Queen Elizabeth footing the bill for a huge wardrobe of motley. Read the list sometime. The fools Robert Greene, Jack Green, and Mr. Shenstone. An Italian named Monarcho. A little Blackamoor. Thomasina the Dwarf — oh, I'd like to have seen her — and Ipolyta the Tartarian. And Clod. Clod — bless him — Clod is even chided by his Queen for not criticizing her sharply enough. Royal displeasure at his failure to play his role. Not quick enough in his hits upon Glorianna, can you imagine?" He warmed to his own tired lecture style, feeling how safely he could dissemble under its fey pedantry as others gathered around him. "The Fool is with us, you see? With them, I suppose I should say," he added hastily, "but I mean, abroad. That's important. Abroad. As the Lord of Misrule, as the Comte de Permission, guilty of 'Flearing and making of mouths.' He is fed on crow's meat, they say, and monkey flesh. Or he eats only what the dogs have tasted, and so they serve the dogs great delicacies for the Fool's sake. An odd, rarified life, you realize. Terribly indulgent, but at the same time terribly mangy. It says of Will Sommers, for instance, Henry the Eighth's great fool, that he 'laid himself down among the spaniels to sleep' after he'd pleased his Harry with a riddle. A silly riddle at that. Damnably silly. 'What is it that, being borne without life, head, lip, or eye, yet doth run roaring through the world till it die?'"

He looked quickly around him hoping for someone to answer. It was so easy, but they all seemed to give up. He felt the silliness take an oddly dreadful hold upon him, and spoke as lightly as he could.

"'Why, quoth Will, it is a fart.'"

He knew he was the only one laughing — senselessly — yet all their faces were bent up in a way that meant they might be laughing too, if he could only hear them. Desperately he fought his way out of his own shameful laughter.

"The most ridiculous bawdry. Not funny at all. Just not funny. Very weak. Very. But you see — I think we can sense in it — the Fool's familiarity." He wormed loose again. "To an Elizabethan, Jacobean audience. What I mean is, that the Fool might have more reality for these people than Lear, even though they did know kings too. They wouldn't expect to go into the narrow streets at Bankside and find Lear walking abroad. But they could very well expect to find the Fool. That, actually, is how fools were found. They existed, you see. Naturals."

He stopped, hoping he was nearer sense now. "Fascinating idea," his friend said, but he knew that was coddling. He must be more careful, he realized, much more careful, even with friends, and this suddenly enraged him.

"Do you know how to pick a fool?" he burst out. "There was one in Germany named Conrad Pocher — the Count Palatine delighted in him — he was considered ripe for the court's pleasure after he hanged a little boy from a tree. Pocher hanged the little boy because the little boy had scabs. It was a joke that Pocher would hang you if you had scabs too. Beware, all of you who are scabrous — "

He felt his friend's hand grip his shoulder, as if to pinch off what he was saying. His friend said to him, "I'm afraid I still don't see what you're getting at, but good luck with it any-how." The others hastily agreed.

He closed them out and turned abruptly to Nelson. "I'm letting you take all my classes."

The surprise of it dropped his friend's hand from his shoulder. But he couldn't bother to care. He went on to Nelson. "I'd appreciate it if you'd do the exam as well. I'm afraid I'm going to want to be left very much alone."

Now he didn't dare look at his friend. He had as good as abdicated. Nelson was in a fidget of self-effacement. He felt he wouldn't be able to stand that maggoty beard another moment longer. Other friends came up to him. They sug-gested delicately all the wonderful things he had done in the past, and the long life he had ahead in peace and quiet con-templation. In five more minutes, it was over, and he turned from the scattered gathering, found his coat, and went out across the frozen snow that pitched out flat before him like a white heath.

He worked furiously. Every day he was more exhausted, but he fought fatigue with anger, and anger, he found, could keep him going when all his faculties were otherwise ready to fail.

The storm wore on, running in tatters across the stiff snow, almost following his anger. After a ruthless night, it would seem to be dying away, only to regain its ferocity in the late afternoon, cutting icily against the window, closing away what little light there was in the grey sky. But he didn't mind. It kept him alone. He'd taken his card off the door, and nobody bothered him.

The Fool was always decorous. For the most part, he stayed happily in his chair, and thumbed through the books over and over again, timing his flurries to the storm. There were a few pranks. The old man would glance up from his work to find the marotte nodding methodically over his shoulder like a wizened scholar whose head had been shrunk, the Fool pressed right up against the back of his chair. It made him jump, but no more. Or he would come in to find a paper full of meaningless inkblots, almost like writing, lying among his notes. Yet he could never quite be sure it wasn't a scrap he'd used himself to test his pen. The tricks kept him on edge, but they were nothing beside the threat he felt in the Fool's patience. The Fool seemed somehow able to wait without ever losing a moment. Nothing could exhaust his empty loyalty. He was there forever. Or not. It made no difference to him. Only to those in quest of differences.

But he could admit none of this. Not to himself, certainly not to the Fool. Not even by the fleet tribute of another eye-blink that might drop him into an unguarded sleep.

Instead, he settled into a fixed wakefulness, embarking on what he sensed would be some final test of his scholarship. He had already made a beginning, so it was only a matter of shifting his emphasis. Under the pretense of still pursuing his studies of *Lear* — to whom, he wondered, to whom? — he set out to study the Fool himself. He felt certain that if he could only read up on the Fool, chivvy his motley image through the bramble of source material and first mentions and oblique references and analogues, hunt him down like startled sense at bay behind a faulty and obscure text, he would save him. As simple a thing as fixing the Fool's dates properly might trap him, he was half convinced. He was depending upon his last reliable habit of mind. Somewhere among the disputed readings, the incunabula, the endless exegesis, he felt he was bound to come upon the right page. Then, all he would need to do — all he could ever do to end this gest — was somehow to rip out that page.

He began working through the literature. Other scholars had been there before him, but they had no sense of the menace — he could tell that from the bloodless measure they took in their writings — the menace that lay within the sweet hollow of folly. None of them, obviously, had ever kept a fool. Yet any simpleton writing a pet manual, would at least know his German Shepherd or his Siamese or his box turtle. He pushed impatiently through their treacly rationality to the primary sources, testimony from the great warders who had once kept real fools to fondle like favored apes.

He searched constantly for a touchstone. He picked finically even among the original Latinisms in hopes of finding a proper one. *Stultus. Morio. Fatuus. Sannio.* They all fitted, yet none quite, really. He set the legends alongside his own Fool for measure. Til Eulenspiegel, the owl glass, the wise mirror, but still a brute. At Til's graveside, a cord snapped, and his coffin tipped upright into the broken earth. "Leave him as he is, he was strange in this life, he wants to be after his death." So they buried him standing straight up and stole his estate, which proved his last mockery, being only a box of stones. His own Fool could have inherited, yes, easily inherited that owlishness, that false legacy of stones. But much more his own Fool favored Marcolf, the jester who watched Solomon dispense justice to the two women who claimed one child, and as the king calmly lowered the threatening sword to his side again and judged so wisely, jeered at him for trusting a woman's tears. Ah, how that fitted. That exactly, the same jeering laughter that so harrowed him, turning his own subtlety of mind suddenly as sluggish as the clapper in a frozen bell.

Yet legend could not satisfy him. Legendary fools were vagrant in time, and his own Fool carried his days upon his back — a hunch to his motley shoulders that meant he stooped under the hour, not under a proverb. He came from a rich period. The old man relished such labor, and early on, among the many sotties he dug up, he found Robert Armin's own *Nest of Ninnies.* The actor-clown's account of the fools of his day. "Simply of themselves without Compound." Just what was wanted — "without Compound" — and reaching into that nest — down among Jemy Camber, the fat fool a yard wide and a nail high, and Jack Oates, eating a hot quince pie while standing in the moat and drinking from it to cool his tongue, and Will Sommers, capping Cardinal Woolsey's rhymes — he felt the quick flutter of his own Fool's ninny soul cross his fingertips.

He reached again, but then drew back quickly from that mock grin, the glissando that ran down the coxcomb bells in chilling welcome.

He pushed deeper into the documents. Account books of royal households, pamphlet Lives of fools, ha' penny street ballads and mock Last Wills & Testaments, extracts from court diaries, an actual letter to James I from his fool away in Spain with Philip II's court. Some of them were on microfilm, and he turned to this newfangled apparatus for momentary escape. He could leave his Fool behind, yet pursue him still, more at his ease, studying the little scrolls as they unrolled beneath the thumbing white light of the scanner. But he soon found this another mockery. The glare of the machine, blowing up the quaint Elizabethan printing into an illusory page pressed without substance against the cold, milky glass, was too much for his weak, old eyes, and somehow for his sense of reality. He could not stand the ghostliness of it. He felt he must be able to turn the actual page, crumble a chip out of its browned edge, smell its acrid, bookish dust, if he were ever going to find it. What was there to tear out here. He hated the skimping artifice that robbed him of the feel of a book, and imagined the scanner as some great Worm that had invested the castle of his learning. Like Spenser's Error, only too uncreatured a thing to spew forth black ink, or disgorge the books it had swallowed. Its only malice, a pale flush of cold light producing an incubus of a page. He knew how ridiculous he was being, possibly senile, and he drove himself to take meticulous notes, as usual. But he only breathed freely again in the staleness of his closed-up study, back within the pied ambiance of his Fool.

By then, he had all his facts. He was now thoroughly familiar with, something of an authority on, a good man in the field of. Oh, he understood his own qualifications all too well. It only remained for him to think things through to the entrapment, to perform the sacred rites of abstraction, and in a curious way, he sought to cleanse himself for them. He stripped away his last ragged pretenses to any venerability, all the shoddy of his professorial airs, and bared himself, in all but intellect, for a naked, failing old man.

It ended so many qualms. He could talk to himself freely. He mumbled and muttered as he pleased, and if his mouth grew wet, he wiped it on his sleeve without shame. When he caught the Fool imitating him in some palsied fumble, he hardly cared. Once he watched the Fool's great, dirty tongue loll almost to the floor before he sensed the coldness at his own cheek and brushed away a long, loose string of saliva. Unimportant. All that mattered was the careful tightening of his logic as it closed around the Fool.

"Decide whether natural or artificial," he thought or said or wrote down somewhere. "Could be a mute. Idiot boy sold by a rustic to some great house in exchange for a few acres grazing land free of enclosure. Such happens. But looks brighter than that. Silence too sly. Vacancy too coy. Hidden wits. I see him offering the egg. Like Will Sommers again, asking the King to let him give an egg to every cuckold in England, and permission granted, hands the first egg to Harry himself. What is he here to hand me? What's in his hand? What's in my hand? A page? A page?"

He glanced down at his hand, but there was only the back of it, covered with liver spots, and he realized that the ambuscade, so carefully laid up in his notes, had missed its elusive quarry yet again.

But he started once more, reciting a tale. "Will Sommers loudly broke wind, and glared at the lady by his side. Then he smiled at her and said for all to hear, 'Don't worry. I'll say it was me.' Clever fool. Rich fool. But this is a poor fool. Violent? Often they are insane. No attack yet. But if it comes...Bawdry? A scurrilous fool? Behind that dumb-show, what cess of mind, waiting to pour over me like a chamber pot? Gardyloo!" And then an old man's decrepit giggle, like beans rattling in a bladder, caught him off guard, sucked up from some grossness he'd suddenly remembered from his long study of folly. Again and again, he broke away from that giggle, forcing his way back to the needed date or reference that would repair the break where flatulence and scurrility had escaped from his thinking.

He even allowed himself little threats now. Never quite to the Fool's face, but, "Take heed," he would mumble, "the whip. The whip."

Then suddenly he felt the grip of it in his hand.

Carefully he let go, and gathered up his notecards to give his hands something else to do. He tried to reshuffle them for the hundredth time, but found that they were at last, by some fluke, in a correct order. Irrefutably that order imposed itself upon him. Sequential, exact, conclusive. This time, all his learning told him, there was no escape. Tapping each card nervously on his blotter, searching for error, he tried to think how many days it had been, how many stormy hours had hawked at his chill window to tumble this sudden, random knowledge upon him. He counted slowly — days, hours, cards — and imagined the Fool at his back, counting too, with great pulls at his gross fingers, unable, like himself, to arrive at any sensible number.

But he did not turn around. He saw that he could corner the Fool now with a mere glance, that he could positively identify him beyond any quibble to his colleagues, much more, that he could whip him, rip him out, do with him as he pleased. He had all that certainty, but once again it seemed to be forcing him to the verge of that same opulent unknown over which he had tottered so often, so perilously...

Only now, at the Fool's warning titter, he deliberately stared down into its black gulf. He referred back and back, as far as his mind would take him, and knowledge did not come to him so much as it physically seized him. The brush of the long ass's ears around his own cheeks. The plucking up of his whole spine into a rich, red comb, topped with bells. The whirligig of his coat plaids turning to lozenges. His grip on the whip thinning, loosening to a fragile, foolish hold upon the stick of a marotte. One foot jingled beneath him, and quite suddenly he could feel just where the whip was going to cut.

He did the one thing possible in the moment left before the black gulf itself turned over and sat upon his head for a cap. He jumped into it at last.

"Stay!" he shouted to the Fool. "Stay right here! Right by my side! Right here with me!"

Then he whirled around and doubled over in laughter, jeering widely at the suddenly defeated jangling thing in the chair.

"Right?" he whispered. "Right, right?"

The Fool's vacant stare was afire like a bone pit, but his marotte nodded its eternal grin.

IV

He was still laughing when the knock came at his door. Very cautiously he judged his surprise at it. No, it was no longer an interruption of his solitude. It was an intrusion upon their intimacy. The Fool shook both fists as if beating back at the door, letting loose a rage of bells.

"Who is it?" he asked, smiling at the angry Fool.

"Nelson, sir. Are you all right?"

He and the Fool shrugged at each other, both repressing laughter this time. He was still a little bit in awe of his own triumph, the confidence they had so suddenly found in each other. But then why, he wondered, had it taken so long to see what the Fool was there for?

"Sir?"

Young Nelson was anxious. He chortled to himself. The Fool immediately understood him and giggled into his two ass's ears which he had crossed gleefully over his mouth.

"I heard — well, laughing, sir. I just wondered if everything's all right. I thought I heard..." Nelson left off.

He hesitated because he wanted to savor this moment, the superb jest it had finally turned out to be. With this to top it off.

"No, I'm perfectly fine. Excellent fettle." He winked at the Fool. "Come in, if you've a moment."

The door eased open, just far enough for Nelson to squirm around it, braving everything with his shadow first. He nodded from it, smiling, while his eyes flicked nervously around the room. His stare scurried into every corner, and then he flushed, realizing he had absolutely no excuse.

"No, really. Sit down, sit down."

Nelson gratefully moved over to the chair and plumped down in it. The Fool bounced up just in time. He shook his bells angrily, and scowled. The old man chuckled good-naturedly. Nelson joined him in chuckling, out of deference.

"I'm really sorry, sir." He shifted once, twice in the chair. "Honestly, it sounded like you were in here laughing yourself silly."

"No, no. I was just — " How to put it, how to put it? "I've

just finished up my work on *Lear*, you see, and I was having a good laugh over it."

Nelson grew terribly puzzled, but only above the eyebrows. The Fool caught it, and took off this sedate puzzlement with a mock petite frown of his own. An irresistible bit of fleering. Again the old man chuckled, worrying Nelson into joining him again. The frown looked even more ridiculous over the polite chuckle.

"Oh, I must fill you in," he said. "It's just that this whole business with *Lear* has turned out to be, after all — well, a pretty big joke."

"I'm sorry about that," Nelson said elaborately. "Really very sorry."

He looked at the young instructor sharply. He'd caught something, just for a second. Nelson *was* sorry for him, of course. Flamboyantly sorry. Poor old codger. But there was something more, edging in, smacking distinctly of derringdo. He glanced at the Fool, who was leaning with both elbows on the back of Nelson's chair. The Fool poked two saucy fingers up for ears behind Nelson's head, and blew his lips flatulently.

"But I can see how it might come out that way," Nelson went on. "*Lear* is such a difficult play — and...*disappointing*, don't you think?"

Had he jumped? He felt sure the Fool had. But the skittishness was not so much in them, he sensed, as in Nelson. Was he about to skip and run for it on his own?

"Perhaps you've found — " Nelson paused at a near stutter and then hurdled, "what *I've* always found." The Fool stared, and then lifted himself on the chair back, kicking his bells together at the heels in muffled joy. "In the end, it really all comes to nothing, doesn't it? Dr. Johnson may have been right."

"Then you *have* been..."

He saw instantly that Nelson was going to misinterpret him. There would now be a painstaking mending of fences, he could tell, which would only delay the real point. Only the Fool had the patience for it. His greedy eyes puddled, and that same inane grin sank down once more into the vapid face like water crumbling sand.

"No, no," said Nelson, starting in on his fences. "I honestly haven't. I was leaving that all to you. I touch on the play, yes, but only with reference to some work I'm trying to do on the older play. *Leir.*" He leaned forward, and for an awful moment the old man thought that from the undermining of the grin, the Fool's face had at last caved in entirely and fallen upon Nelson's own. But then he saw it was only a great, watery leer. "But if you *are* giving up on your own work — I mean, if you're leaving the field free again — and that's the only way I'd want to have it, frankly — I think I might try to treat the two plays together."

"What *exactly* is it you're going to show?" Besides this abruptness, this, this...

"It'll be tough sledding, but I'm pretty clear now that *Leir* is infinitely the better play. At least, in my own mind. You see, sir..."

Then the flights and dips and swoops and long drifts of a young, excited mind swept over him. A swift, ignorant, sweet bird beating its new wings in the heart of an old storm. He listened as carefully as he could, and tried not to look at the Fool. He was afraid that if he did, he would not be able to account for his tears. Why was it so irretrievably sad? All that he heard was challenging and clever and zealous. But it depended upon so many certainties that weren't really there. The dimness, the vagueness, the lack of distinction that blurred every final thought, every last, best guess — he saw that the young man did not even feel their menace. Perhaps, on some midnight balance of his secret fears, Nelson allowed himself to know he might be wrong, but did he ever allow himself to know he might not even be that?

The old man's gaze drifted in mute appeal to the Fool. Then it simply drifted, caught up in the aimless wandering of the Fool's vacuous stare. Just in time, he saw his mistake. He looked quickly away before the Fool had a chance to throw his own lugubriousness back at him, and pulled himself together, alert to danger. He cursed his own stupidity. How very much, he realized bitterly, my very own.

He was losing his Fool.

"Nelson." He said it for once affectionately, as a first name, not a last. "How sure are you of all these things?" He meant the question to be only cautionary, but he could see it had gone hopelessly wrong. Nelson's face hardened a bit, and the gleeful Fool twirled the marotte over Nelson's head, badgering the old man for — what? — simply an old man, what more. He tried to think of a way to make his words less discouraging, less cantankerous. "I mean, it all sounds very wonderful, but is this to be a whole-hearted plunge into — " Into what? He knew the word he wanted to use, but also what irreparable damage it would do his little contact with the young man. And whose fault is it, he asked himself, the contact is so little? How very much, he thought bitterly again, my very own.

"A plunge into what, sir?"

A plunge into Folly. That's what he wanted to say. There was the Fool behind the chair, with as large a charter as the wind, to blow on whom he pleased. No man could hold him back. *Numerus stultorum est infinitus.*

"Let me put it this way, Nelson. I can't tell you how to do your work. Nobody can." He stopped helplessly. The Fool had turned and lifted one fat buttock at him, dropping the marotte down between his motley legs. The tiny head wig-wagged at him like a phallus with an obscene, upside-down grin. He forced himself ahead. "Do you have any idea what it's really like to work your way to the limits of something?" Limits? Limits of what? "I don't mean just setting out to settle a moot point. I mean plunging in so far that you can't — can never succeed — succeed in getting out again."

He pressed his hands together for steadiness. He saw the Fool imitate him, turning it into a silly prayerful gesture.

"You're alone. But accompanied. It's funny, but your companions are all there to help you feel alone. Because you don't, you mustn't admit they're there." He smiled. "That's the funny part about it. Once you admit — "

The Fool shook like a Sunday morning of church bells.

"Once you admit — " He looked hard at Nelson. There was nothing in his face but sufferance. Deferential sufferance. "Think of Lear on the heath, Nelson. Who are his companions? Who? The boundaries of his loneliness, really. Aren't they?"

He waited now. The burden was on the other.

"I'm pretty sure of my ground, I think, sir. Others have had the same idea bout *Leir*, I'm sure you're aware. Tolstoi, for instance, gave it my interpretation. What I should say is, I'm taking up *his*."

So the harlequinade will go on, he thought helplessly. He did not even look about for his Fool. He tried to keep his weak eyes fixed on a single, groomed tuft of Nelson's beard.

"I appreciate all your advice, and I'd like to come to you for some help, if that's all right with you. But for the moment. . ."

He didn't hear the rest. They said things near the door, but to him, it was an absolutely wordless parting. He could not be sure, but he thought that something scuttled hastily between his knees as he shut himself in.

He stepped over to his window. It was still snowing, as if forever. Across the flurry he could see Nelson trudging away. A shadow — only a shadow — scurried and scraped about him in the storm with grotesque, unhallowed gestures. With great pain, he admitted they were gestures of fondness. Finally he thought he saw it leap up on the man's back, like a loving thing, and that bowed his own head to the cold window pane.

He knew. Deserted now, even by his own measure of solitude, he knew what he would never know again. Any boundary to his own loneliness. He supposed, since he was still alive, that he must take this to be wisdom.

Robert Phillips
Middle Age:
A Nocturne

The silver tea service
assembles, stands at attention
when you walk by.
Like some lost regiment,
it wears tarnished coats.

The grand piano bares
yellowed teeth as you
give it the brush-off.
You no longer tickle its fancy.
The feeling is mutual.

The liquor cabinet chokes
on dusty bottles. You're forbidden.
In the wines sediment
settles like sentiment,
like expectations.

You visit your children's rooms.
In their sleep they breathe
heavily. In their waking
they bear new adulthood
easily. They don't need you.

In her dreams your wife sheds
responsibilities like cellulite,
acquires a new habit.
A gaunt nun of the old order,
she bends to a mystical flame.

All the pictures have been
looked at, all the books read.
Your former black mistress,
the telephone, hangs around;
there's no one you want to call.

      But early this morning,
      in the upper field:
      seven young deer
      grazing in the rain!

Randall Jarrell
A Quilt-Pattern

The blocked-out Tree
Of the boy's Life is gray
On the tangled quilt: the long day
Dies at last, after many tales.
Good me, bad me, the Other
Black out, and the humming stare
Of the woman — the good mother —
Drifts away; the boy falls
Through darkness, the leagues of space
Into the oldest tale of all.

All the graves of the forest
Are opened, the scaling face
Of a woman — the dead mother —
Is square in the steam of a yard
Where the cages are warmed all night for the rabbits,
All small furry things
That are hurt, but that never cry at all —
That are skinned, but that never die at all.
Good me, bad me
Dry their tears, and gather patiently
Through the loops of the chicken-wire of the cages
Blackberries, the small hairy things
They live on, here in the wood of the dream.

Here a thousand stones
Of the trail home shine from their strings
Like just-brushed, just-lost teeth.
All the birds of the forest
Sit brooding, stuffed with crumbs.
But at home, far, far away
The white moon shines from the stones of the chimney,
His white cat eats up his white pigeon.

But the house hums, "We are home." Good me, bad me
Sits wrapped in his coat of rabbit-skin
And looks for some little living thing
To be kind to, for then it will help him —
There is nothing to help; good me
Sits twitching the rabbit's-fur of his ears
And says to himself, "My mother is basting
Bad me in the bath-tub — "
                                    the steam rises,
A washcloth is turned like a mop in his mouth.
He stares into the mouth
Of the whole house: there in it is waiting —
No, there is nothing.

He breaks a finger
From the window and lifts it to his —
"Who is nibbling at me?" says the house.
The dream says, "The wind,
The heaven-born wind";
The boy says, "It is a mouse."
He sucks at the finger; and the house of bread
Calls to him in its slow singing voice:
"Feed, feed! Are you fat now?
Hold out your finger."
The boy holds out the bone of the finger.
It moves, but the house says, "No, you don't know.
Eat a little longer."

The taste of the house
Is the taste of his —
                    "I don't know,"
Thinks the boy. "No, I don't *know*!"

His whole dream swells with the steam of the oven
Till it whispers, "You are full now, mouse —
Look, I have warmed the oven, kneaded the dough:
Creep in — ah, ah, it is warm! —
Quick, we can slip the bread in now," says the house.
He whispers, "I do not know
How I am to do it."
                    "Goose, goose," cries the house,
"It is big enough — just look!
See, if I bend a little, so — "

He has moved. . . . He is still now, and holds his breath.
If something is screaming itself to death
There in the oven, it is not the mouse
Nor anything of the mouse's. Bad me, good me
Stare into each other's eyes, and timidly
Smile at each other: it was the Other.

But they are waking, waking; the last stair creaks —
Out there on the other side of the door
The house creaks, "How is my little mouse? Awake?"
It is she.
He says to himself, "I will never wake."
He says to himself, not breathing:
"Go away. Go away. Go away."

And the footsteps go away.

Ralph Waldo Emerson
Demonology

THE NAME DEMONOLOGY covers dreams, omens, coincidences, luck, sortilege, magic, and other experiences which shun rather than court inquiry, and deserve notice chiefly because every man has usually in a lifetime two or three hints in this kind which are specially impressive to him. They also shed light on our structure.

The witchcraft of sleep divides with truth the empire of our lives. This soft enchantress visits two children lying locked in each other's arms, and carries them asunder by wide spaces of land and sea, and wide intervals of time....

'Tis superfluous to think of the dreams of multitudes, the astonishment remains that one should dream; that we should resign so quietly this deifying Reason, and become the theatre of delirious shows, wherein time, space, persons, cities, animals, should dance before us in merry and mad confusion; a delicate creation outdoing the prime and

---

☞ Mr. Emerson's course of lectures, on *Human Life*, will commence on WEDNESDAY EVENING, 5th December, at 7 o'clock, at the Masonic Temple.

Tickets to the Course, or to the single Lecture, may be had at C. C. Little & James Brown's, No 112, and at James Munroe & Co's, 134, Washington Street.

flower of actual nature, antic comedy alternating with horrid pictures. Sometimes the forgotten companions of childhood reappear:

> They come, in dim procession led,
> The cold, the faithless, and the dead,
> As warm each hand, each brow as gay,
> As if they parted yesterday. [Sir Walter Scott]

Or we seem busied for hours and days in peregrinations over seas and lands, in earnest dialogues, strenuous actions for nothings and absurdities, cheated by spectral jokes and waking suddenly with ghastly laughter, to be rebuked by the cold, lonely, silent midnight, and to rake with confusion in memory among the gibbering nonsense to find the motive of this contemptible cachinnation. Dreams are jealous of being remembered; they dissipate instantly and angrily if you try to hold them. When newly awaked from lively dreams, we are so near them, still agitated by them, still in their sphere, — give us one syllable, one feature, one hint, and we should repossess the whole; hours of this strange entertainment would come trooping back to us; but we cannot get our hand on the first link or fibre, and the whole is lost. There is a strange wilfulness in the speed with which it disperses and baffles our grasp.

A dislocation seems to be the foremost trait of dreams. A painful imperfection almost always attends them. The fairest forms, the most noble and excellent persons, are deformed by some pitiful and insane circumstance. The very landscape and scenery in a dream seem not to fit us, but like a coat or cloak of some other person to overlap and encumber the wearer; so is the ground, the road, the house, in dreams, too long or too short, and if it served no other purpose would show us how accurately nature fits man awake.

There is one memory of waking and another of sleep. In our dreams the same scenes and fancies are many times associated, and that too, it would seem, for years. In sleep one shall travel certain roads in stage-coaches or gigs, which he recognizes as familiar, and has dreamed that ride a dozen times; or shall walk alone in familiar fields and meadows, which road or which meadow in waking hours he never looked upon. This feature of dreams deserves more attention from its singular resemblance to that obscure yet startling experience which almost every person confesses in daylight, that particular passages of conversation and action have occurred to him in the same order before, whether dreaming or waking; a suspicion that they have been with precisely these persons in precisely this room, and heard precisely this dialogue, at some former hour, they know not when.

Animals have been called "the dreams of nature." Perhaps for a conception of their consciousness we may go to our own dreams. In a dream we have the instinctive obedience, the same torpidity of the highest power, the same unsurprised assent to the monstrous as these metamorphosed men exhibit. Our thoughts in a stable or in a menagerie, on the other hand, may well remind us of our dreams. What compassion do these imprisoning forms awaken! You may catch the glance of a dog sometimes which lays a kind of claim to sympathy and brotherhood. What! somewhat of me down there? Does he know it? Can he too, as I, go out of himself, see himself, perceive relations? We fear lest the poor brute should gain one dreadful glimpse of his condition, should learn in some moment the tough limitations of this fettering organization. It was in this glance that Ovid got the hint of his metamorphoses; Calidasa of his transmigration of souls. For these fables are our own thoughts carried out. What keeps those wild tales in circulation for thousands of years? What but the wild fact to which they suggest some approximation of theory? Nor is the fact quite solitary, for in varieties of our own species where organization seems to predominate over the genius of man, in Kalmuck or Malay or Flathead Indian, we are sometimes pained by the same feeling; and sometimes too the sharp-witted prosperous white man awakens it. In a mixed assembly we have chanced to see not only a glance of Abdiel, so grand and keen, but also in other faces the features of the mink, of the bull, of the rat, and the barn-door fowl. You think, could the man overlook his own condition, he could not be restrained from suicide.

Dreams have a poetic integrity and truth. This limbo and dust-hole of thought is presided over by a certain reason, too. Their extravagance from nature is yet within a higher nature. They seem to us to suggest an abundance and fluency of thought not familiar to the waking experience. They pique us by independence of us, yet we know ourselves in this mad crowd, and owe to dreams a kind of divination and wisdom. My dreams are not me; they are not Nature, or the Not-me: they are both. They have a double consciousness, at once sub- and ob-jective. We call the phantoms that rise, the creation of our fancy, but they act like mutineers, and fire on their commander; showing that every act, every thought, every cause, is bi-polar, and in the act is contained the counteraction. If I strike, I am struck; if I chase, I am pursued.

Wise and sometimes terrible hints shall in them be thrown to the man out of a quite unknown intelligence. He shall be startled two or three times in his life by the justice as well as the significance of this phantasmagoria. Once or twice the conscious fetters shall seem to be unlocked, and a freer utterance attained. A prophetic character in all ages has haunted them. They are the maturation often of opinions not consciously carried out to statements, but whereof we already possessed the elements. Thus, when awake, I know the character of Rupert, but do not think what he may do. In dreams I see him engaged in certain actions which seem preposterous, — out of all fitness. He is hostile, he is cruel, he is frightful, he is a poltroon. It turns out prophecy a year later. But it was already in my mind as character, and the sibyl dreams merely embodied it in fact. Why then should not symptoms, auguries, forebodings be, and, as one said, the moanings of the spirit?

We are let by this experience into the high region of Cause, and acquainted with the identity of very unlike-seeming effects. We learn that actions whose turpitude is very differently reputed proceed from one and the same affection. Sleep takes off the costume of circumstance, arms us with terrible freedom, so that every will rushes to a deed. A skilful man reads his dreams for his self-knoweldge; yet not the details, but the quality. What part does he play in them, — a cheerful, manly part, or a poor drivelling part? However monstrous and grotesque their apparitions, they have a substantial truth. The same remark may be extended to the omens and coincidences which may have astonished us. Of all it is true that the reason of them is always latent in the individual. Goethe said: "These whimsical pictures, inasmuch as they originate from us, may well have an analogy with our whole life and fate."

The soul contains in itself the event that shall presently befall it, for the event is only the actualizing of its thoughts. It is no wonder that particular dreams and presentiments should fall out and be prophetic. The fallacy consists in selecting a few insignificant hints when all are inspired with the same sense. As if one should exhaust his astonishment at the economy of his thumb-nail, and overlook the central causal miracle of his being a man. Every man goes through the world attended with innumerable facts prefiguring (yes, distinctly announcing) his fate, if only eyes of sufficient heed and illumination were fastened on the sign. The sign is always there, if only the eye were also; just as under every tree in the speckled sunshine and shade no man notices that every spot of light is a perfect image of the sun, until in some hour the moon eclipses the luminary; and then first we notice that the spots of light have become crescents, or annular, and correspond to the changed figure of the sun. Things are significant enough, Heaven knows; but the seer of the sign, — where is he? We doubt not a man's fortune may be read in the lines of his hand, by palmistry; in the lines of his face, by physiognomy; in the outlines of the skull, by craniology: the lines are all there, but the reader waits.

• • • • •

It is not the tendency of our times to ascribe importance to whimsical pictures of sleep, or to omens. But the faith in peculiar and alien power takes another form in the modern mind, much more resembling the ancient doctrine of the guardian genius. The belief that particular individuals are attended by a good fortune which makes them desirable associates in any enterprise of uncertain success, exists not only among those who take part in political and military projects, but influences all joint action of commerce and affairs, and a corresponding assurance in the individuals so distinguished meets and justifies the expectation of others by a boundless self-trust. "I have a lucky hand, sir," said Napoleon to his heistating Chancellor; "those on whom I lay it are fit for anything." This faith is familiar in one form, — that often a certain abdication of prudence and foresight is an element of success; that children and young persons come off safe from casualties that would have proved dangerous to wiser people. We do not think the young will be forsaken; but he is fast approaching the age when the sub-miraculous external protection and leading are withdrawn and he is committed to his own care. The young man takes a leap in the dark and alights safe. As he comes into manhood he remembers passages and persons that seem, as he looks at them now, to have been supernaturally deprived of injurious influence on him. His eyes were holden that he could not see. But he learns that such risks he may no longer run. He observes, with pain, not that he incurs mishaps here and there, but that his genius, whose invisible benevolence was tower and shield to him, is no longer present and active.

In the popular belief, ghosts are a selecting tribe, avoiding millions, speaking to one. In our tradition, fairies, angels and saints show the like favoritism; so do the agents and the means of magic, as sorcerers and amulets. This faith in a doting power, so easily sliding into the current belief everywhere, and, in the particular of lucky days and fortunate persons, as frequent in America today as the faith in incantations and philters was in old Rome, or the wholesome potency of the sign of the cross in modern Rome, — this supposed power runs athwart the recognized agencies, natural and moral, which science and religion explore. Heeded though it may be in many actions and partnerships, it is not the power to which we build churches, or make liturgies and prayers, or which we regard in passing laws, or found college professorships to expound. Goethe has said in his Autobiography what is much to the purpose: —

I believed that I discovered in nature, animate and inanimate, intelligent and brute, somewhat which manifested itself only in contradiction, and therefore could not be grasped by a conception, much less by a word. It was not god-like, since it seemed unreasonable; not human, since it had no understanding; not devilish, since it was beneficent; not angelic, since it is often a marplot. It resembled chance, since it showed no sequel. It resembled Providence, since it pointed at connection. All which limits us seemed permeable to that. It seemed to deal at pleasure with the necessary elements of our constitution; it shortened time and extended space. Only in the impossible it seemed to delight, and the possible to repel with contempt. This, which seemed to insert itself between all other things, to sever them, to bind them, I named the Demoniacal, after the example of the ancients, and of those who had observed the like.

Although every demoniacal property can manifest itself in the corporeal and incorporeal, yes, in beasts too in a remarkable manner, yet it stands specially in wonderful relations with men, and forms in the moral world, though not an antagonist, yet a transverse element, so that the former may be called the warp, the latter the woof. For the phenomena which hence originate there are countless names, since all philosophies and religions have attempted in prose or in poetry to solve this riddle, and to settle the thing once for all, as indeed they may be allowed to do.

But this demonic element appears most fruitful when it shows itself as the determining characteristic in an individual. In the course of my life I have been able to observe several such, some near, some farther off. They are not always superior persons, either in mind or in talent. They seldom recommend themselves through goodness of heart. But a monstrous force goes out from them, and they

exert an incredible power over all creatures, and even over
the elements; who shall say how far such an influence may
extend? All united moral powers avail nothing against
them. In vain do the clear-headed part of mankind discredit
them as deceivers or deceived, — the mass is attracted.
Seldom or never do they meet their match among their con-
temporaries; they are not to be conquered save by the
universe itself, against which they have taken up arms. Out
of such experiences doubtless arose the strange, monstrous
proverb, 'Nobody against God but God.'

It would be easy in the political history of every time to furnish examples of this irregular success, men having a force
which without virtue, without shining talent, yet makes
them prevailing. No equal appears in the field against them.
A power goes out from them which draws all men and
events to favor them. The crimes they commit, the ex-
posures which follow, and which would ruin any other man,
are strangely overlooked, or do more strangely turn to their
account.

I set down these things as I find them, but however poetic
these twilights of thought, I like daylight, and I find
somewhat wilful, some play at blindman's buff, when men
as wise as Goethe talk mysteriously of the demonological.
The insinuation is that the known eternal laws of morals and
matter are sometimes corrupted or evaded by this gipsy
principle, which chooses favorites and works in the dark for
their behoof; as if the laws of the Father of the universe were
sometimes balked and eluded by a meddlesome Aunt of the
universe for her pets. You will observe that this extends the
popular idea of success to the very gods; that they foster a
success to you which is not a success to all; that fortunate
men, fortunate youths exist, whose good is not virtue or the
public good, but a private good, robbed from the rest. It is a
midsummer-madness, corrupting all who hold the tenet.
The demonologic is only a fine name for egotism; an exag-
geration namely of the individual, whom it is Nature's
settled purpose to postpone. "There is one world common
to all who are awake, but each sleeper betakes himself to one

of his own." [Heraclitus] Dreams retain the infirmities of our character. The good genius may be there or not, our evil genius is sure to stay. The Ego partial makes the dream; the Ego total the interpretation. Life is also a dream on the same terms.

• • • • •

Before we acquire great power we must acquire wisdom to use it well. Animal magnetism inspires the prudent and moral with a certain terror; so the divination of contingent events, and the alleged second-sight of the pseudo-spiritualists. There are many things of which a wise man might wish to be ignorant, and these are such. Shun them as you would the secrets of the undertaker and the butcher. The best are never demoniacal or magnetic; leave this limbo to the Prince of the power of the air. The lowest angel is better. It is the height of the animal; below the region of the divine. Power as such is not known to the angels.

Great men feel that they are so by sacrificing their selfishness and falling back on what is humane; in renouncing family, clan, country, and each exclusive and local connection, to beat with the pulse and breathe with the lungs of nations. A Highland chief, an Indian sachem or a feudal baron may fancy that the mountains and lakes were made specially for him Donald, or him Tecumseh; that the one question for history is the pedigree of his house, and future ages will be busy with his renown; that he has a guardian angel; that he is not in the roll of common men, but obeys a high family destiny; when he acts, unheard-of success evinces the presence of rare agents; what is to befall him, omens and coincidences foreshow; when he dies banshees will announce his fate to kinsmen in foreign parts. What more facile than to project this exuberant selfhood into the region where individuality is forever bounded by generic and cosmical laws? The deepest flattery, and that to which we can never be insensible, is the flattery of omens.

We may make great eyes if we like, and say of one on whom the sun shines, "What luck presides over him!" But we know that the law of the Universe is one for each and for all. There is as precise and as describable a reason for every fact occurring to him, as for any occurring to any man. Every fact in which the moral elements intermingle is not the less under the dominion of fatal law. Lord Bacon uncovers the magic when he says, "Manifest virtues procure reputation; occult ones, fortune." Thus the so-called fortunate man is one who, though not gifted to speak when the people listen, or to act with grace or with understanding to great ends, yet is one who, in actions of a low or common pitch, relies on his instincts, and simply does not act where he should not, but waits his time, and without effort acts when the need is. If to this you add a fitness to the society around him, you have the elements of fortune; so that in a particular circle and knot of affairs he is not so much his own man as the hand of nature and time. Just as his eye and hand work exactly together, — and to hit the mark with a stone he has only to fasten his eye firmly on the mark and his arm will swing true, — so the main ambition and genius being bestowed in one direction, the lesser spirits and involuntary aids within his sphere will follow. The fault of most men is that they are busybodies; do not wait the simple movement of the soul, but interefere and thwart the instructions of their own minds.

Coincidences, dreams, animal magnetism, omens, sacred lots, have great interest for some minds. They run into this twilight and say, "There's more than is dreamed of in your philosophy." Certainly these facts are interesting, and deserve to be considered. But they are entitled only to a share of attention, and not a large share. . . . Let their value as exclusive subjects of attention be judged of by the infallible test of the state of mind in which much notice of them leaves us. . . . They who love them say they are to reveal to us a world of unknown, unsuspected truths. But suppose a diligent collection and study of these occult facts were made, they are merely physiological, semi-medical, related to the machinery of man, opening to our curiosity how we live, and no aid on the superior problems why we live, and what we do. While the dilettanti have been prying into the humors and muscles of the eye, simple men will have helped themselves and the world by using their eyes.

• • • • •

Meantime far be from me the impatience which cannot brook the supernatural, the vast: far be from me the lust of explaining away all which appeals to the imagination, and the great presentiments which haunt us. Willingly I too say, Hail! to the unknown awful powers which transcend the ken of the understanding. And the attraction which this topic has had for me and which induces me to unfold its parts before you is precisely because I think the numberless forms in which this superstition has re-appeared in every time and every people indicates the inextinguishableness of wonder in man; betrays his conviction that behind all your explanations is a vast and potent and living Nature, inexhaustible and sublime, which you cannot explain. He is sure no book, no man has told him all. He is sure the great Instinct, the circumambient soul which flows into him as into all, and is his life, has not been searched. He is sure that intimate relations subsist between his character and his fortunes, between him and his world; and until he can adequately tell them he will tell them wildly and fabulously. Demonology is the shadow of Theology.

The whole world is an omen and a sign. Why look so wistfully in a corner? Man is the Image of God. Why run after a ghost or a dream? The voice of divination resounds everywhere and runs to waste unheard, unregarded, as the mountains echo with the bleatings of cattle.

Emily Dickinson
Two Poems

410

The first Day's Night had come —
And grateful that a thing
So terrible — had been endured —
I told my Soul to sing —

She said her Strings were snapt —
Her Bow — to Atoms blown —
And so to mend her — gave me work
Until another Morn —

And then — a Day as huge
As Yesterdays in pairs,
Unrolled its horror in my face —
Until it blocked my eyes —

My Brain — began to laugh —
I mumbled — like a fool —
And tho' 'tis Years ago — that Day —
My Brain keeps giggling — still.

And Something's odd — within —
That person that I was —
And this One — do not feel the same —
Could it be Madness — this?

419

We grow accustomed to the Dark —
When Light is put away —
As when the Neighbor holds the Lamp
To witness her Goodbye —

A Moment — We uncertain step
For newness of the night —
Then — fit our Vision to the Dark —
And meet the Road — erect —

And so of larger — Darknesses —
Those Evenings of the Brain —
When not a Moon disclose a sign —
Or Star — come out — within —

The Bravest — grope a little —
And sometimes hit a Tree
Directly in the Forehead —
But as they learn to see —

Either the Darkness alters —
Or something in the sight
Adjusts itself to Midnight —
And Life steps almost straight.

William Goyen
Bridge of Music, River of Sand

D O YOU REMEMBER the bridge that we crossed over the river to get to Riverside? And if you looked over yonder you saw the railroad trestle? High and narrow? Well that's what he jumped off of. Into a nothing river. "River!" I could laugh. I can spit more than runs in that dry bed. In some places it's just a little damp, but that's it. That's your grand and rolling river: a damp spot. That's your remains of the grand old Trinity. Where can so much water go? I at least wish they'd do something about it. But what can they do? What can anybody do? You can't replace a *river*.

Anyway, if there'd been water, maybe he'd have made it, the naked diver. As it was, diving into the river as though there were water in it, he went head first into moist sand and drove into it like an arrow into flesh and was found in a position of somebody on their knees, headless, bent over looking for something. Looking for where the river vanished to? I was driving across the old river bridge when I said to myself, wait a minute I believe I see something. I almost ran into the bridge railing. I felt a chill come over me.

What I did was when I got off the bridge to draw my car off to the side of the road and get out and run down the river bank around a rattlesnake that seemed to be placed there as a deterrent (the banks are crawling with them in July), and down; and what I came upon was a kind of avenue that the river had made and paved with gleaming white sand, wide and grand and empty. I crossed this ghostly thoroughfare of the river halfway, and when I got closer, my Lord Jesus God Almighty damn if I didn't see that it was half a naked human body in what would have been midstream were there water. I was scared to death. What ought I to do? Try to pull it out? I was scared to touch it. It was a heat-stunned afternoon. The July heat throbbed. The blue, steaming air waved like a veil. The feeling of something missing haunted me: it was the lost life of the river — something so powerful that it had haunted the countryside for miles around; you could feel it a long time before you came to it. In a landscape that was un-natural — flowing water was missing — everything else seemed unnatural. The river's vegetation was thin and starved-looking; it lived on the edge of sand instead of water; it seemed out of place.

If only I hadn't taken the old bridge. I was already open to a fine of five thousand dollars for driving across it, according to the sign, and I understood why. (Over yonder arched the shining new bridge. There was no traffic on it.) The flapping of loose boards and the quaking of the iron beams was terri-fying. I almost panicked in the middle when the whole construction swayed and made such a sound of crackling and clanking. I was surprised the feeble structure hadn't more than a sign to prohibit passage over it — it should have been barricaded. At any rate, it was when I was in the middle of this rocking vehicle that seemed like some mad carnival ride that I saw the naked figure diving from the old railroad trestle. It was as though the diver were making a flamboyant leap into the deep river below — until to my horror I realized that the river was dry. I dared not stop my car and so I maneuvered my way on, mechanical with terror, enchanted by the melodies that rose from the instruments of the melodious bridge that played like some orchestra of xylophones and drums and cellos as I moved over it. Who would have known that the dead bridge, condemned and closed away from human touch, had such music in it? I was on the other side now. Behind me the music was quieter now, lowering into something like chime sounds and harness sounds and wagons; it shook like bells and tolled like soft, deep gongs.

His hands must have cut through the wet sand, carving a path for his head and shoulders. He was sunk up to his mid-waist and had fallen to a kneeling position: a figure on its knees with its head buried in the sand, as if it had decided not to look at the world any more. And then the figure began to sink as if someone underground were pulling it under. Slowly the stomach, lean and hairy, vanished; then the loins, thighs. The river, which had swallowed half this body, now seemed to be eating the rest of it. For a while the feet lay, soles up, on the sand. And then they went down, arched like a dancer's.

Who was the man drowned in a dry river? eaten by a dry river? devoured by sand? How would I explain, describe what had happened? I'd be judged to be out of my senses. And why would I tell somebody — the police or — anybody? There was nothing to be done, the diver was gone, the naked leaper was swallowed up. Unless somebody had pushed him over the bridge and he'd assumed a diving posi-tion to try to save himself. But what evidence was there? Well, I *had* to report what I'd seen, what I'd witnessed. Witness? To what? Would anybody believe me? There was no evidence anywhere. Well, I'd look, I'd search for evidence. I'd go up on the railroad trestle.

I climbed up. The trestle was perilously narrow and high. I could see a long ways out over Texas, green and steaming in July. I could see the scar of the river, I could see the healed-looking patches that were the orphaned bottomlands. I could see the tornado-shaped funnel of bilious smoke that twisted out of the mill in Riverside, enriching the owner and poisoning him, his family and his neighbors. And I could see the old bridge which I'd just passed over and still trembling under my touch, arching perfect and precious, golden in the sunlight. The music I had wrought out of it was now stilled except, it seemed, for a low, deep hum that rose from it. It seemed impossible that a train could move on these narrow tracks now grown over with weeds. As I walked, grass-hoppers flared up in the dry heat.

I saw no footprints in the weeds, no sign of anybody hav-ing walked on the trestle — unless they walked on the rails or the ties. Where were the man's clothes? Unless he'd left them on the bank and run out naked onto the trestle. This meant searching on both sides of the trestle — Christ, what was I caught up in? It could also mean that he was a suicide, my mind went on dogging me; or insane; it could also mean that nobody else was involved. Or it could mean that I was suffering a kind of bridge madness, or the vision that sometimes comes from going home again, of going back to places haunted by deep feeling?

Had anyone ever told me the story of a man jumping into the river from the trestle? Could this be some tormented spirit doomed forever to re-enact his suicide? And if so, must he continue it, now that the river was gone? This thought struck me as rather pitiful.

How high the trestle was! It made me giddy to look down at the riverbed. I tried to find the spot where the diver had hit the dry river. There was absolutely no sign. The mouth of sand that had sucked him down before my very eyes had closed and sealed itself. The story was over, so far as I was concerned. Whatever had happened would be my secret. I had to give it up, let it go. You can understand that I had no choice, that that was the only thing I could do.

That was the summer I was making a sentimental trip through home regions, after fifteen years away. The bridge over the beloved old river had been one of my most touching memories — an object that hung in my memory of childhood like a precious ornament. It was a fragile creation, of iron and wood, and so poetically arched, so slender, half a bracelet (the other half underground) through which the green river ran. The superstructure was made more for a minaret than a bridge. From a distance it looked like an ornate pier, in Brighton or early Santa Monica; or, in the summer heat haze, a palace tower, a creation of gold. Closer, of course, it was an iron and wooden bridge of unusual beauty, shape and design. It had always been an imperfect bridge, awry from the start. It had been built wrong — an engineering mistake: the ascent was too steep and the descent too sharp. But its beauty endured. And despite its irregularity, traffic had used the bridge at Riverside, without serious mishap, for many years. It was just an uncomfortable trip, and always somewhat disturbing, this awkward, surprising and somehow mysterious crossing.

Some real things happened on this practical, if magical, device for crossing water. For one thing, since it swayed, my mother, in our childhood days, would refuse to ride across it. She would remove herself from the auto and walk across, holding onto the railing, while my father, cursing, drove the rest of us across. My sister and I peered back at the small figure of our mother laboring darkly and utterly alone on the infernal contraption which was her torment. I remember my father getting out of the car, on the other side, waiting at the side of the road, looking toward the bridge, watching my mother's creeping progress. When she arrived, pale, she declared, as she did each time, "I vow to the Lord if my sister Sarah didn't live in Riverside I'd never to my soul come near this place." "Well you could lie down in the back seat, put the cotton in your ears that you always bring, and never know it, as I keep telling you," said my father. "I'd still know it," my mother came back. "I'd still know we was on this infernal bridge." "Well then take the goddamn train from Palestine. Train trestle's flat." And, getting in the car and slamming the door, "Or stay home and just *write* to your damned sister Sarah. Married to a horse's ass, anyway."

"Mama," said my sister, trying to pacify the situation. "Tell us about the time you almost drowned in the river and Daddy had to jump in and pull you out."

"Well, it was just right over yonder. We'd been fishing all morning, and . . ."

"Aw for Christ's sake," my father said.

On the other side of the bridge, after a crossing of hazards and challenges, there was nothing more than a plain little town of mud streets and weather-faded shacks. The town of poor people lived around an ugly mill that puffed out like talcum something called Fuller's Earth over it. This substance lay on rooftops, on the ground and in lungs. It smelled sour and bit the eyes.

As I drove away toward that town, haunted by the vision of the leaping man and now so shaken in my very spirit, lost to fact but brought to some odd truth which I could not yet clear for myself, I saw in the mirror the still image of the river bridge that had such hidden music in it, girdling the ghost of what it had been created for, that lost river that held in its bosom of sand the diving figure of the trestle that I was sure I had seen. I was coming into Riverside and already the stinging fumes of the mill brought tears to my eyes.

Maxine Kumin
Insomnia

—To hear the owl is the poet's prerogative.

In the hand-me-down of dead hours
I hear him moving up the mountain
tree by tree insistent as
a paranoid calling out his one verse
raising the break-bone alarm like
those quaint East European churches
that tolled their non-Sunday bells
to usher in the pogrom.

Finally he settles in my basswood.
We both doze listening for each other.
Going out to help my horse up
in the first light I see him
hurry into the haymow
furtive as an old boarder
flapping along the corridor
to tell his secret to the toilet.

O red eye! Sit tight
up in the rafters.
Hang on
safe as a puffball.
Tonight
another chapter —
the promise of hatchets.

A Hundred Nights

Dark came first and settled in
the pin oak rubbing on my screen.
Ten lightning bugs sealed in a milk
jar on my bureau winked and sulked.
I washed into a dream of a hunchback
chasing me with an empty mail sack

until the terrible mouse with wings
notched like bread knives came skittering
down the chimney next to my bed;
rudderless, raving, flapped and shied
against the ceiling, bedclothes, table.
I screamed as soon as I was able.

Father in a union suit
came a hundred sultry nights,
came like an avenging ghost.
He waved a carpetbeater, trussed
with scrolls of hearts and cupid wings,
a racket with rococo strings.

Two uncles one floor up ran down
a hundred nights to cheer and groan
as Father swore and chipped the plaster,
a game he never cared to master.
My father had his principles.
He smacked to stun them, not to kill.

Frozen underneath the sheets,
I heard the bats mew when he hit.
I heard them drop like squashing fruit.
I heard him test them with his foot.
I knew when he unlatched the screen
and sent them skimming by one wing.

The fall revived them, so he said.
I cried. I wished that they were dead.
I begged him stuff the chimney stack.
I pinched my lips to stay awake
to keep those flapping rats outside,
sang to myself, told riddles, prayed.

I memorized those crepey nights
with dying fireflies for lights:
the heave of wings come down horn-mad
to thump and thwack against the shade.
No matter that my parents said
it only happened twice that way

and all the rest are in my head.
Once, before my father died,
I meant to ask him why he chose
to loose those furies at my bed.

Mary Oliver
Last Days

Things are
  changing; things are starting to
    spin, snap, fly off into
      the blue sleeve of the long
        afternoon. *Oh* and *ooh*
come whistling out of the perished mouth
  of the grass, as things
turn soft, boil back
  into substance and hue. As everything,
    forgetting its own enchantment, whispers:
      I too love oblivion why not it is full
        of second chances. *Now,*
hiss the bright curls of the leaves. *Now!*
  booms the muscle of the wind.

Bats

In the blue air
the bats float
touching no leaf.

Science
has shown how they capture
their prey —

moths, mosquitoes — in
the middle of flight
in the fold of a wing,

and how they hang
by the millions,
socially, in caves.

But in the night
still comes
the unexplained figure

slipping in and out
of bedrooms, in and out
the soft throats of women.

For science is only
the golden boat
on the dark river

of blood, where women dream
such fur on the cheeks, such teeth
behind the kiss.

The Night Traveler

Passing by, he could be anybody:
A thief, a tradesman, a doctor
On his way to a worried house.
But when he stops at your gate,
Under the room where you lie half-asleep,
You know it is not just anyone —
It is the Night Traveler.

You lean your arms on the sill
And stare down. But all you can see
Are bits of wilderness attached to him —
Twigs, loam and leaves,
Vines and blossoms. Among these
You feel his eyes, and his hands
Lifting something in the air.

He has a gift for you, but it has no name.
It is windy and woolly.
He holds it in the moonlight, and it sings
Like a newborn beast,
Like a child at Christmas,
Like your own heart as it tumbles
In love's green bed.
You take it, and he is gone.

All night — and all your life, if you are willing —
It will nuzzle your face, cold-nosed,
Like a small white wolf;
It will curl in your palm
Like a hard blue stone;
It will liquefy into a cold pool
Which, when you dive into it,
Will hold you like a mossy jaw.
A bath of light. An answer.

Ned Rorem
Being Alone

THE CLICHÉ THAT CLICHÉS ARE CLICHÉ only because their truth is self-evident would seem self-evident. Yet from birth we're taught that things are not as simple as they seem. The wise man's work is to undo complications: things *are* simple, truth blazes ("brightness falls from the air"), and the obvious way to prevent wars is not to fight. Thus, when I proclaim that I am never less alone than when I'm by myself, and am met with a glazed stare, the stare is from one who abhors a vacuum — the look of nature. But I'm complicating matters.

Comfortable rainy darkness has for days fit over the city like a mammoth tea cozy or winding sheet so that the lights of spring gleam unperceived. Earlier this evening, on my way to dine at mother and father's, I stopped into Julius's Bar, as very occasionally I do, for a mug of soda. Standing there among the stricken I gape through the window at the drizzling golden streetlamps, and at the women over there in Djuna's Bookshop thumbing magazines. The bistro itself is unchanged from when we drank here, merry and bloody and hot, thirty summers ago: same careful dust, same wobbly stools, same hearty smell of ale and hamburger, same drowsy jukebox emitting heart-piercing sevenths. Except tonight I am dead sober, there are no "possibilities," I know nobody and nobody knows me, and, like a Jean Rhys heroine, I feel lonely in a not unpleasant way. The seagreen reflections from the mirror in my soda seem somehow sadder than any Irish keening. But at least there are no carnal emanations, so after ten minutes I flee.

With pleasure am reading *Walden* finally after three decades of urging from mother. Less disturbed than amused by a fallacy which jumps from every page, like McLuhan writing that writing is obsolete. If all is vanity, and the amassing of worldly goods and the longing for great place and posterity are demeaning, so too is the need to document one's vanity. Art's the biggest vanity: the assumption that one's view of peace or fright or beauty is permanently communicable. I keep a diary about the uselessness of keeping a diary, but the desire is strong and I am vain. Nor am I counter vanity. And the old man for whom nothing counted but *les merveilleux nuages* is recalled only because Baudelaire solidified him.

Sunlight rushes through the house like wind. Yellow brooks defy gravity flowing up the stairs and over the ceiling. Rooms glimmer with optimism. What joy to get out of bed on such mornings. Yet by mid-afternoon the pall's begun, and when night falls now by five o'clock the stultifying loneliness has retaken hold. Little reason to go on. The reason for the lack of reason is no longer on my list.

Walk careless and lively over the room through sunlight — blood of the day — soaking profligate into rugs. Then dissolve in wonderment that this too ends in death. Sly Death, coming on little cat feet, fooling all of the people all of the time, arranging for man — Earth's one rational beast — irrationally to persist in hoping for a life after You. On the other hand, if the world after ten milleniums finally concedes to equality of the sexes then anything is possible, even life after death.

If, as is now suspected, trillions of lifeless galaxies will be forever turning up, why does this leave us feeling lonely, we who despise our neighbors? Astronomer Bernard Lovell declares chillingly (warningly?) that Earthlings are unique, the expansion rate of the cosmos having had to be just so, right after that Big Bang. "If the rate had been less by an almost insignificant amount in the first second, then the universe would have collapsed long before any biological evolution could have taken place. Conversely, if the rate had been marginally greater, then the expansion would have reached such magnitudes that no gravitationally bound systems (that is, galaxies and stars) could have formed." There appears also to be, beyond "us," super-universes and an ever vaster chain of Big Bangs eternally.

Now, if there is no consciousness outside ourselves, no witness of these stellar procedures, then (except to us) does the universe exist? or did we literally invent it all, including the facts of life? JH: the theory of Does-a-falling-tree-make-a-noise-if-nobody's-there-to-hear-it is puzzling only because of hazy terms. If sound means displacement of air then of course the tree makes a noise, but if sound is what's received through the aural sense then of course the tree makes no noise.

Suppose the universe as it is, but that for some reason we are all asleep — unconscious. Does the universe then exist?

Although the dentist appointment was for two, at 1:30 I was still garbed in only a towel when the doorbell rang, and suddenly Sergeant David Durk, who lives downstairs, stood before me. Did I know anyone who might (he wanted to know) take over his lease, since he and his family are moving away forever? I explained that I had to dress for the dentist at two, but would think about it. Yet he lingered. Was it that he was too filled with his fame to spot the incongruity of a naked composer and a holstered cop in stalemated converse about real estate? Two cultured adults who speak good English but with nothing in common. It's not that Babel was polyglot but that values were dispersed. People of different tongues and classes can be in close accord, while peers feud.

Rushing to the bathroom I grabbed the first book that came to hand, which turned out to be *The Age of Innocence*. There I read again those masterful (hmmm. . .mistressful isn't quite the word either) last paragraphs where Archer withdraws from a longed-for reunion ''lest that last shadow of reality should lose its edge'' — remembering when I'd first read them a quarter-century ago. It would have been an autumn afternoon (like today in Nantucket, warm and russet) on a café terrace, Rue Galilée, and I closed the book, moved, and filled with a Paris evoked by Wharton some thirty years earlier, fictional even then, and so real.

We have the choice, the passing choice, of returning and ruining, or of refraining and keeping. If we keep too long the living person in our heart (imagining that person in a firelit room across the ocean), that person will die. Which is the case with my Paris now. I can go back and rekindle in that same cafe the rekindling that fired me twenty-five years ago as I evoked Archer rekindling his past. But I cannot close the book — that physically same book — and rise to keep my date with Marie Laure (who was tolerant of lateness only when the need of a book retained her date), because Marie Laure lies underground. Yet, maybe fortunately, for me the power of places has always been stronger than the power of persons.

The older I get the aloner I feel. (But one can grow only so old.) The solitude, classically divorced from company or place, is hinged to a knowledge, recognized even by children, that we rise to heaven unaided. *Car le joli printemps / C'est le temps d'une aiguille,* sang Fombeure through Poulenc's lips. Our springtime's but a point, a needle point, in time, but rich and poor can pass with equal ease, though forever single file, through the needle's eye. (I never knew whether that needle's eye was the same as Gide's *Porte étroite* — the ''straight gate'' to paradise? — mentioned by Saint Matthew.) Those hundreds who perished ''simultaneously''at Guyana really died, as the clock ticks, separately.

Long weekend in Philadelphia to supervise the concert of my music at Curtis in whose hallowed halls I'd not set foot for 144 seasons.

Tea chez Henry McIlleny with Stephen Spender.We talk of Saul Bellow. I mention that Bellow is, well, a bit too heterosexual for me, if you know what I mean. Spender answers: "Yes, Bellow does treat women horribly, doesn't he!" then goes on to equate male homosexuality with the feminine side of man's nature. Stephen being Stephen, this is surely not stupidity so much as academic hypocrisy.

Yet you *can* turn back the clock and recall cleanly as a photo each minute of a finite past. How *deja vu* like old movies our hours are numbered even as we enjoy them heedlessly. To relive a great love — *quelle horreur.* Only the smoky smell of erstwhile roses makes a useful difference.

And you *can* go home again. Write of PQ's visit wherein the dread gave way to sympathy, though the fact that friendship can withstand decades of separation, while cheering, limns the notion of death more sharply than if there were no returns. Is a reunion really a return?

Twenty years last summer since PQ approached along Cannes' Croisette and asked *Vous etes en vacances?* Thirteen years since last we met, in Marseilles. And now, better (not worse) than my memory, he's come at fifty-one for his first excursion (professional, for ecology in Saint Louis) to an America which had never appealed to him as an idea. I see the city through his eyes, and oh, our natives are plain. The golden youth from the U.S.A., for whom the Frenchman, licking his chops, lay in ambush during every holiday of the early post-war years, has vanished. Search amid the millions, day after sodden day, in the subway or Sardi's, for one beguiling face, and search in vain. Why? PQ says it's urban living. (In his Marseilles apparently beauty still reigns, as here, emptyheaded, in California). JH says it's the achiever complex indigenous to Manhattan. Or is it from that lack of physical narcism that comes from money? Unlike Romans, Americans don't need to be beautiful.

Americans, wrote Tennessee Williams in 1949, suffer from "a misconception of what it means to be...any kind of creative artist. They feel it is something to adopt *in the place of* actual living." Could not the reverse be posited? The act of making art *is* the artist's actual living, and the hum-drum needs of life are a by-product of that art. The best artists, by and large, lead what outsiders would find dull lives; those whose "actual living" is overly gaudy just haven't the time for art, even when such living forms the art's very material.

Reperusing with distaste the transcribed conversation taped years ago for the Dance Collection of the Library of Performing Arts. What disparity in meaning between the spoken and the written word! Transcriptions of this sort in their "spontaneity" are less true than the "artifice" of the pen. All that I utter, in an urge to be clever and valid, turns thin and dull, except for one phrase about the aloneness of Martha Graham. Greatness has no playmates. Creative artists are no more lonely than real people, but to get work done they obviously need to be alone more than salesmen or bankers. Even love is expensive for an artist: the time love takes is thrilling, but not instructive — not even for writing about love. Greatness has no playmates, that is true. Alas, it's also true that the dispenser of tenth-rate art must dispense with playmates.

Martha is the only giant I can think of who has never been denied by her successors. She has authored perhaps 150 ballets, most of them with original scores. Yet with one or two exceptions she has caused no topnotch music to exist. Neither, except for Vivian Fine on one occasion, has Martha used music by women. Nor have I noticed that women composers among themselves are magnanimous. They are more anxious to be taken seriously by men than by their sisters.

Insomnia, colored not by private anxieties but cluttered by passing concerns. TV dominates. Julia Child mixed with Guyana horrors churning with oil prices climbing. Cut to Melville's *Pierre,* uncomfortably verbose. Back to the screen. Anxious to hear (see) Tashi play Takemitsu's new *Quatrain* on WNET but not wanting to miss Stockard Channing on "Rock Hour" scheduled simultaneously, I switch from channel to channel. "Rock Hour" is *no less good* than the Takemitsu which is merely six sound-effects in search of a coherer. Insomnia.

Ruth Kligman, ever avid for the full life, exclaims: "I've found the most divine pill. It puts you to sleep for only fifteen minutes, and you wake up thoroughly refreshed so that you can *live* and be *conscious* and *savor experiences* and...."

Jane Frielicher: "I have trouble just staying awake for fifteen minutes."

We who are to be destroyed are first made sane by our Lord.

Did I still keep a diary 'twould not serve to reveal secret sex and cake recipes. The disease and dying of dear friends ever more preoccupies us all, and wonder at the cheerlessness we come to.

Is my entire *oeuvre* an *oeuvre*? In that case I do not repeat myself, since each piece is part of a continuing whole. (And although such stuff as dreams are made on generally turns out to be sheer twaddle in the morning, my sleeping hours, unlike Ruth Kligman's, feel no less urgent than the waking.)

Tonight while reworking a choral version of Hardy's "The Oxen" composed twenty-four years ago (around the time I was reading Wharton), I feel for the thousandth time how time freezes during focus on the act. Musically the inspirational shove seems identical: I may have more or less energy (more technique, less facility), but the expressive line's the same, and also the special piquant secundal harmonic clots that make me wince nicely while imagining that I and only I have ever thought up such combinations. But further still, in this icy today on America's seventieth street, I find my very body resurrounded by those vases of vastly odoriferous tuberoses which graced the Noailles salon where once I labored on that evening of June 21st, 1954. It is enough to pore over the metro map of Paris to be transported there, back through the ether and years, smells above all. That is one way to learn a city, through odors, as through cruising parks and pissotières, the hardboiled egg stench, the rotten seaweed stench, the dimple on the ruddy chin of that policeman, the etc. Why must we move through time, since time, whatever it is, says the same thing perpetually?

Occasionally a stranger in the mail attests to how much my music has meant to him. Why does this trouble me? Why am I made anxious and not elated at seeing my books in a store, name in a program? (Vicious letters or negative reviews are no more terrible than pleasant ones.) Because the damage is done, the work is removed and leading its own life, influencing (or not) the unknown quantities while the maker could be dead, left with my own vile body.

People are always asking, "How do you remember all that stuff? Me, I forget things as soon as they happen." But why live if that which occurs makes no impression, can't be used, even the endless boredom? Why live if only to forget having lived? This said, my notorious total recall is abetted by date books and diaries, and by recalling the months, and divisions thereof, of returns to America, of an affair with a certain person, of the impulse for a certain piece. To live is to improvise variations on our own theme, yet those improvisations are not random but (unbeknownst to us at the moment) formal and collective. How does one manage *not* to have total recall? of this unique rhubarb tart, that red hot torso, these November leaves, all the wars, those dying friends?
   Other people are always saying, "How can you live in the past?" But the present *is* the past (as Marcel was hardly the first to show), and the older we grow the more past we have. Our shriveling future may be all that we make of it, but so is our past which changes perspective with each new dawn. Life is awfully nice, yes, and keeps getting nicer, but never nice enough, surely not enough to have been born for. And is life short? To die at seventy-five will mean that eight thousand nights stretch on ahead. How to fill them? By using them through what's been learned so far? Now, on the contrary, could it be that the past grows smaller, like a blood-

flavored popsicle on which we gnaw self-cannibalistically, and when it's melted utterly, we...? Owls and tigers commence their flights and prowls at dusk, and thus might symbolize Death were it not that they too, God's creatures, prey upon their own pasts, their shrinking pasts. Endless, the future? Certainly not, since by definition the future does not exist.

Thomas Dekker
On Sleep

Do BUT CONSIDER what an excellent thing sleep is: it is so inestimable a jewel that, if a tyrant would give his crown for an hour's slumber, it cannot be bought: of so beautiful a shape is it, that though a man lie with an Empress, his heart cannot beat quiet till he leaves her embracements to be at rest with the other: yea, so greatly indebted are we to this kinsman of death, that we owe the better tributary, half our life to him: and there is good cause why we should do so: for sleep is the golden chain that ties health and our bodies together. Who complains of want? of wounds? of cares? of great men's oppressions? of captivity? whilst he sleepeth? Beggars in their beds take as much pleasure as kings: can we therefore surfeit of this delicate ambrosia?

Walt Whitman
The Sleepers

I WANDER all night in my vision,
Stepping with light feet, swiftly and noiselessly stepping
    and stopping,
Bending with open eyes over the shut eyes of sleepers,
Wandering and confused, lost to myself, ill-assorted,
    contradictory,
Pausing, gazing, bending, and stopping.

How solemn they look there, stretch'd and still,
How quiet they breathe, the little children in their cradles.

The wretched features of ennuyés, the white features of
    corpses, the livid faces of drunkards, the sick-gray
    faces of onanists,
The gash'd bodies on battle-fields, the insane in their
    strong-door'd rooms, the sacred idiots, the
    new-born emerging from gates, and the dying
    emerging from gates,
The night pervades them and infolds them.

The married couple sleep calmly in their bed, he with his
    palm on the hip of the wife, and she with her palm on
    the hip of the husband,

The sisters sleep lovingly side by side in their bed,
The men sleep lovingly side by side in theirs,
And the mother sleeps with her little child carefully wrapt.

The blind sleep, and the deaf and dumb sleep,
The prisoner sleeps well in the prison, the runaway son
    sleeps,
The murderer that is to be hung next day, how does he
    sleep?
And the murder'd person, how does he sleep?

The female that loves unrequited sleeps,
And the male that loves unrequited sleeps,
The head of the money-maker that plotted all day sleeps,
And the enraged and treacherous dispositions, all,
    all sleep.

I stand in the dark with drooping eyes by the worst-
    suffering and the most restless,
I pass my hands soothingly to and fro a few inches
    from them,
The restless sink in their beds, they fitfully sleep.

Now I pierce the darkness, new beings appear,
The earth recedes from me into the night,
I saw that it was beautiful, and I see that what is not the
    earth is beautiful.

I go from bedside to bedside, I sleep close with the other
    sleepers each in turn,
I dream in my dream all the dreams of the other dreamers,
And I become the other dreamers.

I am a dance — play up there! the fit is whirling me fast!

I am the ever-laughing — it is new moon and twilight,

I see the hiding of douceurs, I see nimble ghosts which-
	ever way I look,
Cache and cache again deep in the ground and sea, and
	where it is neither ground nor sea.

Well do they do their jobs those journeymen divine,
Only from me can they hide nothing, and would not if
	they could,
I reckon I am their boss and they make me a pet besides,
And surround me and lead me and run ahead when
	I walk,
To lift their cunning covers to signify me with stretch'd
	arms, and resume the way;
Onward we move, a gay gang of blackguards! with mirth-
	shouting music and wild-flapping pennants of joy!

I am the actor, the actress, the voter, the politician,
The emigrant and the exile, the criminal that stood in the
	box,
He who has been famous and he who shall be famous
	after to-day,
The stammerer, the well-form'd person, the wasted or
	feeble person.

I am she who adorn'd herself and folded her hair
	expectantly,
My truant lover has come, and it is dark.

Double yourself and receive me darkness,
Receive me and my lover too, he will not let me go
	without him.

I roll myself upon you as upon a bed, I resign myself to
	the dusk.

He whom I call answers me and takes the place of
	my lover,

He rises with me silently from the bed.

Darkness, you are gentler than my lover, his flesh was
    sweaty and panting,
I feel the hot moisture yet that he left me.

My hands are spread forth, I pass them in all directions,
I would sound up the shadowy shore to which you are
    journeying.

Be careful darkness! already what was it touch'd me?
I thought my lover had gone, else darkness and he are
    one,
I hear the heart-beat, I follow, I fade away.

2

I descend my western course, my sinews are flaccid,
Perfume and youth course through me and I am their
    wake.

It is my face yellow and wrinkled instead of the old
    woman's,
I sit low in a straw-bottom chair and carefully darn my
    grandson's stockings.

It is I too, the sleepless widow looking out on the
    winter midnight,
I see the sparkles of starshine on the icy and pallid earth.

A shroud I see and I am the shroud, I wrap a body and lie
    in the coffin,
It is dark here under ground, it is not evil or pain here, it
    is blank here, for reasons.

(It seems to me that every thing in the light and air ought
    to be happy,

Whoever is not in his coffin and the dark grave let him
    know he has enough.)

3

I see a beautiful gigantic swimmer swimming naked
    through the eddies of the sea,
His brown hair lies close and even to his head, he strikes
    out with courageous arms, he urges himself with his
    legs,
I see his white body, I see his undaunted eyes,
I hate the swift-running eddies that would dash him head-
    foremost on the rocks.

What are you doing you ruffianly red-trickled waves?
Will you kill the courageous giant? will you kill him in the
    prime of his middle age?

Steady and long he struggles,
He is baffled, bang'd, bruis'd, he holds out while his
    strength holds out,
The slapping eddies are spotted with his blood, they bear
    him away, they roll him, swing him, turn him,
His beautiful body is borne in the circling eddies, it is con-
    tinually bruis'd on rocks,
Swiftly and out of sight is borne the brave corpse.

4

I turn but do not extricate myself,
Confused, a past-reading, another, but with darkness yet.

The beach is cut by the razory ice-wind, the wreck-guns
    sound,
The tempest lulls, the moon comes floundering through
    the drifts.

I look where the ship helplessly heads end on, I hear the
  burst as she strikes, I hear the howls of dismay, they
  grow fainter and fainter.

I cannot aid with my wringing fingers,
I can but rush to the surf and let it drench me and freeze
  upon me.

I search with the crowd, not one of the company is
  wash'd to us alive,
In the morning I help pick up the dead and lay them in
  rows in a barn.

5

Now of the older war-days, the defeat at Brooklyn,
Washington stands inside the lines, he stands on the
  intrench'd hills amid a crowd of officers,
His face is cold and damp, he cannot repress the weeping
  drops,
He lifts the glass perpetually to his eyes, the color is
  blanch'd from his cheeks,
He sees the slaughter of the southern braves confided to
  him by their parents.

The same at last and at last when peace is declared,
He stands in the room of the old tavern, the well-belov'd
  soldiers all pass through,
The officers speechless and slow draw near in their turns,
The chief encircles their necks with his arm and kisses
  them on the cheek,
He kisses lightly the wet cheeks one after another, he
  shakes hands and bids good-by to the army.

6

Now what my mother told me one day as we sat at dinner
  together,

Of when she was a nearly grown girl living home with her
    parents on the old homestead.

A red squaw came one breakfast-time to the old
    homestead,
On her back she carried a bundle of rushes for rush-
    bottoming chairs,
Her hair, straight, shiny, coarse, black, profuse, half-
    envelop'd her face,
Her step was free and elastic, and her voice sounded
    exquisitely as she spoke.

My mother look'd in delight and amazement at the
    stranger,
She look'd at the freshness of her tall-borne face and full
    and pliant limbs,
The more she look'd upon her she loved her,
Never before had she seen such wonderful beauty and
    purity,
She made her sit on a bench by the jamb of the fireplace,
    she cook'd food for her,
She had no work to give her, but she gave her remem-
    brance and fondness.

The red squaw staid all the forenoon, and toward the
    middle of the afternoon she went away,
O my mother was loth to have her go away,
All the week she thought of her, she watch'd for her many
    a month,
She remember'd her many a winter and many a summer,
But the red squaw never came nor was heard of there
    again.

7

A show of the summer softness — a contact of something
    unseen — an amour of the light and air,

I am jealous and overwhelm'd with friendliness,
And will go gallivant with the light and air myself.

O love and summer, you are in the dreams and in me,
Autumn and winter are in the dreams, the farmer goes
    with his thrift,
The droves and crops increase, the barns are well-fill'd.

Elements merge in the night, ships make tacks in the
    dreams,
The sailor sails, the exile returns home,
The fugitive returns unharm'd, the immigrant is back
    beyond months and years,
The poor Irishman lives in the simple house of his child-
    hood with the well-known neighbors and faces,
They warmly welcome him, he is barefoot again, he
    forgets he is well off,
The Dutchman voyages home, and the Scotchman and
    Welshman voyage home, and the native of the Medi-
    terranean voyages home,
To every port of England, France, Spain, enter well-fill'd
    ships,
The Swiss foots it toward his hills, the Prussian goes his
    way, the Hungarian his way, and the Pole his way,
The Swede returns, and the Dane and Norwegian return.

The homeward bound and the outward bound,
The beautiful lost swimmer, the ennuyé, the onanist, the
    female that loves unrequited, the money-maker,
The actor and actress, those through with their parts and
    those waiting to commence,
The affectionate boy, the husband and wife, the voter, the
    nominee that is chosen and the nominee that has
    fail'd,
The great already known and the great any time after
    to-day,

The stammerer, the sick, the perfect-form'd, the homely,
The criminal that stood in the box, the judge that sat and
    sentenced him, the fluent lawyers, the jury, the
    audience,
The laugher and weeper, the dancer, the midnight widow,
    the red squaw,
The consumptive, the erysipalite, the idiot, he that is
    wrong'd,
The antipodes, and every one between this and them in
    the dark,
I swear they are averaged now — one is no better than the
    other,
The night and sleep have liken'd them and restored them.

I swear they are all beautiful,
Every one that sleeps is beautiful, every thing in the dim
    light is beautiful,
The wildest and bloodiest is over, and all is peace.

Peace is always beautiful,
The myth of heaven indicates peace and night.

The myth of heaven indicates the soul,
The soul is always beautiful, it appears more or it appears
    less, it comes or it lags behind,
It comes from its embower'd garden and looks pleasantly
    on itself and encloses the world,
Perfect and clean the genitals previously jetting, and
    perfect and clean the womb cohering,
The head well-grown proportion'd and plumb, and the
    bowels and joints proportion'd and plumb.

The soul is always beautiful.
The universe is duly in order, every thing is in its place,
What has arrived is in its place and what waits shall be in
    its place,

The twisted skull waits, the watery or rotten blood waits,
The child of the glutton or venerealee waits long, and the
child of the drunkard waits long, and the drunkard
himself waits long,
The sleepers that lived and died wait, the far advanced are
to go on in their turns, and the far behind are to come
on in their turns,
The diverse shall be no less diverse, but they shall flow
and unite — they unite now.

8

The sleepers are very beautiful as they lie unclothed,
They flow hand in hand over the whole earth from east to
west as they lie unclothed,
The Asiatic and African are hand in hand, the European
and American are hand in hand,
Learn'd and unlearn'd are hand in hand, and male and
female are hand in hand,
The bare arm of the girl crosses the bare breast of her
lover, they press close without lust, his lips press her
neck,
The father holds his grown or ungrown son in his arms
with measureless love, and the son holds the father in
his arms with measureless love,
The white hair of the mother shines on the white wrist of
the daughter,
The breath of the boy goes with the breath of the man,
friend is inarm'd by friend,
The scholar kisses the teacher and the teacher kisses the
scholar, the wrong'd is made right,
The call of the slave is one with the master's call, and the
master salutes the slave,
The felon steps forth from the prison, the insane becomes
sane, the suffering of sick persons is reliev'd,
The sweatings and fevers stop, the throat that was

unsound is sound, the lungs of the consumptive are
    resumed, the poor distress'd head is free,
The joints of the rheumatic move as smoothly as ever, and
    smoother than ever,
Stiflings and passages open, the paralyzed become supple,
The swell'd and convuls'd and congested awake to
    themselves in condition,
They pass the invigoration of the night and the chemistry
    of the night, and awake.

I too pass from the night,
I stay a while away O night, but I return to you again and
    love you.

Why should I be afraid to trust myself to you?
I am not afraid, I have been well brought forward by you,
I love the rich running day, but I do not desert her in
    whom I lay so long,
I know not how I came of you and I know not where I go
    with you, but I know I came well and shall go well.

I will stop only a time with the night, and rise betimes,
I will duly pass the day O my mother, and duly return
    to you.

A Clear Midnight

This is thy hour O Soul, thy free flight into the
  wordless,
Away from books, away from art, the day erased, the
  lesson done,
Thee fully forth emerging, silent, gazing, pondering the
  themes thou lovest best,
Night, sleep, death and the stars.

Frederick Morgan
Death Mother

for Hayden Carruth

You came as sleep, warily:
when I woke
things had a deep-blue look.

You disguised yourself as night, but
behind the stars
I saw dark flashes of your body.

And as for dreams —
how many you tried me with!
It seems you never weary of your
hopeful grim deceptions

as though I stood in need of such
visions of filth and blood
to move me to acknowledge your
dominion, mother.

2
Lady, when you were born —
frail, blue-veined from the womb
but destined by a god —

the proud man dashed you down.
You died before you lived

yet from the detested corpse
a raging spirit strode up into heaven,
and the man fell shuddering
seeing his death at large.

Now in the night sky
with breasts like elephants,
all circleted in moonbeams,
dark-skinned, in your delicate dark skirt
you dance out our black age.

3
Death is the least of things to be feared
because while we are it is not
and when it comes we are not
and so we never meet it at all.

That was a Greek way of avoiding the issue —
which is, that ever since the blood-drenched moment
of primal recognition,
death has lived all times in us
and we in her, commingled,
and not to recognize her is
not to recognize ourselves.

The lovely body is composed of what was dead
and will be dead again. Death
gives us birth, we live in her.

4
I cornered the thief in the garage at dusk.
Small, furry, with quick-darting eyes
he made no sound but watched his chance.

He had none. I took hold of a heavy stick
and when he rushed me, struck him once
and crushed his skull. There on the cement floor

all at once that life came to an end.
Out of the nostrils blood was oozing,
the right eye dripped down from its socket.

I felt revulsion at myself and him.
The dog edged up and nosed the body.
Later, in the dark, I dug a quiet grave,
laid him in it and covered him over,
and all was almost as if he had never been.

5
The breasts of the loving mothers flow with milk:
quiet in the streamside grove
they suckle the sacred children.
Sit, rest yourself for a moment in the cool of those trees
for it seems (on such a day) love must prevail.

But the Mother is playful and sportive,
she of the burial grounds:
at nightfall Helen the fair
in paroxysm of change
shrivels, a hag with withered dugs.

Do not think to escape her
by calling her fortunate name!
From her mouth blood pours in a torrent,
her girdle is human hands,
she frees one in a hundred-thousand —
the rest she holds to the game.

6

There was no bulldozer handy, so
we shoveled the corpses into the pit —
twenty of us on detail.

I can't remember which month it was, April or May.
The sun was out, a small breeze was blowing as usual.
It meant wading into a complex mass of rot,
they were so many and so putrefied,
with here and there a leg, an arm, a head.
We wore masks, but gagged even so —
several passed out.

Afterwards, where we filled the earth in, it bubbled,
and on the march back Kröger said, "My God,
I'd rather die than do that again."
But he didn't die. None of us did, just then.

7

You cast me from your filthy womb
where snails, worms, and leeches grow
and when I've finished out my time
back down your great gorge I'll go
into your black and stinking gut
and crouch there centuries and rot
and be excreted, or reborn —
it's all the same, it's you I'm from,
your stench, your blood, your pain and lust,
your beauty raising up my pride,
your eyes that gleam in murderous jest,
your ancient sluice that I've enjoyed.
How, mother mine, shall I grow free
of you who keep remaking me?

8
Is it useful to have a mythology of death
or handier just to get along with the bare idea,
the barer the better? Such as
a plain black nothingness: easy to think of
like a light going out. Why
get into talk of legends and deities
with all their paraphernalia?

I deny that consolation is the answer.
The greatest consolation (as Epicurus knew)
is the light going out. All notions
of continuance build up in us expectancy —
and *that* is perhaps the answer: life
as lived, responsive to its fiercest surge,
assumes its own indefinite extension. . .
He has not fully lived, Lorenzo de' Medici said,
who has not felt that other life to come —
and yet one must not dwell on it too much
or put on airs. The light goes out for sure

and all the rest is images — in whose mind?

9
One sweltering Sunday afternoon in August,
walking through the back-meadows as was my custom
I grew sleepy, and lay down in a patch of shade
to rest. Drowsed off; and had this dream I can't forget.

I saw a gigantic woman striding toward me
across the fields: glad eyes in a grim face
and crests of huge dark wings that loomed behind her.
She held in one hand a dripping sword, in the other —
dangling from the intermingled hair —
a thousand human heads confused and bunched.
I was the only person left alive,

and as she neared and looked into my eyes
I saw in hers my own self, burning bright.
This frightened me — my heart shook — and I woke.

10
Who will laugh
in coldest glee
when earth darkens once for all?

When graveyard meats
are the only food,
who will eat the dead men's faces?

And who rides free
in the night sky
holding the mirror that holds the world?

Is it not I
deep in the heart,
I who died before I lived?

Black one,
naked dancer on corpses,
with you as Mother
how shall we fear death.

Carlos Fuentes
The Doll Queen

To María Pilar and José Donoso

I WENT BECAUSE THAT CARD — such a strange card — reminded me of her existence. I found it in a forgotten book whose pages had revived the specter of a childish calligraphy. For the first time in a long while I was rearranging my books. I met surprise after surprise, since some, placed on the highest shelves, had not been read for a long time. So long a time that the edges of the leaves were grainy, and a mixture of gold dust and grayish scale fell on my open palm, reminiscent of the lacquer covering certain bodies glimpsed first in dreams and later in the deceptive reality of the first ballet performance to which we're taken. It was a book from my childhood — perhaps from the childhood of many children — that related a series of more or less truculent exemplary tales which had the virtue of precipitating us onto our elders' knees to ask them, over and over again: Why? Children who are ungrateful to their parents; maidens kidnapped by splendid horsemen and returned home in shame — as well as those who happily abandon hearth and home; old men who in exchange for an overdue mortgage demand the hand of the sweetest, most long-suffering daughter of the threatened family...Why? I do not recall their answers. I only know that from among the stained pages came fluttering a white card in Amilamia's atrocious hand: *Amilamia wil not forget her good friend — com see me here wher I draw it.*

And on the other side was that sketch of a path starting from an X that indicated, doubtlessly, the park bench where I, an adolescent rebelling against prescribed and tedious education, forgot my classroom schedule to spend some hours reading books which, if not in fact written by me, seemed to be: who could doubt that only from my imagination could spring all those corsairs, those couriers of the tsar, those boys slightly younger than I who floated all day down a great American river on a raft. Clutching the side of the park bench as if it were the bow of a magic saddle, at first I didn't hear the sound of the light steps that stopped behind me after running down the graveled garden path. It was Amilamia, and I don't know how long the child would have kept me company in silence had not her mischievous spirit one afternoon chosen to tickle my ear with down from a dandelion she blew toward me, her lips puffed out and her brow furrowed in a frown.

She asked my name, and after considering it very seriously, she told me hers with a smile which, if not candid, was not too rehearsed. Quickly I realized that Amilamia had discovered, if discovered is the word, a form of expression midway between the ingenuousness of her years and the forms of adult mimicry that well-brought-up children have to know, particularly for the solemn moments of introduction and of leave-taking. Amilamia's seriousness was, rather, a gift of nature, whereas her moments of spontaneity, by contrast, seemed artificial. I like to remember her, afternoon after afternoon, in a succession of images that in their totality sum up the complete Amilamia. And it never ceases to surprise me that I cannot think of her as she really was, or remember how she actually moved — light, questioning, constantly looking around her. I must remember her fixed forever in time, as in a photograph album. Amilamia in the distance, a point at the spot where the hill began its descent from a lake of clover toward the flat meadow where I, sitting on the bench, used to read: a point of fluctuating shadow and sunshine and a hand that waved to me from high on the hill. Amilamia frozen in her flight down the hill, her white skirt ballooning, the flowered panties gathered on her legs with elastic, her mouth open and eyes half closed against the streaming air, the child crying with pleasure. Amilamia sitting beneath the eucalyptus trees, pretending to cry so that I would go over to her. Amilamia lying on her stomach with a flower in her hand: the petals of a flower which I discovered later didn't grow in this garden but somewhere else, perhaps in the garden of Amilamia's house, since the pocket of her blue-checked apron was often filled with those white blossoms. Amilamia watching me read, holding with both hands to the slats of the green bench, asking questions with her gray eyes: I recall that she never asked me what I was reading, as if she could divine in my eyes the images born of the pages. Amilamia laughing with pleasure when I lifted her by the waist and whirled her around my head; she seemed to discover a new perspective on the world in that slow flight. Amilamia turning her back to me and waving goodbye, her arm held high, the fingers moving excitedly. And Amilamia in the thousand postures she affected around my bench, hanging upside down, her bloomers billowing; sitting on the gravel with her legs crossed and her chin resting on her fist; lying on the grass, baring her belly button to the sun; weaving tree branches, drawing animals in the mud with a twig, licking the slats of the bench, hiding under the seat, breaking off the loose bark from the ancient tree trunks, staring at the horizon beyond the hill, humming with her eyes closed, imitating the voices of birds, dogs, cats, hens, horses. All for me, and yet nothing. It was her way of being with me, all these things I remember, but also her way of being alone in the park. Yes, perhaps my memory of her is fragmentary because reading alternated with my contemplation of the chubby-cheeked child with smooth hair that changed in the reflection of the light: now wheat-colored, now burnt chestnut. And it is only today that I think how Amilamia in that moment established the other point of support for my life, the one that created the tension between my own irresolute childhood and the wide world, the promised land that was beginning to be mine through my reading.

Not then. Then I dreamed about the women in my books, about the quintessential female — the word disturbed me —

who assumed the disguise of Queen to buy the necklace in secret, about the imagined beings of mythology — half recognizable, half white-breasted, damp-bellied salamanders — who awaited monarchs in their beds. And thus, imperceptibly, I moved from indifference toward my childish companion to an acceptance of the child's grace and seriousness and from there to an unexpected rejection of a presence that became useless to me. She irritated me, finally. I who was fourteen was irritated by that child of seven who was not yet memory or nostalgia, but rather the past and its reality. I had let myself be dragged along by weakness. We had run together, holding hands, across the meadow. Together we had shaken the pines and picked up the cones that Amilamia guarded jealously in her apron pocket. Together we had constructed paper boats and followed them, happy and gay, to the edge of the drain. And that afternoon, amid shouts of glee, when we tumbled together down the hill and rolled to a stop at its foot, Amilamia was on my chest, her hair between my lips; but when I felt her panting breath in my ear and her little arms sticky from sweets around my neck, I angrily pushed away her arms and let her fall. Amilamia cried, rubbing her wounded elbow and knee, and I returned to my bench. Then Amilamia went away and the following day she returned, handed me the card without a word, and disappeared, humming, into the woods. I hesitated whether to tear up the card or keep it in the pages of the book: *Afternoons on the Farm.* Even my reading had become infantile because of Amilamia. She did not return to the park. After a few days I left on my vacation, and when I returned it was to the duties of the first year of prep school. I never saw her again.

II

And now, almost rejecting the image that is unfamiliar without being fantastic, but is all the more painful for being so real, I return to that forgotten park and stopping before the grove of pines and eucalyptus I recognize the smallness of the bosky enclosure that my memory has insisted on drawing with an amplitude that allows sufficient space for

the vast swell of my imagination. After all, Michel Strogoff
and Huckleberry Finn, Milady de Winter and Geneviève de
Brabant were born, lived, and died here: in a little garden
surrounded by mossy iron railings, sparsely planted with
old, neglected trees, scarcely adorned by a concrete bench
painted to look like wood which forces me to think that my
beautiful wrought-iron green bench never existed, or was
part of my ordered, retrospective delirium. And the hill...
How believe the promontory Amilamia ascended and descended in her daily coming and going, that steep slope we
rolled down together, was *this*. A barely elevated patch of
dark stubble with no more height and depth than what my
memory had created.

Com see me here wher I draw it. So I would have to cross the
garden, leave the woods behind, descend the hill in three
loping steps, cut through that narrow grove of chestnuts —
it was here, surely, where the child gathered the white
petals — open the squeaking park gate and instantly
recall... know... find oneself in the street, realize that every
afternoon of one's adolescence, as if by a miracle, one had
succeeded in suspending the beat of the surrounding city,
annulling that flood tide of whistles, bells, voices, sobs,
engines, radios, imprecations. Which was the true magnet,
the silent garden or the feverish city?

I wait for the light to change, and cross to the other side,
my eyes never leaving the red iris detaining the traffic. I
consult Amilamia's card. After all, that rudimentary map is
the true magnet of the moment I am living, and just thinking
about it disturbs me. I was obliged, after the lost afternoons
of my fourteenth year, to follow the channels of discipline;
now I find myself, at twenty-nine, duly certified with a
diploma, owner of an office, assured of a moderate income, a
bachelor still, with no family to maintain, slightly bored with
sleeping with secretaries, scarcely excited by an occasional
outing to the country or to the beach, feeling the lack of a
central attraction such as my books, my park, and Amilamia
once afforded me. I walk down the street of this gray suburb.
The one-story houses, doorways peeling paint, succeed each
other monotonously. Faint neighborhood sounds barely

interrupt the general uniformity: the squeal of a knife sharpener here, the hammering of a shoe repairman there. The neighborhood children are playing in the dead-end streets. The music of an organ grinder reaches my ears, mingled with the voices of children's rounds. I stop a moment to watch them, with the sensation, as fleeting, that Amilamia must be among these groups of children, immodestly exhibiting her flowered panties, hanging by her knees from some balcony, still fond of acrobatic excesses, her apron pocket filled with white petals. I smile, and for the first time I am able to imagine the young lady of twenty-two who, even if she still lives at this address, will laugh at my memories, or who perhaps will have forgotten the afternoons spent in the garden.

The house is identical to all the rest. The heavy entry door, two grilled windows with closed shutters. A one-story house, topped by a false neoclassic balustrade that probably conceals the practicalities of the roof terrace: clothes hanging on a line, tubs of water, servants' quarters, a chicken coop. Before I ring the bell, I want to rid myself of any illusion. Amilamia no longer lives here. Why would she stay fifteen years in the same house? Besides, in spite of her precocious independence and aloneness, she seemed to be a well-brought-up, well-behaved child, and this neighborhood is no longer elegant; Amilamia's parents, without doubt, have moved. But perhaps the new tenants will know where.

I press the bell and wait. I ring again. Here is another contingency: no one is home. And will I feel the need to look again for my childhood friend? No. Because it will not happen a second time that I open a book from my adolescence and find Amilamia's card. I'll return to my routine, I'll forget the moment whose importance lay in its fleeting surprise.

I ring once more. I press my ear to the door and am startled: I can hear harsh, irregular breathing on the other side; the sound of labored breathing, accompanied by the disagreeable odor of stale tobacco, filters through the cracks in the door.

"Good afternoon. Could you tell me...?"

When he hears my voice, the person moves away with heavy and unsure steps. I press the bell again, shouting this time: "Hey! Open up! What's the matter? Don't you hear me?"

No response. I continue to ring, with no result. I move back from the door, still staring at the tiny cracks, as if distance might give me perspective, or even penetration. With my attention fixed on that damned door, I cross the street, walking backward. A piercing scream, followed by a prolonged and ferocious blast of a whistle, saves me in time. Dazed, I seek the person whose voice has just saved me. I see only the automobile moving down the street and I hang on to a lamppost, a hold that more than security offers me support as icy blood rushes through my burning, sweaty skin. I look toward the house that had been, that was, that must be, Amilamia's. There, behind the balustrade, as I had known there would be, are fluttering clothes hung out to dry. I don't know what else is hanging there — skirts, pajamas, blouses — I don't know. All I see is that starched little blue-checked apron, clamped by clothespins to the long cord swinging between an iron bar and a nail in the white wall of the terrace.

III

In the Bureau of Records I have been told that the property is in the name of a Señor R. Valdivia, who rents the house. To whom? That they don't know. Who is Valdivia? He is down as a businessman. Where does he live? Who are *you?* the young woman asked me with haughty curiosity. I haven't been able to show myself calm and assured. Sleep has not relieved my nervous fatigue. Valdivia. As I leave the Bureau, the sun offends me. I associate the aversion provoked by the hazy sun sifting through the clouds — thus all the more intense — with a desire to return to the humid, shaded park. No. It is only a desire to know if Amilamia lives in that house and why they won't let me enter. But what I must reject is the absurd idea that kept me awake all night. Having seen the apron drying on the flat roof, the apron in which she kept the flowers, I had begun to believe that in that house lived a seven-year-old girl I had known fourteen or fifteen years before...She must have a little girl! Yes. Amilamia, at twenty-two, is the mother of a girl who perhaps dresses the same, looks the same, repeats the same games, and — who knows — maybe even goes to the same park. And deep in thought, I arrive once more at the door of the house. I ring the bell and wait for the labored breathing on the other side of the door. I am mistaken. The door is opened by a woman who can't be more than fifty. But wrapped in a shawl, dressed in black and in flat black shoes, with no makeup and her salt-and-pepper hair pulled into a knot, she seems to have abandoned all illusion or pretense of youth. She observes me with eyes so indifferent they seem almost cruel.

"You want something?"

"Señor Valdivia sent me." I cough and run my hand over my hair. I should have picked up my briefcase at the office. I realize that without it I cannot play my role very well.

"Valdivia?" the woman asks without alarm, without interest.

"Yes. The owner of this house."

One thing is clear. The woman will reveal nothing by her face. She looks at me, impassive.

"Oh, yes. The owner of the house."

"May I come in?"

In bad comedies, I think, the traveling salesman sticks a foot in the door so they can't close the door in his face. I do the same, but the woman steps back and with a gesture of her hand invites me to come into what must have been a garage. On one side there is a glass-paneled door, its paint faded. I walk toward the door over the yellow tiles of the entryway and ask again, turning toward the woman, who follows me with tiny steps: "This way?"

I notice for the first time that in her pale hands she carries a chaplet, which she toys with ceaselessly. I haven't seen one of those old-fashioned rosaries since my childhood and I want to say something about it, but the brusque, decisive manner with which the woman opens the door precludes any gratuitous conversation. We enter a long, narrow room. The woman quickly opens the shutters. But because of four large perennials growing in glass-encrusted porcelain pots the room remains in shadow. The only other objects in the room are an old high-backed cane sofa and a rocking chair. But it is neither the plants nor the sparseness of the furniture that holds my attention.

The woman asks me to sit on the sofa before she sits down in the rocking chair. Beside me, on the cane arm of the sofa, there is an open magazine.

"Señor Valdivia sends his apologies for not having come himself."

The woman rocks, unblinking. I peer at the comic book out of the corner of my eye.

"He sends greetings and..."

I stop, waiting for a reaction from the woman. She continues to rock. The magazine is covered with red scribbles.

"...and asks me to inform you that he must disturb you for a few days..."

My eyes search the room rapidly.

"...A reassessment of the house must be made for tax purposes. It seems it hasn't been done for...You have been living here since...?"

Yes. That is a stubby lipstick lying under the chair. If the woman smiles, it is while the slow-moving hands caress the chaplet. I sense, for an instant, a swift flash of ridicule that does not quite disturb her features. She still does not answer.

"...for at least fifteen years, isn't that so?"

She does not agree. She does not disagree. And on the pale thin lips there is not the least trace of lipstick...

"...you, your husband, and...?"

She stares at me, never changing expression, almost daring me to continue. We sit a moment in silence, she playing with the rosary, I leaning forward, my hands on my knees. I rise.

"Well then, I'll be back this afternoon with the papers. . ."

The woman nods and in silence picks up the lipstick and the comic book and hides them in the folds of her shawl.

IV

The scene has not changed. This afternoon, as I write sham figures in my notebook and feign interest in determining the value of the dull floorboards and the length of the living room, the woman rocks, the three decades of the chaplet whispering through her fingers. I sigh as I finish the supposed inventory of the living room and ask for permission to see the rest of the house. The woman rises, bracing her long black-clad arms on the seat of the rocking chair and adjusting the shawl on her narrow, bony shoulders.

She opens the frosted-glass door and we enter a dining room with very little additional furniture. But the aluminum-legged table and the four aluminum-and-plastic chairs lack even the hint of distinction of the living-room furniture. The other window, with wrought-iron grill and closed shutters, must sometime illuminate this bare-walled dining room, devoid of either shelves or sideboards. The only object on the table is a plastic fruit dish with a cluster of black grapes, two peaches, and a buzzing corona of flies. The woman, her arms crossed, her face expressionless, stops behind me. I take the risk of breaking the order of things: clearly, these rooms will not tell me anything I really want to know.

"Couldn't we go up to the roof?" I ask. "That might be the best way to measure the total area."

The woman's eyes light up as she looks at me, or perhaps it is only the contrast with the shadows of the dining room.

"What for?" she says at last. "Señor. . .Valdivia. . .knows the dimensions very well."

And those pauses, before and after the owner's name, are the first indication that something has at last begun to trouble the woman, forcing her, in self-defense, to resort to a kind of irony.

"I don't know." I make an effort to smile. "Perhaps I prefer to go from top to bottom and not" — my false smile drains away — "from bottom to top."

"You will go the way I show you," the woman says, her arms crossed over her chest, a silver crucifix dangling over her dark belly.

Before smiling weakly, I force myself to realize that in these shadows my gestures are of no use, aren't even symbolic. I open the notebook with a creak of the cardboard cover and continue making notes with the greatest possible speed, never glancing up, taking down numbers and estimates for a job whose fiction — the light flush in my cheeks and the perceptible dryness of my tongue tell me — is deceiving no one. And as I cover the graph paper with absurd signs, with square roots and algebraic formulas, I ask myself what is keeping me from getting to the point, from asking about Amilamia and getting out of here with a satisfactory answer. Nothing. And yet I am certain, even if I obtained a response, I would not have the truth. My slim, silent companion is a person I wouldn't look at twice in the street, but in this almost uninhabited house with the coarse furniture, she ceases to be an anonymous face in the crowd and is converted into a stock character of mystery. Such is the paradox, and if memories of Amilamia have once again aroused my appetite for the imaginary, I shall follow the rules of the game, I shall exhaust appearances, and not rest until I have the answer — perhaps simple and clear-cut, immediate and obvious — that lies beyond the veils the señora of the rosary unexpectedly places in my path. Do I bestow a gratuitous strangeness on my reluctant hostess? If so, I'll only take greater pleasure in the labyrinths of my own invention. And the flies are still buzzing around the fruit dish, occasionally pausing on the damaged end of the peach, a nibbled bite — I lean closer, using the pretext of my notes — where little teeth have left their mark in the velvety skin and ocher flesh of the fruit. I do not look toward the señora. I pretend I am taking notes. The fruit seems to be bitten but not touched. I crouch down to see better, rest my hands on the table, move my lips closer as if wishing to repeat the act of biting without touching. I look down and see another sign near my feet: the track of two tires that seem to be bicycle tires, the print of two rubber tires that come as far as the edge of the table and then lead away, growing fainter, the length of the room, toward the senora...

I close my notebook.

"Let us go on, señora."

When I turn toward her, I find her standing with her hands resting on the back of a chair. Seated before her, coughing from the smoke of his black cigarette, is a man with heavy shoulders and hidden eyes: those eyes, scarcely visible behind swollen, wrinkled lids as thick and drooped as the neck of an ancient turtle, seem nevertheless to follow my every movement. The half-shaven cheeks, criss-crossed by a thousand gray furrows, sag from protruding cheekbones, and his greenish hands are folded under his arms. He is wearing a coarse blue shirt, and his rumpled hair is so curly it looks like the bottom of a barnacle-covered ship. He does not move, and the only sign of his existence is that difficult whistling breathing (as if every breath must breach a floodgate of phlegm, irritation, and abuse) I had already heard through the chinks of the door.

Ridiculously, he murmurs: "Good afternoon..." and I am disposed to forget everything: the mystery, Amilamia, the assessment, the bicycle tracks. The apparition of this asthmatic old bear justifies a prompt retreat. I repeat "Good afternoon," this time with an inflection of farewell. The turtle's mask dissolves into an atrocious smile: every pore of that flesh seems fabricated of brittle rubber, of painted, peeling oilcloth. The arm reaches out and detains me.

"Valdivia died four years ago," says the man in a distant, choking voice that issues from his belly instead of his larynx: a weak, high-pitched voice.

In the grip of that strong, almost painful, claw, I tell myself it is useless to pretend. But the waxen, rubber faces observing me say nothing, and so I am able, in spite of everything, to pretend one more time, to pretend I am speaking to myself when I say: "Amilamia..."

Yes; no one will have to pretend any longer. The fist that

clutches my arm affirms its strength for only an instant, immediately its grip loosens, then it falls, weak and trembling, before lifting to take the waxen hand touching his shoulder: the señora, perplexed for the first time, looks at me with the eyes of a violated bird and sobs with a dry moan that does not disturb the rigid astonishment of her features. Suddenly the ogres of my imagination are two solitary, abandoned, wounded old people, scarcely able to console themselves in this shuddering clasp of hands that fills me with shame. My fantasy has brought me to this stark dining room to violate the intimacy and the secret of two human beings exiled from life by something I no longer have the right to share. I have never despised myself more. Never have words failed me so clumsily. Any gesture of mine would be in vain: shall I come closer, shall I touch them, shall I caress the woman's head, shall I ask them to excuse my intrusion? I return the notebook to my jacket pocket. I toss into oblivion all the clues in my detective story: the comic book, the lipstick, the nibbled fruit, the bicycle tracks, the blue-checked apron...I decide to leave the house without saying anything more. The old man, from behind his thick eyelids, must have noticed.

The high breathy voice says: "Did you know her?"

The past, so natural, used by them every day, finally shatters my illusions. There is the answer. Did you know her? How long? How long must the world have lived without Amilamia, assassinated first by my forgetfulness, and then revived, scarcely yesterday, by a sad impotent memory? When did those serious gray eyes cease to be astonished by the delight of an always solitary garden? When did those lips cease to pout or press together thinly in that ceremonious seriousness with which, I now realize, Amilamia must have discovered and consecrated the objects and events of a life that, she perhaps knew intuitively, was fleeting?

"Yes, we played together in the park. A long time ago."

"How old was she?" says the old man, his voice even more muffled.

"She must have been about seven. No, older than that."

The woman's voice rises, as she lifts her arms, seemingly to implore: "What was she like, senor? Tell us what she was like, please."

I can close my eyes. "Amilamia is a memory for me, too. I can only picture her through the things she touched, the things she brought, what she discovered in the park. Yes. Now I see her, coming down the hill. No. It isn't true that it was a scarcely elevated patch of stubble. It was a hill, with grass, and Amilamia's comings and goings had traced a path, and she waved to me from the top before she started down, accompanied by the music, yes, the music I saw, the painting I smelled, the tastes I heard, the odors I touched... my hallucination..." Do they hear me? "She came waving, dressed in white, in a blue-checked apron...the one you have hanging on the roof terrace..."

They take my arm and still I do not open my eyes.

"What was she like, señor?"

"Her eyes were gray and the color of her hair changed in the reflection of the sun and the shadow of the trees..."

They lead me gently, the two of them. I hear the man's labored breathing, the crucifix on the rosary hitting against the woman's body.

"Tell us, please..."

"The air brought tears to her eyes when she ran; when she reached my bench her cheeks were silvered with happy tears..."

I do not open my eyes. Now we are going upstairs. Two, five, eight, nine, twelve steps. Four hands guide my body.

"What was she like, what was she like?"

"She sat beneath the eucalyptus and wove garlands from the branches and pretended to cry so I would stop reading and go over to her..."

Hinges creak. The odor overpowers everything else: it routs the other senses, it takes its seat like a yellow Mongol upon the throne of my hallucination; heavy as a coffin, insinuating as the slither of draped silk, ornamented as a Turkish scepter, opaque as a deep, lost vein of ore, brilliant as a dead star. The hands no longer hold me. More than the sobbing, it is the trembling of the old people that envelops me. Slowly, I open my eyes: first through the dizzying liquid of my corneas, then through the web of my eyelashes, the room suffocated in that gigantic battle of perfumes is disclosed, effluvia and frosty, almost flesh-like petals; the presence of the flowers is so strong here they seem to take on the quality of living flesh — the sweetness of the jasmine, the nausea of the lilies, the tomb of the tuberose, the temple of the gardenia. Illuminated through the incandescent wax lips of heavy, sputtering candles, the small windowless bedroom with its aura of wax and humid flowers assaults the very center of my plexus, and from there, only there at the solar center of life, am I able to come to, and perceive beyond the candles, amid the scattered flowers, the plethora of used toys: the colored hoops and wrinkled balloons, cherries dried to transparency, wooden horses with scraggly manes, the scooter, blind hairless dolls, bears spilling their sawdust, punctured oilcloth ducks, moth-eaten dogs, frayed jumping ropes, glass jars of dried candy, worn-out shoes, the tricycle (three wheels? no, two, and not a bicycle's — two parallel wheels below), little wool and leather shoes; and, facing me, within reach of my hand, the small coffin supported on blue crates decorated with paper flowers, flowers of life this time, carnations and sunflowers, poppies and tulips, but like the others, the ones of death, all part of a compilation created by the atmosphere of this funeral hothouse in which reposes, inside the silvered coffin, between the black silk sheets, on the pillow of white satin, that motionless and serene face framed in lace, highlighted with rose-colored tints, eyebrows traced by the lightest pencil, closed lids, real eyelashes, thick, that cast a tenuous shadow on cheeks as healthy as in the park days. Serious red lips, set almost in the angry pout that Amilamia feigned so I would come to play. Hands joined over her breast. A chaplet, identical to the mother's, strangling that waxen neck. Small white shroud on the clean prepubescent, docile body.

The old people, sobbing, are kneeling.

I reach out my hand and run my fingers over the porcelain face of my little friend. I feel the coldness of those painted features, of the doll queen who presides over the pomp of this royal chamber of death. Porcelain, wax, cotton. *Amilamia wil not forget her good friend — com see me here wher I draw it.*

I withdraw my fingers from the sham cadaver. Traces of my fingerprints remain where I touched the skin of the doll.

And nausea crawls in my stomach where the candle smoke and the sweet stench of the lilies in the enclosed room have settled. I turn my back on Amilamia's sepulcher. The woman's hand touches my arm. Her wildly staring eyes bear no relation to the quiet, steady voice.

"Don't come back, señor. If you truly loved her, don't come back again."

I touch the hand of Amilamia's mother. I see through nauseous eyes the old man's head buried between his knees, and I go out of the room and to the stairway, to the living room, to the patio, to the street.

V

If not a year, nine or ten months have passed. The memory of that idolatry no longer frightens me. I have forgotten the odor of the flowers and the image of the petrified doll. The real Amilamia has returned to my memory and I have felt, if not content, sane again: the park, the living child, my hours of adolescent reading, have triumphed over the specters of a sick cult. The image of life is the more powerful. I tell myself that I shall live forever with my real Amilamia, the conqueror of the caricature of death. And one day I dare look again at that notebook with graph paper in which I wrote down the data of the spurious assessment. And from its pages, once again, Amilamia's card falls out, with its terrible childish scrawl and its map for getting from the park to her house. I smile as I pick it up. I bite one of the edges, thinking that, in spite of everything, the poor old people might accept this gift.

Whistling, I put on my jacket and straighten my tie. Why not go see them and offer them this card with the child's own writing?

I am almost running as I approach the one-story house. Rain is beginning to fall in large isolated drops, bringing out of the earth with magical immediacy the odor of dewy benediction that stirs the humus and quickens all that lives with its roots in the dust.

I ring the bell. The rain gets heavier and I become insistent. A shrill voice shouts: "I'm coming!" and I wait for the mother with her eternal rosary to open the door for me. I turn up the collar of my jacket. My clothes, my body, too, smell different in the rain. The door opens.

"What do you want? How wonderful you've come!"

The misshapen girl sitting in the wheelchair places one hand on the doorknob and smiles at me with an indecipherable, wry grin. The hump on her chest makes the dress into a curtain over her body, a piece of white cloth that nonetheless lends an air of coquetry to the blue-checked apron. The little woman extracts a pack of cigarettes from her apron pocket and quickly lights a cigarette, staining the end with orange-painted lips. The smoke causes the beautiful gray eyes to squint. She fixes her coppery, wheat-colored, permanent-waved hair, all the time staring at me with a desolate, inquisitive, hopeful — but at the same time fearful — expression.

"No, Carlos. Go away. Don't come back."

And from the house, at the same moment, I hear the high labored breathing of the old man, coming closer.

"Where are you? Don't you know you're not supposed to answer the door? Get back! Devil's spawn! Do I have to beat you again?"

And the rain trickles down my forehead, over my cheeks, and into my mouth, and the little frightened hands drop the comic book onto the wet paving stones.

— *translated by Margaret S. Peden from the Spanish*

Yannis Ritsos
Suddenly

Quiet night. Quiet. And you had stopped
waiting. It was peaceful almost.
And suddenly on your face the touch, so vivid,
of the one who is absent. He'll come. Then
the sound of shutters banging on their own.
Now the wind has come up. And a little farther, the sea
was drowning in its own voice.

— translated by Edmund Keeley from the Greek

Circus

Night circus, the lights, the music,
the sparkling cars along the full length of the avenue.
When the lights go out in the neighborhood,
when the last note has fallen like a dry leaf,
the facade of the circus seems
a huge set of false teeth. Then
the brass instruments sleep in their cases,
the animals are heard bellowing over the city,
the tiger in its cage fixes on its own shadow,
the animal-tamer takes off his costume and smokes a
    cigarette.

And every now and then the neighborhood lights up
when the eyes of the lions sparkle behind their bars.

— translated by Edmund Keeley from the Greek

Insomnia

This relentless repetition of the same illegible text —
at the top of the sheet the rusted hole from the thumbtack,
at the bottom two drops of black blood. The two — he said
    — the two,
the double, the double sound, the double meaning. I'm
    tired of doors
closed and open with the dead or women. Lefteris
got going in a hurry before it started raining.
Afterwards he came back with the damp blanket and the
    cap belonging to the one who was executed.

— translated by Edmund Keeley from the Greek

Wallace Stevens
Anecdote of the Prince of Peacocks

In the moonlight
I met Berserk,
In the moonlight
On the bushy plain.
Oh, sharp he was
As the sleepless!

And, "Why are you red
In this milky blue?"
I said.
"Why sun-colored,
As if awake
In the midst of sleep?"

"You that wander,"
So he said,
"On the bushy plain,
Forget so soon.
But I set my traps
In the midst of dreams."

I knew from this
That the blue ground
Was full of blocks
And blocking steel.
I knew the dread
Of the bushy plain,
And the beauty
Of the moonlight
Falling there,
Falling
As sleep falls
In the innocent air.

Henry David Thoreau
Solitude

THIS IS A DELICIOUS EVENING, when the whole body is one sense, and imbibes delight through every pore. I go and come with a strange liberty in Nature, a part of herself. As I walk along the stony shore of the pond in my shirt sleeves, though it is cool as well as cloudy and windy, and I see nothing special to attract me, all the elements are unusually congenial to me. The bullfrogs trump to usher in the night, and the note of the whippoorwill is borne on the rippling wind from over the water. Sympathy with the fluttering alder and poplar leaves almost takes away my breath; yet, like the lake, my serenity is rippled but not ruffled. These small waves raised by the evening wind are as remote from the storm as the smooth reflecting surface. Though it is now dark, the wind still blows and roars in the wood, the waves still dash, and some creatures lull the rest with their notes. The repose is never complete. The wildest animals do not repose, but seek their prey now; the fox, and skunk, and rabbit, now roam the fields and woods without fear. They are Nature's watchmen, — links which connect the days of animated life.

When I return to my house I find that visitors have been there and left their cards, either a bunch of flowers, or a wreath of evergreen, or a name in pencil on a yellow walnut leaf or a chip. They who come rarely to the woods take some little piece of the forest into their hands to play with by the

way, which they leave, either intentionally or accidentally.
One has peeled a willow wand, woven it into a ring, and
dropped it on my table. I could always tell if visitors had
called in my absence, either by the bended twigs or grass, or
the print of their shoes, and generally of what sex or age or
quality they were by some slight trace left, as a flower
dropped, or a bunch of grass plucked and thrown away,
even as far off as the railroad, half a mile distant, or by the
lingering odor of a cigar or pipe. Nay, I was frequently
notified of the passage of a traveller along the highway sixty
rods off by the scent of his pipe.

There is commonly sufficient space about us. Our horizon
is never quite at our elbows. The thick wood is not just at our
door, nor the pond, but somewhat is always clearing,
familiar and worn by us, appropriated and fenced in some
way, and reclaimed from Nature. For what reason have I this
vast range and circuit, some square miles of unfrequented
forest, for my privacy, abandoned to me by men? My nearest
neighbor is a mile distant, and no house is visible from any
place but the hill-tops within half a mile of my own. I have
my horizon bounded by woods all to myself; a distant view
of the railroad where it touches the pond on the one hand,
and of the fence which skirts the woodland road on the
other. But for the most part it is as solitary where I live as on
the prairies. It is as much Asia or Africa as New England. I
have, as it were, my own sun and moon and stars, and a little
world all to myself. At night there was never a traveller
passed my house, or knocked at my door, more than if I were
the first or last man; unless it were in the spring, when at
long intervals some came from the village to fish for pouts, —
they plainly fished much more in the Walden Pond of their
own natures, and baited their hooks with darkness, — but
they soon retreated, usually with light baskets, and left "the
world to darkness and to me," and the black kernel of the
night was never profaned by any human neighborhood. I
believe that men are generally still a little afraid of the dark,
though the witches are all hung, and Christianity and
candles have been introduced.

Yet I experienced sometimes that the most sweet and

tender, the most innocent and encouraging society may be found in any natural object, even for the poor misanthrope and most melancholy man. There can be no very black melancholy to him who lives in the midst of Nature and has his senses still. There was never yet such a storm but it was Aeolian music to a healthy and innocent ear. Nothing can rightly compel a simple and brave man to a vulgar sadness. While I enjoy the friendship of the seasons I trust that nothing can make life a burden to me. The gentle rain which waters my beans and keeps me in the house to-day is not drear and melancholy, but good for me too. Though it prevents my hoeing them, it is of far more worth than my hoeing. If it should continue so long as to cause the seeds to rot in the ground and destroy the potatoes in the low lands, it would still be good for the grass on the uplands, and, being good for the grass, it would be good for me. Sometimes, when I compare myself with other men, it seems as if I were more favored by the gods than they, beyond any deserts that I am conscious of; as if I had a warrant and surety at their hands which my fellows have not, and were especially guided and guarded. I do not flatter myself, but if it be possible they flatter me. I have never felt lonesome, or in the least oppressed by a sense of solitude, but once, and that was a few weeks after I came to the woods, when, for an hour, I doubted if the near neighborhood of man was not essential to a serene and healthy life. To be alone was something unpleasant. But I was at the same time conscious of a slight insanity in my mood, and seemed to foresee my recovery. In the midst of a gentle rain while these thoughts prevailed, I was suddenly sensible of such sweet and beneficent society in Nature, in the very pattering of the drops, and in every sound and sight around my house, an infinite and unaccountable friendliness all at once like an atmosphere sustaining me, as made the fancied advantages of human neighborhood insignificant, and I have never thought of them since. Every little pine needle expanded and swelled with sympathy and befriended me. I was so distinctly made aware of the presence of something kindred to me, even in the scenes which we are accustomed to call wild and dreary, and also that the nearest of blood to me and humanest was not a person nor a villager, that I thought no place could ever be strange to me again. —

> "Mourning untimely consumes the sad;
> Few are their days in the land of the living,
> Beautiful daughter of Toscar."

Some of my pleasantest hours were during the long rain storms in the spring or fall, which confined me to the house for the afternoon as well as the forenoon, soothed by their ceaseless roar and pelting; when an early twilight ushered in a long evening in which many thoughts had time to take root and unfold themselves. In those driving northeast rains which tried the village houses so, when the maids stood ready with mop and pail in front entries to keep the deluge out, I sat behind my door in my little house, which was all entry, and thoroughly enjoyed its protection. In one heavy thunder shower the lightning struck a large pitch-pine across the pond, making a very conspicuous and perfectly regular spiral groove from top to bottom, an inch or more deep, and four or five inches wide, as you would groove a walking-stick. I passed it again the other day, and was struck with awe on looking up and beholding that mark, now more distinct than ever, where a terrific and resistless bolt came down out of the harmless sky some eight years ago. Men frequently say to me, "I should think you would feel lonesome down there, and want to be nearer to folks; rainy and snowy days and nights especially." I am tempted to reply to such, — This whole earth which we inhabit is but a point in space. How far apart, think you, dwell the two most distant inhabitants of yonder star, the breadth of whose disk cannot be appreciated by our instruments? Why should I feel lonely? Is not our planet in the Milky Way? This which you put seems to me not to be the most important question. What sort of space is that which separates a man from his fellows and makes him solitary? I have found that no exertion of the legs can bring two minds much nearer to one another. What do we want most to dwell near to? Not to many men surely, the depot, the post-office, the bar-room, the meeting-house, the school-house, the grocery, Beacon Hill, or the Five Points, where men most congregate, but to the perennial source of our life, whence in all our experience we have found that to issue, as the willow stands near the water and sends out its roots in that direction. This will vary with different natures, but this is the place where a wise man will dig his cellar. . . . I one evening overtook one of my townsmen, who has accumulated what is called "a handsome property," — though I never got a *fair* view of it, — on the Walden road, driving a pair of cattle to market, who inquired to me how I could bring my mind to give up so many of the comforts of life. I answered that I was very sure I liked it passably well; I was not joking. And so I went home to my bed, and left him to pick his way through the darkness and the mud to Brighton, — or Bright-town, — which place he would reach some time in the morning.

Any prospect of awakening or coming to life to a dead man makes indifferent all times and places. The place where that may occur is always the same, and indescribably pleasant to all our senses. For the most part we allow only outlying and transient circumstances to make our occasions. They are, in fact, the cause of our distraction. Nearest to all things is that power which fashions their being. *Next* to us the grandest laws are continually being executed. *Next* to us is not the workman whom we have hired, with whom we love so well to talk, but the workman whose work we are.

"How vast and profound is the influence of the subtile powers of Heaven and of Earth!"

"We seek to perceive them, and we do not see them; we seek to hear them, and we do not hear them; identified with the substance of things, they cannot be separated from them."

"They cause that in all the universe men purify and sanctify their hearts, and clothe themselves in their holiday garments to offer sacrifices and oblations to their ancestors. It is an ocean of subtile intelligences. They are everywhere, above us, on our left, on our right; they environ us on all sides."

We are the subjects of an experiment which is not a little

interesting to me. Can we not do without the society of our gossips a little while under these circumstances, — have our own thoughts to cheer us? Confucius says truly, "Virtue does not remain as an abandoned orphan; it must of necessity have neighbors."

With thinking we may be beside ourselves in a sane sense. By a conscious effort of the mind we can stand aloof from actions and their consequences; and all things, good and bad, go by us like a torrent. We are not wholly involved in Nature. I may be either the drift-wood in the stream, or Indra in the sky looking down on it. I *may* be affected by a theatrical exhibition; on the other hand, I *may not* be affected by an actual event which appears to concern me much more. I only know myself as a human entity; the scene, so to speak, of thoughts and affections; and am sensible of a certain doubleness by which I can stand as remote from myself as from another. However intense my experience, I am conscious of the presence and criticism of a part of me, which, as it were, is not a part of me, but spectator, sharing no experience, but taking note of it; and that is no more I than it is you. When the play, it may be the tragedy, of life is over, the spectator goes his way. It was a kind of fiction, a work of the imagination only, so far as he was concerned. This doubleness may easily make us poor neighbors and friends sometimes.

I find it wholesome to be alone the greater part of the time. To be in company, even with the best, is soon wearisome and dissipating. I love to be alone. I never found the companion that was so companionable as solitude. We are for the most part more lonely when we go abroad among men than when we stay in our chambers. A man thinking or working is always alone, let him be where he will. Solitude is not measured by the miles of space that intervene between a man and his fellows. The really diligent student in one of the crowded hives of Cambridge College is as solitary as a dervis in the desert. The farmer can work alone in the field or the woods all day, hoeing or chopping, and not feel lonesome, because he is employed; but when he comes home at night he cannot sit down in a room alone, at the mercy of his thoughts, but must be where he can "see the folks," and recreate, and as he thinks remunerate, himself for his day's solitude; and hence he wonders how the student can sit alone in the house all night and most of the day without ennui and "the blues;" but he does not realize that the student, though in the house, is still at work in *his* field, and chopping in *his* woods, as the farmer in his, and in turn seeks the same recreation and society that the latter does, though it may be a more condensed form of it.

Society is commonly too cheap. We meet at very short intervals, not having had time to acquire any new value for each other. We meet at meals three times a day, and give each other a new taste of that old musty cheese that we are. We have had to agree on a certain set of rules, called etiquette and politeness, to make this frequent meeting tolerable and that we need not come to open war. We meet at the post-office, and at the sociable, and about the fireside every night; we live thick and are in each other's way, and stumble over one another, and I think that we thus lose some respect for one another. Certainly less frequency would suffice for all important and hearty communications. Consider the girls in a factory, — never alone, hardly in their dreams. It would be better if there were but one inhabitant to a square mile, as where I live. The value of a man is not in his skin, that we should touch him.

I have heard of a man lost in the woods and dying of famine and exhaustion at the foot of a tree, whose loneliness was relieved by the grotesque visions with which, owing to bodily weakness, his diseased imagination surrounded him, and which he believed to be real. So also, owing to bodily and mental health and strength, we may be continually cheered by a like but more normal and natural society, and come to know that we are never alone.

I have a great deal of company in my house; especially in the morning, when nobody calls. Let me suggest a few comparisons, that some one may convey an idea of my situation. I am no more lonely than the loon in the pond that laughs so loud, or than Walden Pond itself. What company has that lonely lake, I pray? And yet it has not the blue devils, but the blue angels in it, in the azure tint of its waters. The sun is alone, except in thick weather, when there sometimes appear to be two, but one is a mock sun. God is alone, — but the devil, he is far from being alone; he sees a great deal of company; he is legion. I am no more lonely that a single mullein or dandelion in a pasture, or a bean leaf, or sorrel, or a horse-fly, or a humble-bee. I am no more lonely than the Mill Brook, or a weathercock, or the north star, or the south wind, or an April shower, or a January thaw, or the first spider in a new house.

I have occasional visits in the long winter evenings, when the snow falls fast and the wind howls in the wood, from an old settler and original proprietor, who is reported to have dug Walden Pond, and stoned it, and fringed it with pine woods; who tells me stories of old time and of new eternity; and between us we manage to pass a cheerful evening with social mirth and pleasant views of things, even without apples or cider, — a most wise and humorous friend, whom I love much, who keeps himself more secret than ever did Goffe or Whalley; and though he is thought to be dead, none can show where he is buried. An elderly dame, too, dwells in my neighborhood, invisible to most persons, in whose odorous herb garden I love to stroll sometimes, gathering simples and listening to her fables; for she has a genius of unequalled fertility, and her memory runs back farther than mythology, and she can tell me the original of every fable, and on what fact every one is founded, for the incidents occurred when she was young. A ruddy and lusty old dame, who delights in all weathers and seasons, and is likely to outlive all her children yet.

The indescribable innocence and beneficence of Nature, — of sun and wind and rain, of summer and winter, — such health, such cheer, they afford forever! and such sympathy have they ever with our race, that all Nature would be affected, and the sun's brightness fade, and the winds would sigh humanely, and the clouds rain tears, and the woods shed their leaves and put on mourning in midsummer, if any man should ever for a just cause grieve. Shall I not have intelligence with the earth? Am I not partly leaves and vegetable mould myself?

What is the pill which will keep us well, serene, contented? Not my or thy great-grandfather's, but our great-grandmother Nature's universal, vegetable, botanic medicines, by which she has kept herself young always, outlived so many old Parrs in her day, and fed her health with their decaying fatness. For my panacea, instead of one of those quack vials of a mixture dipped from Acheron and the Dead Sea, which come out of those long shallow black-schooner looking wagons which we sometimes see made to carry bottles, let me have a draught of undiluted morning air. Morning air! If men will not drink of this at the fountain-head of the day, why, then, we must even bottle up some and sell it in the shops, for the benefit of those who have lost their subscription ticket to morning time in this world. But remember, it will not keep quite till noonday even in the coolest cellar, but drive out the stopples long ere that and follow westward the steps of Aurora. I am no worshipper of Hygeia, who was the daughter of that old herb-doctor Aesculapius, and who is represented on monuments holding a serpent in one hand, and in the other a cup out of which the serpent sometimes drinks; but rather of Hebe, cupbearer to Jupiter, who was the daughter of Juno and wild lettuce, and who had the power of restoring gods and men to the vigor of youth. She was probably the only thoroughly sound-conditioned, healthy, and robust young lady that ever walked the globe, and wherever she came it was spring.

Robert Bly
Six Winter Privacy Poems

1

About four, a few flakes.
I empty the teapot out in the snow,
            feeling shoots of joy in the new cold.
By nightfall, wind,
the curtains on the south sway softly.

2

My shack has two rooms; I use one.
The lamplight falls on my chair and table
and I fly into one of my own poems —
I can't tell you where —
as if I appeared where I am now,
in a wet field, snow falling.

3

More of the fathers are dying each day.
It is time for the sons.
Bits of darkness are gathering around them.
The darkness appears as flakes of light.

4
Sitting Alone

There is a solitude like black mud!
Sitting in this darkness singing,
I can't tell if this joy
is from the body, or the soul, or a third place.

5
Listening to Bach

There is someone inside this music
who is not well described by the names
of Jesus, or Jehovah, or the Lord of Hosts!

6

When I woke, new snow had fallen.
I am alone, yet someone else is with me,
drinking coffee, looking out at the snow.

Lewis Carroll
Pillow Problems

Calming Calculations

IN PREPARING the second edition of my book *Pillow-Problems Thought Out During Sleepless Nights*, I replaced the words 'sleepless nights' by 'wakeful hours.' The change was made in order to allay the anxiety of kind friends, who had written to me to express their sympathy in my broken-down state of health, believing that I am a sufferer from chronic 'insomnia,' and that it is as a remedy for that exhausting malady that I have recommended mathematical calculation.

The original title was not, I fear, wisely chosen; and it certainly *was* liable to suggest a meaning I did not intend to convey, viz. that my 'nights' are very often *wholly* 'sleepless.' This is by no means the case: I have never suffered from 'insomnia': and the over-wakeful hours, that I have had to spend at night, have often been simply the result of the over-sleepy hours I have spent during the preceding evening! Nor is it as a remedy for *wakefulness* that I have suggested mathematical calculation; but as a remedy for the *harassing thoughts* that are apt to invade a wholly-unoccupied mind.

To state the matter logically, the dilemma which my friends *suppose* me to be in has, for its two horns, the endurance of a sleepless night, and the adoption of some recipe for inducing sleep. Now, so far as *my* experience goes, no such recipe has any effect, unless when you are sleepy, and mathematical calculations would be more likely to delay, than to hasten, the advent of sleep.

The *real* dilemma, which I have had to face, is this: given that the brain is in so wakeful a condition that do what I will, I am *certain* to remain awake for the next hour or so, I must chose between two courses, viz. either to submit to the fruitless self-torture of going through some worrying topic, over and over again, or else to dictate to myself some topic sufficiently absorbing to keep the worry at bay. A mathematical problem *is*, for me, such a topic; and is a benefit, even if it lengthens the wakeful period a little. I believe that an hour of calculation is much better for me than half-an-hour of worry.

Even when it is a matter of the most elementary calculation, the process of arriving at a solution may involve a diverting dialogue, viz. the problem of 'The Two Clocks':

Which is better, a clock that is right only once a year, or a clock that is right twice every day?

'The latter,' you reply, 'unquestionably.' Very good, now attend.

I have two clocks: one doesn't go *at all*, and the other loses a minute a day: which would you prefer? 'The losing one,' you answer, 'without a doubt.' Now observe: the one which loses a minute a day has to lose twelve hours, or seven hundred and twenty minutes before it is right again, consequently it is only right once in two years, whereas the other is evidently right as often as the time it points to comes round, which happens twice a day. You see that the clock is right *at* eight o'clock? Consequently, when eight o'clock comes round your clock is right.

'Yes, I see *that*,' you reply.

Very good, then you've contradicted yourself *twice*: now get out of the difficulty as best you can, and don't contradict yourself again if you can help it.

You *might* go on to ask, 'How am I to know when eight o'clock *does* come? My clock will not tell me.' Be patient: you know that when eight o'clock comes your clock is right, very good; then your rule is this: keep your eye fixed on your clock, and *the very moment it is right* it will be eight o'clock. 'But — ,' you say. There, that'll do; the more you argue the farther you get from the point, so it will be as well to stop.

Here are ten calculations for you to attempt while lying awake at night. The first three are problems, the remainder mere puzzles. The solutions will be found at the end.

1. THE PIGS
Place twenty-four pigs in four sties, so that, as you go round and round, you may always find the number in each sty nearer to ten than the number in the last.

2. THE CHELSEA PENSIONERS
If 70 per cent have lost an eye, 75 per cent an ear, 80 per cent an arm, 85 per cent a leg; what percentage, *at least*, must have lost all four?

3. THE TWO OMNIBUSES
Omnibuses start from a certain point, both ways, every 15 minutes. A traveller, starting on foot along with one of them, meets one in 12½ minutes: when will he be overtaken by one?

4.
> Dreaming of apples on a wall,
> And dreaming often, dear,
> I dreamed that, if I counted all,
> — How many would appear?

5.
> A stick I found that weighed two pound:
> I sawed it up one day
> In pieces eight of equal weight!
> How much did each piece weigh?
> (*Everybody says 'a quarter of a pound':
> which is wrong.*)

6.
> John gave his brother James a box:
> About it there were many locks.
>
> James woke and said it gave him pain;
> So gave it back to John again.

The box was not with lid supplied,
Yet caused two lids to open wide:

And all these locks had never a key —
What kind of a box, then, could it be?

7.   What is most like a bee in May?
        'Well, let me think: perhaps —' you say.
    Bravo! You're guessing well today!

8.   Three sisters at breakfast
                were feeding the cat,
    The first gave it sole
            — Puss was grateful for that:
    The next gave it salmon
            — which Puss thought a treat:
    The third gave it herring
            — which Puss wouldn't eat.
    (Explain the conduct of the cat.)

9.   Said the Moon to the Sun,
           'Is the daylight begun?'
        Said the Sun to the Moon,
           'Not a minute too soon.'

    'You're a Full Moon,' said he.
        She replied with a frown,
    'Well! I never *did* see
        So uncivil a clown!'
    (Query: Why was the moon so angry?)

10. When the King found that his money was nearly all gone, and that he really *must* live more economically, he decided on sending away most of his Wise Men. There were some hundreds of them — very fine old men, and magnificently dressed in green velvet gowns with gold buttons: if they *had* a fault, it was that they always contradicted one another when he asked for their advice — and they certainly ate and drank enormously. So, on the whole, he was rather glad to get rid of them. But there was an old law, which he did not dare disobey, which said that there must always be

'Seven blind of both eyes:
Two blind of one eye:
Four that see with both eyes:
Nine that see with one eye.'
(Query: How many did he keep?)

Magic Numbers

While lying awake in bed consider the curious properties of certain 'magic numbers':

What is remarkable about 12345679 is that you can multiply it by 9, or *any* of the first nine multiples of 9, and you will get an answer which simply consists of a repetition of the same digit. Furthermore, the digit will be the same as the number of 9's in the multiplier.

$$12345679 \times 9 = 111111111$$
$$12345679 \times 18 = 222222222$$
$$12345679 \times 27 = 333333333$$
$$12345679 \times 36 = 444444444$$
$$12345679 \times 45 = 555555555$$
$$12345679 \times 54 = 666666666$$
$$12345679 \times 63 = 777777777$$
$$12345679 \times 72 = 888888888$$
$$12345679 \times 81 = 999999999$$

Multiply 100001 by any five-digit number you like and you will get a ten-digit answer made up of the five digits repeated twice.

$$100001 \times 12345 = 1234512345$$
$$100001 \times 54321 = 5432154321$$
$$100001 \times 67890 = 6789067890$$
$$100001 \times 98765 = 9876598765$$
$$100001 \times 13579 = 1357913579$$
$$100001 \times 24680 = 2468024680$$
$$100001 \times 99999 = 9999999999$$
$$100001 \times 69696 = 6969669696$$
$$100001 \times 10001 = 1000110001$$

142857 is a most magical 'magic number':

$$142857 \times 2 = 285714$$
$$142857 \times 3 = 428571$$
$$142857 \times 4 = 571428$$
$$142857 \times 5 = 714285$$
$$142857 \times 6 = 857142$$

You will notice that in each case the answer to the sum consists of the same six digits as in the original number and, though starting with a different digit each time, they are in the same order.

What happens when you multiply it by 7?

$$142857 \times 7 = 999999$$

999999 is *not* the answer you expected, but having arrived at it, look where it takes you:

142857 multiplied by 7 equals 999999
AND 999999 divided by 9 equals 111111!

285714 multiplied by 7 equals 1999998
AND 1999998 divided by 9 equals 222222!

428571 multiplied by 7 equals 2999997
AND 2999997 divided by 9 equals 333333!

571428 multiplied by 7 equals 3999996
AND 3999996 divided by 9 equals 444444!

714285 multiplied by 7 equals 4999995
AND 4999995 divided by 9 equals 555555!

857142 multiplied by 7 equals 5999994
AND 5999994 divided by 9 equals 666666!

Solutions

1.   Place 8 pigs in the first sty, 10 in the second, nothing in the third, and 6 in the fourth: 10 is nearer ten than 8; nothing is nearer ten than 10; 6 is nearer ten than nothing; and 8 is nearer ten than 6.

2.   Ten. Adding the wounds together, we get 70 + 75 + 80 + 85 = 310, among 100 men; which gives 3 to each, and 4 to 10 men. Therefore the least percentage is 10.

3.   In 6¼ minutes.

4.   Ten.

5.   In Shylock's bargain for the flesh was found
          No mention of the blood that flowed around:
      So when the stick was sawed in eight,
          The sawdust lost diminished from the weight.

6.   As curly-headed Jemmy was sleeping in bed,
      His brother John gave him a blow on the head;
      James opened his eyelids, and spying his brother,
      Doubled his fist, and gave him another.
      This kind of box then is not so rare;
      The lids are the eyelids, the locks are the hair,
      And so every schoolboy can tell to his cost,
      The key to the tangles is constantly lost.

7.   'Twixt 'Perhaps' and 'May be'
          Little difference we see:
      Let the question go round,
          The answer is found.

8.   That salmon and sole Puss should think very grand
          Is no such remarkable thing.
      For more of these dainties Puss took up her stand;
      But when the third sister stretched out her fair hand
          Pray why should Puss swallow her ring?

9.   'In these degenerate days,' we oft hear said,
        'Manners are lost and chivalry is dead!'
    No wonder, since in high exalted spheres
        The same degeneracy, in fact, appears.
    The Moon, in social matters interfering,
        Scolded the Sun, when early in appearing:
    And the rude Sun, her gentle sex ignoring,
        Called her a fool, thus her pretensions flooring.

10.   Five seeing, and seven blind
        Give us twelve, in all, we find;
    But all of these, 'tis very plain,
        Come into account again.
    For take notice, it may be true,
        That those blind of one eye are blind for two;
    And consider contrariwise,
        That to see with your eye you may have your eyes:
    So setting one against the other —
        For a mathematician no great bother —
    And working the sum, you will understand
        That sixteen wise men still trouble the land.

Gottfried Keller
Meret

Fragments from a Pastor's Journal, 1713

Today, having received from the godly and noble Madame de M. the first Quarter's Payment for Board, I did immediately make acknowledgment of it, along with my Report. Further, administered to the Child Meret (Emerentia) her weekly *Correction*, though more rigorous than before, laying her upon the Bench and applying a new Rod, not without Lamentation and Sighings to the Lord God, that He might bring this grievous Task to a good End. Whereby the Child did indeed cry most pitifully and pray in Abasement and Pain for Pardon, yet afterward resumed her former Obstinacy, deriding the Hymn Book which I presented to her to learn from. Therefore I allowed her a short Respite and then locked her in the dark Bacon Larder, where she began to whimper and complain, but then fell silent, till she suddenly set to singing and jubilating not otherwise than the three Blessed Men in the Fiery Furnace, and I, listening to her, heard that she sang those same Psalms in Verse which she did at other times refuse to learn, though in the idle and wanton Fashion as were fitting for foolish and meaningless Rhymes for Children, so that I could not but recognize the Devil at his old Wiles again."

Further:

"A most lamentable Letter from Madame, who is indeed a

most excellent and godly Lady. She had wetted the Letter with her Tears, and told me of the great Sorrow her godly Spouse was in because the Child Meret showed no Betterment. It is in truth a sore Calamity that has befallen this most famous and honorable Family, and I would be so bold as to opine, saving their Respect, that the Sins of the child's Grandfather on her Father's side, who was an Evil-Liver and a great Lecher, will be visited on the head of this wretched little Creature. Have changed my *Method* with the Child and will now essay the Hunger Cure. Have also caused my own Wife to make a Shift of coarse Sackcloth, and have forbidden Meret to wear any other Attire, this penitential Shift being most suited to her. Stubbornness at the same *Puncto*.

"Today was forced to prevent the little Demoiselle from all Association and Play with the Village Children, she having run with them into the Wood and there bathed in the Pool, hanging the penitential Shift I caused to be made for her on the Branch of a Tree and dancing before it naked, provoking even her Playmates to Impudence and Wantonness. Considerable *Correction*."

"Today, a day of stir and hubbub. There came to me a big strong Lad, our Miller's Son, and sought a Quarrel with me because of Meret, whom he declares he hears moaning and crying every Day, and as I was disputing with him, who should come up but the young Schoolmaster, the Dolt, who threatened to take me before the Justice, and fell on the evil Creature's neck, kissing and caressing her, etc., etc. Had the Schoolmaster arrested forthwith and taken before the Magistrate. Will have to deal with the Miller's Son, but he is rich and quarrelsome. Were almost fain to believe myself that the Child is a Witch, if such Opinion were not contrary to Reason. In any case the Devil is in her, and I have taken sore Trouble upon myself."

"This whole week I have had in my house a Painter, sent to me by Madame, who is to paint the Portrait of the little Lady. The afflicted Family is not minded to take the Creature back, but will keep her Picture for the purpose of melancholy Contemplation and because of the Child's great Beauty. Monsieur in particular clings fast to the Notion. My wife serves the Painter two measures of Wine daily, which seems not to satisfy him, for he goes every Evening to the Red Lion, where he plays with the Surgeon. Is a vainglorious Fellow, wherefore I often serve him up a Woodcock or a Pike, the same noted in the quarterly Account for Madame. At first he made much of the Child and at once engaged her Affections, till I warned him that he must not interfere with my *Method*. When we took out from the Chest the Dress and Sunday Finery of the Child, and put it on her with her Crown and Belt, she made show of great Pleasure and began to dance. But this her Joy soon turned to Bitterness when I, upon the order of her Lady Mamma, sent for 1 Skull and placed it in her Hand, she resisting with all her Might, and then holding it in her Hand weeping and trembling, as if it were glowing Iron. The Painter declared that he could paint the Skull by Heart, the same being one of the Elements of his Art, but I would not allow it, Madame having written: 'What the Child suffers, we suffer also, and in her Suffering lies our Opportunity of doing Penance, provided we do it for her Sake; for that reason we would have Your Reverence make no Change in your Care and Education. If, as I hope to the Almighty and Merciful God, the Child shall one Day receive Enlightenment at one Point or other and be saved, she will doubtless rejoice greatly that she has done with a great Deal of her Penance by her present Habit of Stubbornness, which Our inscrutable Lord has been pleased to afflict her with.' With these brave words before me, I considered the time had come to use the Skull as a means of serious Penance for the Child. For that Matter, it was a small, light, Child's Skull, the Painter having complained that, by the Rules of his Art, the big, Man's Skull was too uncouth for the little Hands, and indeed she did hold it more readily after. The Painter also laid a white Rose in her Hand, which I suffered because it can be taken as a favorable *Symbol*.

"Received today sudden Counterorders respecting Portrait and am not to send the same to Town, but to keep it here. 'Tis a pity for the fine Work the Painter has done, for he was delighted beyond Measure by the Child's Gracefulness. Had I but known this before, the Fellow could have painted my own Portrait on the Canvas, seeing that the good Victuals and Payment will be wasted anyhow."

Further:

"I have received Orders to cease all worldly Instruction, especially in the French Language, the same being regarded as no longer necessary, and my Wife is to stop the Spinet Lessons, which seems to sadden the Child. I shall from now on treat her like any other charge, taking care only that she give no more Cause for Public Annoyance.

"The Day before Yesterday, little Meret ran away, and we were in great Fear till she was found today at Noon on the Top of the Beech Hill, where she sat naked on her penitential Shift, warming herself to a Turn in the Sun. She had unplaited her Hair and set a Wreath of Beech Leaves on it, and had draped a Scarf of the same round her Body; she had also a quantity of fine Strawberries lying before her and was quite tight and round from eating of them. When she saw us, she started up again to flee, was ashamed of her Nakedness and would have put on her Shift, this giving us time to capture her. Now she lies sick in Bed and seems confused in Mind, giving no reasonable Answers.

"Great Betterment in the Child Meret, yet she changes more and more and seems bereft of all Sense. The Report of the *Medicus* is that she is losing her Mind or going mad, and that she should be placed in Medical Treatment, he offering himself to undertake such Treatment, and promising to restore the Child to Health if she should be placed in his House. But I have noted that *Monsieur Chirurgeon* hath an eye only for the good Payment and the Presents from Madame, so I replied what I thought best, namely that the Lord seemed about to make an End to His Plan concerning His Creature, and that Human Hands could and should change nothing, as is in Truth so."

Five or six months later:

"The Child seems to enjoy excellent Health in her senseless Condition, having fresh rosy Cheeks. Stays the whole Day now in the Bean Field where we cannot see her, and we trouble no more about her, the more so as she occasions no further Nuisance.

"In the Midst of the Bean Field the Child Meret has arranged a little *Salon*, where the village Children pay their Duties to her, carrying to her Fruit and other Victuals which she has most daintily buried and keeps in Store. And we did also find there that little Child's Skull which was lost long since so that it could not be restored to the Sexton. She has also enticed to her and tamed the Sparrows and other Birds, which have made much Havoc among the Beans, but I dare not shoot into the Bean Field now because of its little Inmate. *Item*, she has played with a poisonous Snake which broke through the Hedge and made its Nest beside her. *In Summa*, we have had perforce to take her into the House again and keep her there.

"The rosy Cheeks have faded from her and the Surgeon declares that she will not be with us long. Have written to the Parents.

"Today, before Daybreak, the poor Child Meret must have escaped from her Bed, crept out to the Beans and died there, for we found her lying there as dead in a little Grave she had dug in the Earth, as if preparing to crawl into it. She was stiff as a Rod and her Hair and Nightgown damp and heavy with Dew, which lay in clear Drops on her faintly rosy Cheeks, as it might be on apple blossom. We were overcome by great Fear, and I myself suffered this Day great Distraction and Confusion because Monsieur and Madame arrived from Town just when my Wife was gone to K. to buy Cakes and other Victuals wherewith to offer them becoming Refreshment. Did not know where to turn, all being at Sixes and Sevens, the Maids having to wash and shroud the little Corpse and at the same time prepare suitable Refreshment. In the End I had the green Ham roasted which my Wife laid in Vinegar a Week since, and Jacob caught three of those tame Trout that still come to our Garden now and then though we had forbidden our blessed (?!) Meret to go to the brook. To my great Happiness, these Dishes brought me some Credit, and Madame ate of them with great Pleasure. Great Mourning; we spent two Hours in Prayer and the Contemplation of Death, and the same in melancholy Discourse of the Sickness which afflicted dead Child, since we must now believe, to our great Consolation, that the same arose from a fatal Disposition of the Blood and Brain. And we also spoke of the Child's great Gifts and of her oft-while ingenious and delightful Conceits and *Caprices*, but we, in our earthly Blindness, could make no Sense of it all. Tomorrow Morning the Child is to have Christian Burial, the Presence of the Parents being most desirable in this Point, since the Villagers would otherwise have refused to suffer it."

"This is the strangest and most dreadful Day, not only since the wretched Creature came to us, but in the whole of my peaceful Life. For when the time was come and ten had struck, we set out behind the little Corpse for the Graveyard while the Sexton tolled the Bell, though not with much Fervor, for it rang most dismally and half of the Sound was swallowed up by a great Wind which raged furiously. And the Sky also was dark and lowering, and the Graveyard empty of People save of our little Company, while outside its Walls all the Villagers had gathered, stretching their Heads curiously over it. But just as we were about to lower the little Coffin into the Grave, a most doleful Cry broke from the Coffin, so that Terror overcame us and the Gravedigger took to his Heels. But the Surgeon, who hastened up to the Grave, removed the lid in all Speed, and the dead Child rose up as if alive and climbed quite nimbly out of the Grave and looked at us. And as at that very moment the Beams of Phoebus broke through the clouds with unaccustomed Power, she looked, in her yellow Brocade and glittering little crown, like an Elfin or a Goblin Child. Her Lady Mother fell forthwith into a deep Swoon and Monsieur dashed himself to the Earth, weeping. I myself stood rooted to the Spot in Wonder and Fear, and did at that moment firmly believe in Witchcraft. But the Child soon regained her Self-Command and scampered away over the Graveyard and out of the Village like a Cat, till all the People fled to their Homes in Horror and bolted their Doors. At that very moment, School came out, and the Children entered the Lane, and when the Little Ones saw this Thing we could not hold them back, but a great company of Children ran after the Corpse and pur-

sued it, with the Schoolmaster and his Birch Rod after them.
But she had twenty paces' start and did not stop until she
reached the Beech Hill, and there fell dead, while the
Children scrabbled about her and caressed her in vain. This
all we learned later as we, in our Terror, had taken refuge in
the Parsonage, remaining there in profound Desolation till
the Corpse was brought back to us. It was laid upon a Mat-
tress, and Monsieur and Madame departed, leaving a small
stone Tablet on which nothing is engraved but the Family
Crest and a Date. And now the Child lies there as dead
again, and we dare not go to Bed for Fear. But the *Medicus* sits
by her Bed, and now believes she has at last found Peace."

"Today the *Medicus* declared, having made many ex-
periments, that the Child is truly dead, and she has now
been buried quietly, and nothing further has happened, etc.,
etc."

— translated from the German by Mary Hottinger

Elizabeth Bishop
Insomnia

The moon in the bureau mirror
looks out a million miles
(and perhaps with pride, at herself,
but she never, never smiles)
far and away beyond sleep, or
perhaps she's a daytime sleeper.

By the Universe deserted,
she'd tell it to go to hell,
and she'd find a body of water,
or a mirror, on which to dwell.
So wrap up care in a cobweb
and drop it down the well

into that world inverted
where left is always right,
where the shadows are really the body,
where we stay awake all night,
where the heavens are shallow as the sea
is now deep, and you love me.

Michael Goldman
You Too

The gorillas are asleep
in the laboratory cages.

Night rests on the dangerous
Pacific wave.

The eyes of the watcher are heavy
by the Manila seismograph;
the bombs are heavy in the sleeping plane.

Why do you lie awake, my friend,
surgings awake
in your head, in your chest?

Under the ocean's faces,
under the swollen figures cast by the night,
down through the consolations of the waves,
in the pit of this peace,
the flattened creatures shift in their dreams
and are still.
What have we to do with the will
who were born to sleep?

Joyce Carol Oates
Lamb of Abyssalia

So GREAT WAS MY JOY at being home that I could not sleep. Not the first night, not the second, not the third. I lay awake in my comfortable bed and could not sleep. The room's fixtures were not familiar. Perhaps darkness distorted them. I scrambled to the top of a hill but the parched, cracked earth beneath my feet would not support me and at the very brink of triumph — at the very brink — I lost my balance and fell backward with a scream.

A small landslide was loosed: rocks, pebbles, chunks of mud.

There were screams. They were not familiar screams. *Lamb of Abyssalia*, the voices pleaded. *Lamb of Abyssalia have mercy on us.*

Quietly I made my way through the sleeping house.

No one heard, no one knew. Everyone was asleep. It was necessary to walk quietly, stealthily. During my eight-months' absence I often thought of home, especially those last several weeks when I was very tired. I thought of myself tip-toeing through the house, silent and invisible, poking my head into every room, checking to see that everyone was safe. I love you, I whispered in my feverish sleep, I will protect you. Now that I was home it seemed that I might encounter myself on the stairs or around a corner — a tall, thin, smiling, featureless person with a slight limp. I love you. I will protect you. But don't wake: don't stir in your sleep. Isn't it enough to know that I am home and that I will never leave you again?

In their rooms, in their beds, my children slept. When I heard their soft, feathery breaths I felt as if I might swoon. How I loved them — ! I would never leave them again. The danger was too great.

I drew near to their beds, trembling. Of course they had forgiven me for being away — they knew no better than to forgive me. My children. My dear ones. Quietly I leaned over to kiss the youngest one's forehead. He stirred in his sleep, he sighed, his breath was sweet. I wiped a thin thread of saliva from his chin. . . . The eldest did not wake when I approached his bed but he began to grind his teeth suddenly, as if the landscape of his dream had unaccountably turned threatening. But only for a moment: only for a moment. Not wishing to wake him I did not risk brushing my lips against his forehead, I merely stared at him in silence, I blessed him in silence, and then backed away. In my daughter's room I stood for some time, motionless, in awe of her beauty. The fair down of her cheeks and arms, the dimple near her mouth, the small snub nose: her beauty frightened me. Her seventh birthday came and went while I was in Abyssalia, in the night-half of the world.

I could not sleep so I slipped from my bed and went downstairs to my study. I thought it prudent to begin work. I had been home now for nearly a week and I had not begun to work.

You will accomplish very important things, my elders told me. One of them shook my hand, covering it with his other hand: I believe there were tears in his eyes. (And he was by no means a sentimental man.) I smiled and stammered my gratitude as always. You will go farther than any of us, my elders said with their bright hopeful smiles. They were not jealous, there was no need for jealousy; they knew how I revered them.

Their prophecies have turned out to be, for the most part, true.

● ● ● ● ●

Once I flew against the sun — eastward against the sun's motion — and I passed beneath the sun and in that way overtook the sun. On my return flight I flew westward beneath the sun and the sun's rays stung and I was drawn by the magnificent tug of the sun westward and it appeared that once again I overtook the sun as I passed beneath the sun but perhaps this was an illusion, like many: perhaps I did not overtake the sun on either flight.

There are eight notebooks, a duffel bag and a knapsack filled with three-by-five cards, and several piles of papers — some of them are rumpled letterheads from the Hotel Bru'jaila, some are merely slips of paper. Twists and bits of paper. I spend my hours smoothing papers with the flat of my hand. The halo of light that falls atop my desk is very intense. I am fearful of insects — fearful that they will flock to the light and hit against the shade and against my face — but I keep on with my work.

On the fourteenth floor of the Hotel Bru'jaila the hoarse-voiced Minister of Finance and Development introduced me to a very curious, very strong but also very sweet — stingingly sweet — drink called Ā-sā. Ā-sā? I am not sure of its pronunciation. It is a brownish purple-red, a claret red. In certain lights. In other lights it is very dark. When I tasted it two wires leapt into life, running up my nostrils and back into my brain. What is Ā-sa made of, I asked the Minister when I was able to speak. He ignored my question; perhaps he did not understand it. You try more, you like, he said flatly, unquestioningly. You will enjoy. He watched as I sipped at the tall iced sugar-rimmed glass on the fourteenth floor of the Hotel Bru'jaila.

● ● ● ● ●

On the banks of the River of Blossoms, and the River of Faith, and the Blessed River of Forgetfulness. Squatting creatures with human characteristics: their great dark bruised eyes, their brain-damaged eyes, seizing me and releasing me in the same instant. I adjusted my sunglasses. I moistened my lips.

The white man is considered by the Abyssalians to be a kind of ghost or "trick" person. A "trick" shadow. Moving my hands slowly before their eyes, this way and that, I noted that their gaze did not follow the movement of my hands.

Certain insects buzzed angrily about my face.

Lamb of Abyssalia pray for us. Lamb of Abyssalia have mercy on us.

I stooped and kissed the child's forehead. Perhaps it was my imagination but his skin felt feverish. I drew my cool fingers across his forehead; I brushed a strand of hair away, noting its silkiness. I forgive you, the child whispered. I love you and I forgive you but you must never leave me again — you must never leave your family again. We wept together. Our cheeks were hot with tears. I was a giant creature crouched over his bed, my face must have been terrifying, so contorted with sorrow, yet the child found it in his heart to forgive me. But you must never leave your family again, he said.

Abyssalia. Bounded by Equatorial Guinea, the Republics of Rambu and Nazaire, and the French Territory of the Barrantes. Area: 114,000 sq. mi. Pop. (1976 est.): 2,800,000. Cap. and largest city: Bru'jaila (pop. 1976 est., 174,000). Language: Abyssalian, Bantu dialects, French. Religion: animist approximately 70%; Muslim and Christian minorities.

You like, you will enjoy. You will learn.

• • • • •

The Lamb of Abyssalia is led from hut to hut, and at each dwelling bits of its fleece are plucked. The hill people are tall and very dark and their cheekbones appear to be pushing through their skin. Their eyes appear to be growing back into their skulls. It is said (and I had no way of confirming) that from 5%–8% of the population lives to be more than 110 years of age.

Infant mortality, however, is high. Very high.

The Lamb of Abyssalia is led in a great circle and is brought back to the little altar before the priest's hut. The Lamb is always a male; it is a very choice lamb, never more than one month old. Music of a sort — gourds, drums, a fife-like pipe — accompanies the Lamb's passage.

I crouched over the narrow bed, I brushed a strand of hair out of the child's eyes. My God I am so frightened. So frightened. But the child slept his deep innocent sleep. My fingers trembled: I pulled a single strand of hair out of his scalp: I yanked it free.

I began to sort the note-cards. Twelve separate piles. And the slips of paper — some of them no more than an inch square. Scrawls in ballpoint and pencil. Some words illegible. Snips and bits of paper. Magic utterances. Twists of words. Syllables missing: I sweated through my clothes there in Abyssalia and my wisdom is therefore fragmentary.

As far as the eye can see, a wave of bodies: a sea of bodies.

Making their way along the banks of the River of Blossoms. So many! I held my sunglasses in place for fear they would fly off.

Why are there so many, I asked, seeing the caved-in eyes, the swollen stomachs, the knobby bones. Where are they going, I asked.

A religious procession, I was told.

One crumpled bit of paper speaks of those gaily colored rags.

Another speaks of the heat, and of course the odor.

Another speaks of the noises: the groans, the grunts, the random shrieks, the occasional outbursts of song. And of laughter? I am not sure.

Still another note, much-folded, speaks of a wraith-like mask hovering above a bright orange rag. *It appeared to be a mask,* the scrawl declares hesitantly. How curious, a kind of death's-head, the eyes, nose, and mouth darkest, as if shaded in by crayon or charcoal. How curious, that it should be trembling. Quivering. Pulsing. I came closer and saw that it was something living: a swarm of dark-glinting insects. Mosquitos. I came closer still and saw that it was a child's face but the face was covered with insects, and the insects were most crowded, most dense, on the eyes and nose and mouth. (I began to shout. I began to scream. I clapped my hands and some of the mosquitos rose from the child, sluggish and heavy with blood, not very disturbed. I could not stop shouting. Perhaps I was screaming. Someone touched my shoulder and drew me away. Stop, they said, you must stop. You'll have sunstroke. You'll be very, very ill. I was still screaming. Insects darted against my face; something had bitten me on the right cheekbone. There was a terrible stench. The child's face was swollen and bleeding and very ugly. Perhaps it was not a child. It wore a twisted orange rag. Come away, they said gently, the mother has abandoned him and death is inevitable. Why do you tire yourself in this heat?)

A detailed description of the Hotel Bru'jaila: its waterfall, its potted trees and flowers, its velvet couches, its marble floors, its marvelous air-conditioning. (Some of the women wore sweaters, in fact. One wore a lynx stole.) The Minister of Finance and Development, the President of the University of Abyssalia, a smiling young black man named Robert, and I, on the fourteenth floor of the hotel, eating native dishes, listening to a combo playing breezy tunes from the American Forties. You'll be very, very ill. In the distance the hills evaporated into a sullen heat-haze the color of sand. Isn't the fourteenth floor of any hotel really the thirteenth floor, I inquired, my breath hot from the Ā-sā I had drunk too quickly. Only Robert caught my meaning. He had played tennis at Harvard with Neville Hughes's son: did I know Neville Hughes? He had done so much for the cause of Abyssalia, for its liberation. In 1957. Surely I knew him? I was joking, surely, to say I did not know him?

I shielded my eyes against the sun but it did no good. Everything caught fire, everything was seared with heat. During the afternoon the sun shook itself like a giant, bumbling, good-natured dog and descended from the sky and dwelt among us and caused us to swim through him — it — *him.* I lay on my cot in my tent, in bedclothes soaked in the River of Faith. Insects threw themselves against the netting.

Something burrowed beneath my fingernails, into my arm-pits, into my left ear. O help me. O God help me. I drank in the evenings, writing in my notebook. The book would grow, the book would blossom, I would rise when my name was called and come to the podium where the President of the Academy of American Letters would shake my hand and present me with a scroll. I would clear my throat nervously. I would give my brief prepared speech. My lips would part in a grateful smile as I stared into the audience, row upon row of applauding individuals. I am very happy, I would say, I am very grateful, I am humble, I am surprised and pleased, I am ill. You must excuse me but I am very, very ill.

The applause would continue, however.

• • • • •

Applause, applause.

Murmurings, shouts, outbursts of song or laughter or — ? Rage, perhaps. Terror. Millions upon millions of creatures with human characteristics, swarming upon a river-bank, splashing in the bright green fetid water, their rags catching fire in the sunshine. Such fine gay brightly dyed colors! The glinting movement of their wings, the fixed precision of their eyes. Swarming. I waved my hands violently, I cried out, but no one listened. Had my foot slipped I would have fallen among them. Beneath them. Had my foot slipped, had the plane's propellors failed to start, I would never have returned home.

Where my joy is so intense that I crouch above the little girl's bed, my face swollen big as the ceiling. O look! A cloud dark with thunder! In my own dreams I run shrieking up a hill, my feet scrambling beneath me, and in utter silence I don't — quite — don't quite — Someone's tiny soft hand reaches out blindly. Someone's fingers tweak my nose. Dad-dy? Daddy? Look at funny Daddy! I am convulsed with a joy that cannot quite translate itself into laughter and when I wake I am not in my bed, not in any of my beds: I am stand-ing, still, above the child's bed, my back stiff and my neck taut with pain. My cheeks glisten in the pale moonlight. My eyes are awash with a stranger's tears.

Lamb of Abyssalia, my lips plead, have mercy on us, pray for us, have mercy. . . .

No one may witness the sacred ceremony, they told me gravely.

It is death to witness the sacred ceremony.

So they told me in Bru'jaila but they turned out to be misinformed — which was so often the case. (They knew less about their own history and the details of their tradition than I; but of course I kept such knowledge to myself.)

We camped on the bank of the River of Blossoms, and then again on the bank of the River of Faith. The Blessed River of Forgetfulness excited my curiosity until I saw it — a squalid muddy stream not much larger than an irrigation ditch, curling through the vegetation. I wished to dip my hand into it, thinking perhaps that I would be blessed with forgetfulness, and as I stooped my hat fell off — did not fall so much as leap — or perhaps it was tugged off by an impish river demon — and though I lunged for it immediately it was lost.

I tied a piece of cloth about my forehead as I had in the days of my youth, running long-distance in the sun.

A bright red rag about my forehead to keep sweat from my eyes.

I grew gay, talkative, spirited. A single swallow of wine was enough to inflate me like a balloon — my eyes fairly bulging with elation. At first the others laughed with me. They grinned and shook their heads from side to side, signifying now *yes*, now *no*, sometimes a noncommital *Yes?* that had no human meaning at all. Afterward they grew silent. Then sullen. Then fearful.

What can be done, I asked, having witnessed the Sacrifice of the Lamb at last, my head awash, my lips rubbery with grinning. What can be done? — who will do it? — what will salvation consist of? — who will be the savior? — will we survive the summer? — will we get back to the capital? — will we be devoured like the Lamb, hairs plucked from our heads and bodies, our eyeballs chewed, our blood splashed on the lovely blank foreheads of children who would rather be somewhere else playing? — our sacred organs anointed with oil, our bones ground down fine for fertilizer? — will we acquiesce to the sacrifice, or will we go berserk at the last moment and fight? — and will we fight bravely, or helplessly, thrashing about like children? What can be done, I cried, unable to sleep for the fourth night, what can be done and who will do it? *Who will do it?*

I spoke of the Blood of the Lamb and though my eyes were glittering with tears and my throat constricted with the desperate need not to cry and my voice trembled foolishly, the audience forgave me; or did not know. They were waiting merely to applaud. They were waiting for the presentation ceremony to end. Afterward there would be conversation, drinks, high spirits — a release from my voice and the queer wet blank stare I fixed upon them. They waited merely to applaud. They were not restless — it was a very courteous and civilized audience.

I would praise them all, I would bless them. I would kiss their parched foreheads. An immense face floating above a crib, lips puckered for a kiss: a ticklish kiss! The child dreams of a swarthy face, a creature from the dark side of the earth; the child groans and twists from side to side. The fetid smell of the river is in the room with us. Why are the windows closed, why have I forgotten to open them? — or are they open? — is the wind blowing from the wrong direction? As far as the eye can see there are bodies. Bodies heaped upon bodies. Some are alive, crawling upon the dead. Some have been devoured by flame and are now ashes that float past us on the sacred stream. As far as the eye can see: the swarming of dark oil-slick bodies. My foot slips, I am falling, I clutch at the sides of the crib but cannot break my fall, the air is rich with the odor of decaying flesh and excrement and something sweet, achingly sweet, like sugar cane; in the distance the holy bells are clamoring. Wait, I cry, what can be done, who will do it —

The audience begins to applaud at last.

Come away, someone says, touching my arm. Come away.

I would resist but I don't want to disturb the boy. I allow myself to be led quietly out of the room.

Can't you sleep? But why? Why can't you sleep? Have you really tried? How many nights has it been? Won't you try a sleeping pill? Won't you see a doctor? How long can this go on? What can I do? What can be done?

Her voice is too soft, the harsh crazy clamor of the holy bells drowns it out. Why don't the bells ring in unison, I asked, surely they are not in competition with one another — ? But they are ringing in unison, I was told. They are ringing in unison.

I'm so afraid, she says. Staring at me. She too is sleepless though she would deny it if I inquired. She is sleepless because she spies on me, listening to my footsteps, following in her mind's eye my passage through the house. Though I walk on tiptoe and have no more weight than a dream-wraith, she can hear me: her eyes are wide with fear. She *knows*.

And yet she can't possibly know.

You're frightening the children, she whispers. You're frightening me. Sometimes I think —

That's ridiculous, I tell her, smiling.

I think you might harm one of us —

Ridiculous.

A very choice lamb it was, a male no more than four weeks old. Led past the excited villagers by an old man who scolded it fondly, tugging at the length of twine tied about its neck, making of its squealing terror a kind of joke. Yes yes yes yes yes! Such foolishness! Such a baby! Bits of its wool were plucked by greedy fingers. And stuck in hair, behind ears, even up nostrils. There was music, there was singing. Everything was gay, noisy, cacophonous. Children screamed with excitement. Women rocked from side to side, clutching their breasts. I stood to the side, staring. I was invisible: no one saw.

I kept a careful journal.

At last the lamb was dragged to the little stone altar at the center of the village and killed with an ordinary knife about the size of a fishing knife: blood was sprinkled liberally in all directions by the old man: and then the villagers were anointed, one by one, on their foreheads and collar bones: and then most of the lamb was devoured raw. (Afterward the lamb's skull was fixed to a tree in a grove of trees outside the village. There were skulls or parts of skulls on most of the trees.)

The people were so happy afterward, I whisper.

She does not hear. She leads me along the darkened hallway, her hand closed tight about mine. As far as the eye can see there are bodies — some with heads balanced precariously upon skeletal necks, their eyes dark and bruised and sightless; some with swollen bellies; some with no bellies at all. I will save you, I tell them. Have faith in me. But my wife leads me past them, stepping daintily around them. We are both barefoot. We are both frightened. If the stench of the bodies sickens my wife, however, she gives no sign.

You must sleep and then you'll be well again, she says. Then you'll be yourself again.

I stoop and kiss the child's forehead. Is he feverish? Is his face swollen?

The people were so happy afterward, so *happy*, I try to explain. There is no fear, no pain, no sorrow, no possibility of being lost — not even in that vast wilderness. Have faith in me. Don't doubt me. My dear one, my love, sweet mouse, sweet baby. Do you hear?

Ted Hughes
Ghost-Crabs

At nightfall, as the sea darkens,
A depth darkness thickens, mustering from the gulfs and
    the submarine badlands,
To the sea's edge. To begin with
It looks like rocks uncovering, mangling their pallor.
Gradually the labouring of the tide
Falls back from its productions,
Its power slips back from glistening nacelles, and they
    are crabs.
Giant crabs, under flat skulls, staring inland
Like a packed trench of helmets.
Ghosts, they are ghost-crabs.
They emerge
An invisible disgorging of the sea's cold
Over the man who strolls along the sands.
They spill inland, into the smoking purple
Of our woods and towns — a bristling surge
Of tall and staggering spectres
Gliding like shocks through water.
Our walls, our bodies, are no problem to them.
Their hungers are homing elsewhere.
We cannot see them or turn our minds from them.

Their bubbling mouths, their eyes
In a slow mineral fury
Press through our nothingness where we sprawl on beds,
Or sit in rooms. Our dreams are ruffled maybe.
Or we jerk awake to the world of possessions
With a gasp, in a sweat burst, brains jamming blind
Into the bulb-light. Sometimes, for minutes, a sliding
Staring
Thickness of silence
Presses between us. These crabs own this world.
All night, around us or through us,
They stalk each other, they fasten on to each other,
They mount each other, they tear each other to pieces,
They utterly exhaust each other.
They are the powers of this world.
We are their bacteria,
Dying their lives and living their deaths.
At dawn, they sidle back under the sea's edge.
They are the moil of history, the convulsion
In the roots of blood, in the cycles of concurrence.
To them, our cluttered countries are empty battleground.
All day they recuperate under the sea.
Their singing is like a thin seawind flexing in the rocks of
      a headland,
Where only crabs listen.

They are God's only toys.

C.G. *Jung*
Dreams

THE DREAM IS A LITTLE HIDDEN DOOR in the innermost and most secret recesses of the soul, opening into that cosmic night which was psyche long before there was any ego-consciousness, and which will remain psyche no matter how far our ego-consciousness extends. For all ego-consciousness is isolated; because it separates and discriminates, it knows only particulars, and it sees only those that can be related to the ego. Its essence is limitation, even though it reach to the farthest nebulae among the stars. All consciousness separates; but in dreams we put on the likeness of that more universal, truer, more eternal man dwelling in the darkness of primordial night. There he is still the whole, and the whole is in him, indistinguishable from nature and bare of all egohood. It is from these all-uniting depths that the dream arises, be it never so childish, grotesque, and immoral.

No amount of scepticism and criticism has yet enabled me to regard dreams as negligible occurrences. Often enough they appear senseless, but it is obviously we who lack the sense and ingenuity to read the enigmatic message from the nocturnal realm of the psyche. Seeing that at least half our psychic existence is passed in that realm, and that consciousness acts upon our nightly life just as much as the unconscious overshadows our daily life, it would seem all the more incumbent on medical psychology to sharpen its senses by a systematic study of dreams. Nobody doubts the importance of conscious experience; why then should we doubt the significance of unconscious happenings? They also are part of our life, and sometimes more truly a part of it for weal or woe than any happenings of the day.

The dream has for the primitive an incomparably higher value than it has for civilized man. Not only does he talk a great deal about his dreams, he also attributes an extraordinary importance to them, so that it often seems as though he were unable to distinguish between them and reality. To the civilized man dreams as a rule appear valueless, though there are some people who attach great significance to certain dreams on account of their weird and impressive character. This peculiarity lends plausibility to the view that dreams are inspirations.

Dream psychology opens the way to a general comparative psychology from which we may hope to gain the same understanding of the development and structure of the human psyche as comparative anatomy has given us concerning the human body.

A dream, like every element in the psychic structure, is a product of the total psyche. Hence we may expect to find in dreams everything that has ever been of significance in the life of humanity. Just as human life is not limited to this or that fundamental instinct, but builds itself up from a multiplicity of instincts, needs, desires, and physical and psychic conditions, etc., so the dream cannot be explained by this or that element in it, however beguilingly simple such an explanation may appear to be. We can be certain that it is incorrect, because no simple theory of instinct will ever be capable of grasping the human psyche, that mighty and mysterious thing, nor, consequently, its exponent, the dream. In order to do anything like justice to dreams, we need an interpretive equipment that must be laboriously fitted together from all branches of the humane sciences.

The dream is often occupied with apparently very silly details, thus producing an impression of absurdity, or else it is on the surface so unintelligible as to leave us thoroughly bewildered. Hence we always have to overcome a certain resistance before we can seriously set about disentangling the intricate web through patient work. But when at last we penetrate to its real meaning, we find ourselves deep in the dreamer's secrets and discover with astonishment that an apparently quite senseless dream is in the highest degree significant, and that in reality it speaks only of important and serious matters. This discovery compels rather more respect for the so-called superstition that dreams have a meaning, to which the rationalistic temper of our age has hitherto given short shrift.

Dreams that form logically, morally, or aesthetically satisfying wholes are exceptional. Usually a dream is a strange and disconcerting product distinguished by many "bad" qualities, such as lack of logic, questionable morality, uncouth form, and apparent absurdity or nonsense. People are therefore only too glad to dismiss it as stupid, meaningless, and worthless.

Dreams are impartial, spontaneous products of the unconscious psyche, outside the control of the will. They are pure nature; they show us the unvarnished, natural truth, and are therefore fitted, as nothing else is, to give us back an attitude that accords with our basic human nature when our consciousness has strayed too far from its foundations and run into an impasse.

As in our waking state, real people and things enter our field of vision, so the dream-images enter like another kind of reality into the field of consciousness of the dream-ego. We do not feel as if we were producing the dreams, it is rather as if the dreams came to us. They are not subject to our control but obey their own laws. They are obviously autonomous psychic complexes which form themselves out of their own material. We do not know the source of their motives, and we therefore say that dreams come from the unconscious. In saying this, we assume that there are independent psychic complexes which elude our conscious control and come and go according to their own laws.

In sleep, fantasy takes the form of dreams. But in waking life, too, we continue to dream beneath the threshold of consciousness, especially when under the influence of repressed or other unconscious complexes.

The dream is specifically the utterance of the unconscious. Just as the psyche has a diurnal side which we call consciousness, so also it has a nocturnal side: the unconscious psychic activity which we apprehend as dreamlike fantasy.

Dreams contain images and thought associations which we do not create with conscious intent. They arise spontaneously without our assistance and are representatives of a psychic activity withdrawn from our arbitrary will. Therefore the dream is, properly speaking, a highly objective, natural product of the psyche, from which we might expect indications, or at least hints, about certain basic trends in the psychic process. Now, since the psychic process, like any other life-process, is not just a causal sequence, but is also a process with a teleological orientation, we might expect dreams to give us certain *indicia* about the objective causality as well as about the objective tendencies, because they are nothing less than self-portraits of the psychic life-process.

• • • • •

The unconscious is the unknown at any given moment, so it is not surprising that dreams add to the conscious psychological situation of the moment all those aspects which are essential for a totally different point of view. It is evident that this function of dreams amounts to a psychological adjustment, a compensation absolutely necessary for properly balanced action. In a conscious process of reflection it is essential that, so far as possible, we should realize all the aspects and consequences of a problem in order to find the right solution. This process is continued automatically in the more or less unconscious state of sleep, where, as experience seems to show, all those aspects occur to the dreamer (at least by way of allusion) that during the day were insufficiently appreciated or even totally ignored — in other words, were comparatively unconscious.

The view that dreams are merely the imaginary fulfilments of repressed wishes is hopelessly out of date. There are, it is true, dreams which manifestly represent wishes or fears, but what about all the other things? Dreams may contain ineluctable truths, philosophical pronouncements, illusions, wild fantasies, memories, plans, anticipations, irrational experiences, even telephathic visions....

As against Freud's view that the dream is essentially a wish-fulfillment, I hold...that the dream is a spontaneous self-portrayal, in symbolic form, of the actual situation in the unconscious.

The psyche is a self-regulating system that maintains its equilibrium just as the body does. Every process that goes too far immediately and inevitably calls forth compensations, and without these there would be neither a normal metabolism nor a normal psyche. In this sense we can take the theory of compensation as a basic law of psychic behaviour. Too little on one side results in too much on the other.

The more one-sided his conscious attitude is, and the further it deviates from the optimum, the greater becomes the possibility that vivid dreams with a strongly contrasting but purposive content will appear as an expression of the self-regulation of the psyche.

• • • • •

Though dreams contribute to the self-regulation of the psyche by automatically bringing up everything that is repressed or neglected or unknown, their compensatory significance is often not immediately apparent because we still have only a very incomplete knowledge of the nature and the needs of the human psyche. There are psychological compensations that seem to be very remote from the problem on hand. In these cases one must always remember that every man, in a sense, represents the whole of humanity and its history. What was possible in the history of mankind at large is also possible on a small scale in every individual. What mankind has needed may eventually be needed by the individual too. It is therefore not surprising that religious compensations play a great role in dreams. That this is increasingly so in our time is a natural consequence of the prevailing materialism of our outlook.

• • • • •

To interpret the dream process as compensatory is in my view entirely consistent with the nature of the biological process in general. Freud's view tends in the same direction, since he too ascribes a compensatory role to dreams in so far as they preserve sleep. . . . As against this, we should not overlook the fact that the very dreams which disturb sleep most — and these are not uncommon — have a dramatic structure which aims logically at creating a highly affective situation, and builds it up so efficiently that it unquestionably wakes the dreamer. Freud explains these dreams by saying that the censor was no longer able to suppress the painful affect. It seems to me that this explanation fails to do justice to the facts. Dreams which concern themselves in a very disagreeable manner with the painful experiences and activities of daily life and expose just the most disturbing thoughts with the most painful distinctness are known to everyone. It would, in my opinion, be unjustified to speak here of the dream's sleep-preserving, affect-disguising function. One would have to stand reality on its head to see in these dreams a confirmation of Freud's view.

• • • • •

Dreams are often anticipatory and would lose their specific meaning on a purely causalistic view. They afford unmistakable information about the analytical situation, the correct understanding of which is of the greatest therapeutic importance.

The causal point of view tends by its very nature towards uniformity of meaning, that is, towards a fixed significance of symbols. The final point of view, on the other hand, perceives in the altered dream-image the expression of an altered psychological situation. It recognizes no fixed meaning of symbols. From this standpoint, all the dream-images are important in themselves, each one having a special significance of its own, to which, indeed, it owes its inclusion in the dream....The symbol in the dream has more the value of a parable; it does not conceal, it teaches.

• • • • •

Considering a dream from the standpoint of finality, which I contrast with the causal standpoint of Freud, does not — as I would expressly like to emphasize — involve a denial of the dream's causes, but rather a different interpretation of the associative material gathered round the dream. The material facts remain the same, but the criterion by which they are judged is different. The question may be formulated simply as follows: What is the purpose of this dream? What effect is it meant to have? These questions are not arbitrary inasmuch as they can be applied to every psychic activity. Everywhere the question of the "why" and the "wherefore" may be raised, because every organic structure consists of a complicated network of purposive functions, and each of these functions can be resolved into a series of individual facts with a purposive orientation.

The prospective function, on the other hand, is an anticipation in the unconscious of future conscious achievements, something like a preliminary exercise or sketch, or a plan roughed out in advance....The occurrence of prospective dreams cannot be denied. It would be wrong to call them prophetic, because at bottom they are no more prophetic than a medical diagnosis or a weather forecast. They are merely an anticipatory combination of probabilities which may coincide with the actual behavior of things but need not necessarily agree in every detail. Only in the latter case can we speak of "prophecy." That the prospective function of dreams is sometimes greatly superior to the combinations we can consciously foresee is not surprising, since a dream results from the fusion of subliminal elements and is thus a combination of all the perceptions, thoughts, and feelings which consciousness has not registered because of their feeble accentuation. In addition, dreams can rely on subliminal memory traces that are no longer able to influence consciousness effectively. With regard to prognosis, therefore, dreams are often in a much more favourable position than consciousness.

Another dream-determinant that deserves mention is telepathy. The authenticity of this phenomenon can no longer be disputed today. It is, of course, very simple to deny its existence without examining the evidence, but that is an unscientific procedure which is unworthy of notice. I have found by experience that telepathy does in fact influence dreams, as has been asserted since ancient times. Certain people are particularly sensitive in this respect and often have telepathically influenced dreams. But in acknowledging the phenomenon of telepathy I am not giving unqualified assent to the popular theory of action at a distance. The phenomenon undoubtedly exists, but the theory of it does not seem to me so simple.

• • • • •

Dreams are as simple or as complicated as the dreamer is himself, only they are always a little bit ahead of the dreamer's consciousness. I do not understand my own dreams any better than any of you, for they are always somewhat beyond my grasp and I have the same trouble with them as anyone who knows nothing about dream interpretation. Knowledge is no advantage when it is a matter of one's own dreams.

• • • • •

It is obvious that in handling "big" dreams intuitive guesswork will lead nowhere. Wide knowledge is required, such as a specialist ought to possess. But no dream can be interpreted with knowledge alone. This knowledge, furthermore, should not be dead material that has been memorized; it must possess a living quality, and be infused with the experience of the person who uses it. Of what use is philosophical knowledge in the head, if one is not also a philosopher at heart?

One would do well to treat every dream as though it were a totally unknown object. Look at it from all sides, take it in your hand, carry it about with you, let your imagination play round it, and talk about it with other people. Primitives tell each other impressive dreams, in a public palaver if possible, and this custom is also attested in late antiquity, for all the ancient peoples attributed great significance to dreams. Treated in this way, the dream suggests all manner of ideas and associations which lead us closer to its meaning. The ascertainment of the meaning is, I need hardly point out, an entirely arbitrary affair, and this is where the hazards begin. Narrower or wider limits will be set to the meaning, according to one's experience, temperament, and taste. Some people will be satisfied with little, for others much is still not enough. Also the meaning of the dream, or our interpretation of it, is largely dependent on the intentions of the interpreter, on what he expects the meaning to be or requires it to do. In eliciting the meaning he will involuntarily be guided by certain presuppositions, and it depends very much on the scrupulousness and honesty of the investigator whether he gains something by his interpretation or perhaps only becomes still more deeply entangled in his mistakes.

So difficult is it to understand a dream that for a long time I have made it a rule, when someone tells me a dream and asks for my opinion, to say first of all to myself: "I have no idea what this dream means." After that I can begin to examine the dream.

The psychological context of dream-contents consists in the web of associations in which the dream is naturally embedded. Theoretically we can never know anything in advance about this web, but in practice it is sometimes possible, granted long enough experience. Even so, careful analysis will never rely too much on technical rules; the danger of deception and suggestion is too great. In the analysis of isolated dreams above all, this kind of knowing in advance and making assumptions on the grounds of practical expectation or general probability is positively wrong. It should therefore be an absolute rule to assume that every dream, and every part of a dream, is unknown at the outset, and to attempt an interpretation only after carefully taking up the context. We can then apply the meaning we have thus discovered to the text of the dream itself and see whether this yields a fluent reading, or rather whether a satisfying meaning emerges.

• • • • •

I call every interpretation which equates the dream images with real objects an *interpretation on the objective level*. In contrast to this is the interpretation which refers every part of the dream and all the actors in it back to the dreamer himself. This I call *interpretation on the subjective level*. Interpretation on the objective level is analytic, because it breaks down the dream content into memory-complexes that refer to external situations. Interpretation on the subjective level is synthetic, because it detaches the underlying memory-complexes from their external causes, regards them as tendencies or components of the subject, and reunites them with that subject....In this case, therefore, all the contents of the dream are treated as symbols for subjective contents.

If our dreams reproduce certain ideas these ideas are primarily *our* ideas, in the structure of which our whole being is interwoven. They are subjective factors, grouping themselves as they do in the dream, and expressing this or that meaning, not for extraneous reasons but from the most intimate promptings of our psyche. The whole dream-work is essentially subjective, and a dream is a theatre in which the dreamer is himself the scene, the player, the prompter, the producer, the author, the public, and the critic.

The relation between conscious and unconscious is compensatory. This is one of the best-proven rules of dream interpretation. When we set out to intepret a dream, it is always helpful to ask: What conscious attitude does it compensate?

If we want to interpret a dream correctly, we need a thorough knowledge of the conscious situation at that moment, because the dream contains its unconscious complement, that is, the material which the conscious situation has constellated in the unconscious. Without this knowledge it is impossible to interpret a dream correctly, except by a lucky fluke.

The real difficulty begins when the dreams do not point to anything tangible, and this they do often enough, especially when they hold anticipations of the future. I do not mean that such dreams are necessarily prophetic, merely that they feel the way, they "reconnoitre." These dreams contain inklings of possibilities and for that reason can never be made plausible to an outsider.

Anyone sufficiently interested in the dream problem cannot have failed to observe that dreams also have a continuity *forwards* — if such an expression be permitted — since dreams occasionally exert a remarkable influence on the conscious mental life of even persons who cannot be considered superstitious or particularly abnormal.

It is not denied in medieval ecclesiastical writings that a divine influx may occur in dreams, but this view is not exactly encouraged, and the Church reserves the right to decide whether a revelation is to be considered authentic or not. In spite of the Church's recognition that certain dreams are sent by God, she is disinclined, and even averse, to any serious concern with dreams, while admitting that some might conceivably contain an immediate revelation. Thus the change of mental attitude that has taken place in recent centuries is, from this point of view at least, not wholly unwelcome to the Church, because it effectively discouraged the earlier introspective attitude which favoured a serious consideration of dreams and inner experiences.

As individuals we are not completely unique, but are like all other men. Hence a dream with a collective meaning is valid in the first place for the dreamer, but it expresses at the same time the fact that his momentary problem is also the problem of other people. This is often of great practical importance, for there are countless people who are inwardly cut off from humanity and oppressed by the thought that nobody else has their problems. Or else they are those all-too-modest souls who, feeling themselves non-entities, have kept their claim to social recognition on too low a level. Moreover, every individual problem is somehow connected with the problem of the age, so that practically every subjective difficulty has to be viewed from the standpoint of the human situation as a whole. But this is permissible only when the dream really is a mythological one and makes use of collective symbols.

If, in addition to this, we bear in mind that the unconscious contains everything that is lacking to consciousness, that the unconscious therefore has a compensatory tendency, then we can begin to draw conclusions — provided, of course, that the dream does not come from too deep a psychic level. If it is a dream of this kind, it will as a rule contain mythological motifs, combinations of ideas or images which can be found in the myths of one's own folk or in those of other races. The dream will then have a collective meaning, a meaning which is the common property of mankind.

It is characteristic that dreams never express themselves in a logical, abstract way but always in the language of parable or simile. This is also a characteristic of primitive languages, whose flowery turns of phrase are very striking. If we remember the monuments of ancient literature, we find that what nowadays is expressed by means of abstractions was then expressed mostly by similes. Even a philosopher like Plato did not disdain to express certain fundamental ideas in this way.

Just as the body bears the traces of its phylogenetic development, so also does the human mind. Hence there is nothing surprising about the possibility that the figurative language of dreams is a survival from an archaic mode of thought.

• • • • •

Nature commits no errors.

I take the dream for what it is. The dream is such a difficult and complicated thing that I do not dare to make any assumptions about its possible cunning or its tendency to deceive. The dream is a natural occurrence, and there is no earthly reason why we should assume that it is a crafty device to lead us astray. It occurs when consciousness and will are to a large extent extinguished. It seems to be a natural product which is also found in people who are not neurotic. Moreover, we know so little about the psychology of the dream process that we must be more than careful when we introduce into its explanation elements that are foreign to the dream itself.

Nature is often obscure or impenetrable, but she is not, like man, deceitful. We must therefore take it that the dream is just what it pretends to be, neither more nor less. If it shows something in a negative light, there is no reason for assuming that it is meant positively.

• • • • •

But in no circumstances may we anticipate that this meaning will fit in with any of our subjective expectations; for quite possibly, indeed very frequently, the dream is saying something surprisingly different from what we would expect. As a matter of fact, if the meaning we find in the dream happens to coincide with our expectations, that is a reason for suspicion; for as a rule the standpoint of the unconscious is complementary or compensatory to consciousness and thus unexpectedly "different."

Every interpretation is an hypothesis, an attempt to read an unknown text. An obscure dream, taken in isolation, can hardly ever be interpreted with any certainty. For this reason I attach little importance to the interpretation of single dreams. A relative degree of certainty is reached only in the interpretation of a series of dreams, where the later dreams correct the mistakes we have made in handling those that went before. Also, the basic ideas and themes can be recognized much better in a dream-series.

Seen purely theoretically, a dream can mean anything or nothing. For that matter, does a thing or a fact ever mean anything in itself? The only certainty is that it is always man who interprets, who assigns meaning. And that is the gist of the matter for psychology.

• • • • •

I have no theory about dreams, I do not know how dreams arise. And I am not at all sure that my way of handling dreams even deserves the name of a "method." I share all your prejudices against dream-interpretation as the quintessence of uncertainty and arbitrariness. On the other hand, I know that if we meditate on a dream sufficiently long and thoroughly, something almost always comes of it. This something is not of course a scientific result to be boasted about or rationalized; but it is an important practical hint which shows the patient what the unconscious is aiming at. Indeed, it ought not to matter to me whether the result of my musings on the dream is scientifically verifiable or tenable, otherwise I am pursuing an ulterior — and therefore auto-erotic — aim. I must content myself wholly with the fact that the result means something to the patient and sets his life in motion again. I may allow myself only one criterion for the result of my labours: does it work? As for my scientific hobby — my desire to know *why* it works — this I must reserve for my spare time.

• • • • •

The evolutionary stratification of the psyche is more clearly discernible in the dream than in the conscious mind. In the dream, the psyche speaks in images, and gives expression to instincts, which derive from the most primitive levels of nature. Therefore, through the assimilation of unconscious contents, the momentary life of consciousness can once more be brought into harmony with the law of nature from which it all too easily departs, and the patient can be led back to the natural law of his own being.

The interpretation of dreams enriches consciousness to such an extent that it relearns the forgotten language of the instincts.

Many people who know something, but not enough, about dreams and their meaning, and who are impressed by their subtle and apparently intentional compensation, are liable to succumb to the prejudice that the dream actually has a moral purpose, that it warns, rebukes, comforts, foretells the future, etc. If one believes that the unconscious always knows best, one can easily be betrayed into leaving the dreams to take the necessary decisions, and is then disappointed when the dreams become more and more trivial and meaningless. Experience has shown me that a slight knowledge of dream psychology is apt to lead to an over-rating of the unconscious which impairs the power of conscious decision. The unconscious functions satisfactorily only when the conscious mind fulfils its tasks to the very limit. A dream may perhaps supply what is then lacking, or it may help us forward where our best conscious efforts have failed.

In each of us there is another whom we do not know. He speaks to us in dreams and tells us how differently he sees us from the way we see ourselves. When, therefore, we find ourselves in a difficult situation to which there is no solution, he can sometimes kindle a light that radically alters our attitude — the very attitude that led us into the difficult situation.

• • • • •

To concern ourselves with dreams is a way of reflecting on ourselves — a way of self-reflection. It is not our ego-consciousness reflecting on itself; rather, it turns its attention to the objective acuality of the dream as a communication or message from the unconscious, unitary soul of humanity. It reflects not on the ego but on the self; it recollects that strange self, alien to the ego, which was ours from the begin-ning, the trunk from which the ego grew. It is alien to us because we have estranged ourselves from it through the aberrations of the conscious mind.

A dream is nothing but a lucky idea that comes to us from the dark, all-unifying world of the psyche. What would be more natural, when we have lost ourselves amid the endless particulars and isolated details of the world's surface, than to knock at the door of dreams and inquire of them the bearings which would bring us closer to the basic facts of human existence? Here we encounter the obstinate prejudice that dreams ar so much froth, they are not real, they lie, they are mere wish-fulfilments. All this is but an excuse not to take dreams seriously, for that would be uncomfortable. Our intellectual hybris of consciousness loves isolation despite all its inconveniences, and for this reason people will do anything rather than admit that dreams are real and speak the truth. There are some saints who had very rude dreams. Where would their saintliness be, the very thing that exalts them above the vulgar rabble, if the obscenity of a dream were a real truth? But it is just the most squalid dreams that emphasize our blood-kinship with the rest of mankind, and most effectively damp down the arrogance born of an atrophy of the instincts. Even if the whole world were to fall to pieces, the unity of the psyche would never be shattered. And the wider and more numerous the fissures on the surface, the more this unity is strengthened in the depths.

Charles Wright
12 Lines at Midnight

Sleep, in its burning garden, sets out the small plants.
Behind me an animal breaks down,
One ear to the moon's brass sigh.

The earth ticks open like a ripe fruit.
The mist, with sleeves of bone, slides out of the reeds,
Everything hushed, the emptiness everywhere.

The breath inside my breath is the breath of the dream.
I lick its charred heart, a piece of the same flaked sky
The badger drags to his hole.

The bread bleeds in the cupboard,
The mildew tightens. The clocks, with their tiny hands,
    reach out,
Inarticulate monitors of the wind.

Julia Randall
Insomnia

See here, children, it's time to sleep.
Alice, pull in your long neck.
Sylvia, sheathe your teeth. And lie down, Maggie,
there's a good girl. And Emily,
turn off the hose, and George,
for godssake don't snore. Dear Charlotte, ghosts
do not visit our shore, you're only pretending.
Miriam, stop beating
that drum, and Joan,
one cannot sleep in a crown.

There, there, Mother will tuck you in. Cleo will prowl the
　　hall
a while, but she's old enough
to make her own decisions. Before you start to drink,
practice at home. Be glad
you had tolerant parents. Ruth, you pray too much.
Virginia, did you wind the watch? No, Jeep,
it's not a man, it's a possum.

　　　　　　　　Oh my own,
will you go to sleep now? will you leave me alone?

Paul Bowles
The Eye

TEN OR TWELVE YEARS AGO there came to live in Tangier a man who would have done better to stay away. What happened to him was in no way his fault, notwithstanding the whispered innuendos of the English-speaking residents. These people often have reactions similar to those of certain primitive groups: when misfortune overtakes one of their number, the others by mutual consent refrain from offering him aid, and merely sit back to watch, certain that he has called his suffering down upon himself. He has become taboo, and is incapable of receiving help. In the case of this particular man, I suppose no one could have been of much comfort; still, the tacit disapproval called forth by his bad luck must have made the last months of his life harder to bear.

His name was Duncan Marsh, and he was said to have come from Vancouver. I never saw him, nor do I know anyone who claims to have seen him. By the time his story reached the cocktail-party circuit he was dead, and the more irresponsible residents felt at liberty to indulge their taste for myth-making.

He came alone to Tangier, rented a furnished house on the slopes of Djamaa el Mokra — they were easy enough to find in those days, and correspondingly inexpensive — and presently installed a teen-age Moroccan on the premises to act as night-watchman. The house provided a resident cook and gardener, but both of these were discharged from their duties, the cook being replaced by a woman brought in at the suggestion of the watchman. It was not long after this that Marsh felt the first symptoms of a digestive illness which over the months grew steadily worse. The doctors in Tangier advised him to go to London. Two months in hospital there helped him somewhat. No clear diagnosis was made, however, and he returned here only to become bedridden. Eventually he was flown back to Canada on a stretcher, and succumbed there shortly after his arrival.

In all this there was nothing extraordinary; it was assumed that Marsh had been one more victim of slow poisoning by native employees. There have been several such cases during my five decades in Tangier. On each occasion it has been said that the European victim had only himself (or herself) to blame, having encouraged familiarity on the part of a servant. What strikes the outsider as strange is that no one ever takes the matter in hand and inaugurates a search for the culprit, but in the total absence of proof there is no point in attempting an investigation.

Two details complete the story. At some point during his illness Marsh told an acquaintance of the arrangements he had made to provide financial aid for his night-watchman in the event that he himself should be obliged to leave Morocco; he had given him a notarized letter to that effect, but apparently the boy never tried to press his claim. The other report came from Dr. Halsey, the physician who arranged for Marsh's removal from the house to the airport. It was this last bit of information which, for me, at least, made the story take on life. According to the doctor, the soles of Marsh's feet had been systematically marked with deep incisions in the form of crude patterns; the cuts were recent, but there was some infection. Dr. Halsey called in the cook and the watchman: they showed astonishment and dismay at the sight of their employer's feet, but were unable to account for the mutilations. Within a few days after Marsh's departure, the original cook and gardener returned to take up residence, the other two having already left the house.

The slow poisoning was classical enough, particularly in the light of Marsh's remark about his provision for the boy's well-being, but the knife-drawn designs on the feet somehow got in the way of whatever combinations of motive one could invent. I thought about it. There could be little doubt that the boy was guilty. He had persuaded Marsh to get rid of the cook that came with the house, even though her wages had to continue to be paid, and to hire another woman (very likely from his own family) to do the cooking. The poisoning process lasts many months if it is to be undetectable, and no one is in a better position to take charge of it than the cook herself. Clearly she knew about the financial arrangement that had been made for the boy, and expected to share in it. At the same time the crosses and circles slashed in the feet were inexplicable. The slow poisoner is patient, careful, methodical; his principal concerns are to keep the dosage effective and to avoid leaving any visible marks. Bravado is unknown to him.

The time came when people no longer told the story of Duncan Marsh. I myself thought of it less often, having no more feasible hypotheses to supply. One evening perhaps five years ago, an American resident here came to me with the news that he had discovered a Moroccan who claimed to have been Marsh's night-watchman. The man's name was Larbi; he was a waiter at Le Fin Bec, a small back-street restaurant. Apparently he spoke poor English, but understood it without difficulty. This information was handed me for what it was worth, said the American, in the event that I felt inclined to make use of it.

I turned it over in my mind, and one night a few weeks later I went down to the restaurant to see Larbi for myself. The place was dimly lit and full of Europeans. I studied the three waiters. They were interchangeable, with wide black moustaches, blue jeans and sport shirts. A menu was handed me; I could scarcely read it, even directly under the glow of the little table lamp. When the man who had brought it returned, I asked for Larbi.

He pulled the menu from my hand and left the table. A moment later another of the triumvirate came up beside me and handed me the menu he carried under his arm. I ordered in Spanish. When he brought the soup I murmured that I was surprised to find him working there. This brought him up short; I could see him trying to remember me.

"Why wouldn't I be working here?" His voice was level, without inflection.

"Of course! Why not? It was just that I thought by now you'd have a bazaar or some sort of shop."

His laugh was a snort. "Bazaar!"

When he arrived with the next course, I begged his pardon for meddling in his affairs. But I was interested, I said, because for several years I had been under the impression that he had received a legacy from an English gentleman.

"You mean Señor Marsh?" His eyes were at last wide open.

"Yes, that was his name. Didn't he give you a letter? He told his friends he had."

He looked over my head as he said: "He gave me a letter."

"Have you ever showed it to anyone?" This was tactless, but sometimes it is better to drive straight at the target.

"Why? What good is it? Señor Marsh is dead." He shook his head with an air of finality, and moved off to another table. By the time I had finished my crème caramel, most of the diners had left, and the place seemed even darker. He came over to the table to see if I wanted coffee. I asked for the check. When he brought it I told him I should like very much to see the letter if he still had it.

"You can come tomorrow night or any night, and I'll show it to you. I have it at home."

I thanked him and promised to return in two or three days. I was confused as I left the restaurant. It seemed clear that the waiter did not consider himself to be incriminated in Duncan Marsh's troubles. When, a few nights later, I saw the document, I no longer understood anything.

It was not a letter; it was a *papier timbré* of the kind on sale at tobacconists. It read, simply: *To Whom It May Concern: I, Duncan Whitelow Marsh, do hereby agree to deposit the sum of One Hundred Pounds to the account of Larbi Lairini, on the first of each month, for as long as I live.* It was signed and notarized in the presence of two Moroccan witnesses, and bore the date June 11, 1966. As I handed it back to him I said: "And it never did you any good."

He shrugged and slipped the paper into his wallet. "How was it going to? The man died."

"It's too bad."

"*Suerte.*" In the Moroccan usage of the word, it means *fate*, rather than simple luck.

At that moment I could have pressed on, and asked him if he had any idea as to the cause of Marsh's illness, but I wanted time for considering what I had just learned. As I rose to leave I said: "I'm sorry it turned out that way. I'll be back in a few days." He held out his hand and I shook it. I had no intentions then. I might return soon or I might never go back.

For as long as I live. The phrase echoed in my mind for several weeks. Possibly Marsh had worded it that way so it would be readily understandable to the *adoul* of Tangier who had affixed their florid signatures to the sheet; yet I could not help interpreting the words in a more melodramatic fashion. To me the document represented the officializing of a covenant already in existence between master and servant: Marsh wanted the watchman's help, and the watchman had agreed to give it. There was nothing upon which to base such an assumption, nevertheless I thought I was on the right track. Slowly I came to believe that if only I could talk to the watchman, in Arabic, and inside the house itself, I might be in a position to see things more clearly.

One evening I walked to Le Fin Bec and without taking a seat motioned to Larbi to step outside for a moment. There I asked him if he could find out whether the house Señor Marsh had lived in was occupied at the moment or not.

"There's nobody living there now." He paused and added: "It's empty. I know the guardian."

I had decided, in spite of my deficient Arabic, to speak to him in his own language, so I said: "Look. I'd like to go with you to the house and see where everything happened. I'll give you fifteen thousand francs for your trouble."

He was startled to hear the Arabic; then his expression

shifted to one of satisfaction. "He's not supposed to let anyone in," he said.

I handed him three thousand francs. "You arrange that with him. And fifteen for you when we leave the house. Could we do it Thursday?"

The house had been built, I should say, in the fifties, when good construction was still possible. It was solidly embedded in the hillside, with the forest towering behind it. We had to climb three flights of stairs through the garden to get to the entrance. The guardian, a squinting Djibli in a brown djellaba, followed close on our footsteps, eyeing me with mistrust.

There was a wide terrace above, with a view to the southeast over the town and the mountains. Behind the terrace a shadowed lawn ended where the forest began. The living room was large and bright, with French doors giving onto the lawn. Odors of damp walls and mildew weighted the air. The absurd conviction that I was about to understand everything had taken possession of me; I noticed that I was breathing more quickly. We wandered into the dining room. There was a corridor beyond, and the room where Marsh had slept, shuttered and dark. A wide curving stairway led down to a level where there were two more bedrooms, and continued its spiral to the kitchen and servants' rooms below. The kitchen door opened onto a small flagstoned patio where high phylodendron covered the walls.

Larbi looked out and shook his head. "That's the place where all the trouble began," he said glumly.

I pushed through the doorway and sat down on a wrought-iron bench in the sun. "It's damp inside. Why don't we stay out here?"

The guardian left us and locked up the house. Larbi squatted comfortably on his heels near the bench.

There would have been no trouble at all, he said, if only Marsh had been satisfied with Yasmina, the cook whose wages were included in the rent. But she was a careless worker and the food was bad. He asked Larbi to find him another cook.

"I told him ahead of time that this woman Meriam had a

little girl, and some days she could leave her with friends and some days she would have to bring her with her when she came to work. He said it didn't matter, but he wanted her to be quiet."

The woman was hired. Two or three days a week she came accompanied by the child, who would play in the patio where she could watch her. From the beginning Marsh complained that she was noisy. Repeatedly he sent messages down to Meriam, asking her to make the child be still. And one day he went quietly around the outside of the house and down to the patio. He got on all fours, put his face close to the little girl's face, and frowned at her so fiercely that she began to scream. When Meriam rushed out of the kitchen he stood up smiling and walked off. The little girl continued to scream and wail in a corner of the kitchen, until Meriam took her home. That night, still sobbing, she came down with a high fever. For several weeks she hovered between life and death, and when she was finally out of danger she could no longer walk.

Meriam, who was earning relatively high wages, consulted one fqih after another. They agreed that "the eye" had been put on the child; it was equally clear that the Nazarene for whom she worked had done it. What they told her she must do, Larbi explained, was to administer certain substances to Marsh which eventually would make it possible to counteract the spell. This was absolutely necessary, he said, staring at me gravely. Even if the señor had agreed to remove it (and of course she never would have mentioned it to him) he would not have been able to. What she gave him could not harm him; it was merely medicine to relax him so that when the time came to undo the spell he would not make any objections.

At some point Marsh confided to Larbi that he suspected Meriam of slipping soporifics into his food, and begged him to be vigilant. The provision for Larbi's well-being was signed as an inducement to enlisting his active support. Since to Larbi the mixtures Meriam was feeding her master were relatively harmless, he reassured him and let her continue to dose him with her concoctions.

Tired of squatting, Larbi suddenly stood up and began to walk back and forth, stepping carefully in the center of each flagstone. "When he had to go to the hospital in London, I told her: 'Now you've made him sick. Suppose he doesn't come back? You'll never break it.' She was worried about it. 'I've done what I could,' she said. 'It's in the hands of Allah.'"

When Marsh did return to Tangier, Larbi urged her to be quick about bringing things to a head, now that she had been fortunate enough to get him back. He was thinking, he said, that it might be better for the señor's health if her treatment were not continued for too long a time.

I asked no questions while he talked; I made a point of keeping my face entirely expressionless, thinking that if he noticed the least flicker of disapproval he might stop. The sun had gone behind the trees and the patio was chilly. I had a strong desire to get up and walk back and forth as he was doing, but I thought even that might interrupt him. Once stopped, the flow might not resume.

Soon Marsh was worse than ever, with racking pains in his abdomen and kidneys. He remained in bed then, and Larbi brought him his food. When Meriam saw that he was no longer able to leave the bed, even to go into the bathroom, she decided that the time had come to get rid of the spell. On the same night that a fqih held a ceremony at her house in the presence of the crippled child, four men from Meriam's family came up to Djamaa el Mokra.

"When I saw them coming, I got onto my motorcycle and went into the city. I didn't want to be here when they did it. It had nothing to do with me."

He stood still and rubbed his hands together. I heard the southwest wind beginning to sound in the trees; it was that time of afternoon. "Come. I'll show you something," he said.

We climbed steps around the back of the house and came out onto a terrace with a pergola over it. Beyond this lay the lawn and the wall of trees.

"He was very sick for the next two days. He kept asking me to telephone the English doctor."

"Didn't you do it?"

Larbi stopped walking and looked at me. "I had to clean everything up first. Meriam wouldn't touch him. It was during the rains. He had mud and blood all over him when I got back here and found him. The next day I gave him a bath and changed the sheets and blankets. And I cleaned the house, because they got mud everywhere when they brought him back in. Come on. You'll see where they had to take him."

We had crossed the lawn and were walking in the long grass that skirted the edge of the woods. A path led off to the right through the tangle of undergrowth, and we followed it, climbing across boulders and fallen treetrunks until we came to an old stone well. I leaned over the wall of rocks around it and saw the small circle of sky far below.

"They had to drag him all the way here, you see, and hold him steady right over the well while they made the signs on his feet, so the blood would fall into the water. It's no good if it falls on the side of the well. And they had to make the same signs the fqih drew on paper for the little girl. That's hard to do in the dark and in the rain. But they did it. I saw the cuts when I bathed him."

Cautiously I asked him if he saw any connection between all this and Marsh's death. He ceased staring into the well and turned around. We started to walk back toward the house.

"He died because his hour had come."

And had the spell been broken? I asked him. Could the child walk afterward? But he had never heard, for Meriam had gone to Kenitra not much later to live with her sister.

When we were in the car, driving back down to the city, I handed him the money. He stared at it for several seconds before slipping it into his pocket.

I let him off in town with a vague sense of disappointment, and I saw that I had not only expected, but actually hoped, to find someone on whom the guilt might be fixed. What constitutes a crime? There was no criminal intent — only a mother moving in the darkness of ancient ignorance. I thought about it on my way home in the taxi.

Sir Thomas Wyatt
They Flee from Me

They flee from me that sometime did me seek,
With naked foot stalking within my chamber.
Once have I seen them gentle, tame, and meek
That now are wild, and do not once remember
That sometime they have put themselves in danger
To take bread at my hand. And now they range,
Busily seeking in continual change.

Thanked be fortune it hath been otherwise
Twenty times better, but once especial:
In thin array, after a pleasant guise,
When her loose gown did from her shoulders fall
And she me caught in her arms long and small,
And therewithal so sweetly did me kiss
And softly said, "Dear heart, how like you this?"

It was no dream, for I lay broad awaking.
But all is turn'd now through my gentleness
Into a bitter fashion of forsaking,
And I have leave to go of her goodness,
And she also to use newfangleness.
But since that I unkindly so am served,
How like you this? What hath she now deserved?

Weldon Kees
Girl at Midnight

Then walk the floor, or twist upon your bed
While bullets, cold and blind, rush backward from the
    target's eye,
And say, "I will not dream that dream again. I will not
    dream
Of long-spent whispers vanishing down corridors
That turn through buildings I have never known;
The snap of rubber gloves; the tall child, blind,
Who calls my name; the stained sheets
Of another girl. And then a low bell,
Sounding through the shadows in the cold,
Disturbs the screen that is my mind in sleep.

"—Your face is never clear. You always stand
In charcoal doorways in the dark. Part of your face
Is gone. You say, 'Just to be through with this damned
    world.
Contagious fogs blow in. Christ, we could die
The way deer sometimes do, their antlers locked,
Rotting in snow.'
                    "And I can never speak.
But have I ever told the truth to you?

I did not ask for this; a new disease threads in.
I want your lips upon my lips, your mouth
Upon my breasts, again, again, again, again;
I want the morning filled with sun.

"But I must dream once more of cities burned away,
Corrupted wood, and silence on the piers.
Love is a sickroom with the roof half gone
Where nights go down in a continual rain.

Heart, heart. I do not live. The lie of peace
Echoes to no end; the clocks are dead.
What we have had we will not have again."

Julia Mishkin
Insomnia

It's three or four in the morning.
There's a bird squawking and beating
its wings in the chimney, louder

than the jealous noise of dreams:
a boy turning into a dog.
The changing profile of a man on the wall.

These have nothing to do
with my life here in bed, next to
this other dreamer: he lifts his head,

looks me in the eye, rows away.
He hears the bird but prefers to think
it's hallucination. I kick the sheets away,

spend the night eliminating
possibilities. I don't want to walk
around with this bird's bad dream.

Anyway, it's another day.
There's dew on the stack of logs.
There's the sound of wings

trying to fly. A strong smell of ash
lifts through the house.
A lime-colored sun wheels through the sky.

Jean Rhys
My Day

M Y DAY STARTS VERY EARLY, usually at three in the morning by my bedside clock. I lie with my eyes closed hoping that I'll sleep again, but no dice. On the contrary, I feel very energetic and have to exercise a certain amount of restraint not to bound out of bed, go into the kitchen, make tea, and smoke. But it'll be four hours before the post comes, or the papers. Too long, it'll mean being sleepy all day.

As something like this happens every night, I'm used to it and have an assortment of literature at the foot of the bed. A thriller, a book called *Lo!* which I'm very fond of, full of marvels and wonders, plagues of grasshoppers, mysterious apparitions, disappearances, and so on. The author also asserts, to my great satisfaction, that the earth is not round but flat. As Somerset Maugham said, "We *believe* the earth is round; we *know* it is flat." Quite so. That applies to a lot of other things. We believe what we have been told, the theory. What we know, we know.

Lo! is for quiet nights. So is the murder story. Not right for when I wake and hear, not the hound of the Baskervilles, as a French critic said of my "life in remote Devon," but the wind moaning and groaning round the house. It's astonishing the noises it makes. Sometimes there's a pause, a silence, then a gust so fierce that you're sure the ramshackle place won't stand up to it, the roof will be blown off, the windows shattered. The whole house creaks and rattles. "Not well built," as people have said to me with relish. But there is something else, not a creak, not a rattle, not the house or the wind, but a heavy thump that sounds from the next room. "You ought to get up and look," I tell myself but of course I don't. Instead, I reach for my cookery book.

Long ago in the 'thirties, when I first began cooking at all, I grew interested, discovered that I liked it and wanted to take lessons from a Frenchman in Sloane Street who was supposed to make you into a *cordon bleu* in twelve easy stages. This was laughed at so I struggled on until one day, by chance, I came upon Marcel Boulestin's book. At once I saw light. How simple, how direct, how easy to understand. With what authority he said: "Do." With what subtle irony he said: "Don't on any account." I saw my way then and flattered myself I could produce quite good meals.

Then came the war and chaos. I lost my Boulestin and ever since have been trying to buy another. Recently as I had to start cooking again, I really searched, nothing else would do. The writers always assume that you are cooking for a large family or have gadgets which you haven't, ingredients impossible to buy. None of them had his directness, his simplicity. When one day a friend rang me up and told me she'd found Boulestin in a second-hand bookshop, I was delighted. The book arrived and it was very thick. I remembered it as a slim paperback. Quality not quantity. The new one was by Marcel Boulestin and a Madame somebody, carefully got up to look very old. The cover, the print, the careful piecing together of various pages, all combined to give the impression that it was published in the early nineteenth century. Talk about ingredients: *"Hachez finement et mélangez une demi-douzaine de cornichons, quelques câpres, quelques échalottes, une cervelle de mouton ou de veau et deux jaunes d'oeuf."*

But the feeling of the book, the touch of it is reassuring. I grow peaceful as I read, *"Les côtelettes devront d'abord mariner pendant vingt-quatre heures dans un plat creux...."* I don't think of the nineteenth century as shut in, prejudiced. To me the nineteenth century is a large mango tree, orchids, sun, heaven, hell — which you could avoid — sudden darkness, huge stars.

Sometimes I sleep again. Or read on quietly until five o'clock when I can get up, make strong tea, relax, smoke, await the light. When I first came to live in the country, when the rest of the house was intolerable, the kitchen was the one place where I could stop feeling anxious and depressed, where the silence was bearable. I can see the sun rise from one corner, the sun set from another. Nothing like the sad, splendid, West Indian sunsets I can remember, but still quite well worth looking at.

When the post comes, the day starts. Sometimes the news is very satisfactory. I'm to be given a tree by Devon County Council. Indeed, they don't say "tree" but "trees." Have I room for "trees"? How far do the roots spread? I must find out. Wouldn't it be marvelous if I had room for several trees and at last could live in a forest, which has always been one of my ambitions. Later on I can plan a long elaborate meal, my first if I'm hungry. Settle for bread, cheese, and a glass of wine, if I'm not. Isn't the sadness of being alone much stressed and the compensations left out?

What happens next depends on the weather. On fine days I feel childishly happy. It takes very little to make me feel happy now, so happy that I jib at doing anything at all, even answering the loud knocks that occasionally thunder on the door. These are women selling brooms, brushes, or rugs or, more often, someone who wants to convert me. Devon is full of ardent sects and their followers, who, once inside, refuse to leave, standing in the passage arguing with me if I am stupid enough to let them in. There are two ways to get rid of them. One is to say that I'm a fervent Catholic, the other, that I'm cooking something which will spoil if I don't watch it. Neither of these excuses is true, but they nearly always do the trick, especially the second one with women. Not always, though. Once two persistent callers carried a large placard which said in black letters: "Has God deserted humanity?" Something about the smugness of their faces annoyed me, so I said loudly: "I should have thought it was the other way round" and saw not only that this had never occurred to them but anyway that it was rank heresy. I shut the door on them at last with great relief.

Then there's Exeter. What to say about Exeter? It's very full, very crowded and must have been a beautiful city once, but they're pulling it down at a great rate and erecting tall cold-looking buildings, technical colleges, and such. What else have I seen there? A West Indian woman (I'm sure she was a West Indian) walking along the street in a hurry. She dragged after her a very carefully dressed little girl. Out of the child's closely fitting white bonnet peered her dark, bewildered, anxious little face. I couldn't forget her for a long time.

Another day I watched an almost completely naked man in the car park tinkering with his car while my driver fumbled with the boot, his parcels, and keys. The man wasn't in the next car, or the next, but the one after that. When for a moment he straightened up and looked round with contempt at the assembled bourgeoisie, his expression was the most arrogant, conceited, and self-satisfied I've ever seen. Stevie Smith said something like this: "It's all very well to talk about the beauty of the human body, but I can think of a whole lot of other things more beautiful." So can I. Lions, cats, horses. What about hummingbirds, butterflies, even goldfish. Endless.

Now the shops. I can buy vegetables, drink, makeup. "It's very 'ot, isn't it?" says the driver. And though he always complains whenever there is a patch of blue sky or a gleam of sun, I, too, am glad when we leave the streets behind and get onto a part of the road where tall trees meet overhead and there is a pattern of light and shadow. After the trees, there's a dull bit enlivened by his remarks about bullocks, red earth, "fine crops," and so on.

When we're home again, he always says, "Safe and sound as the rat-catcher's daughter." I have a feeling of shyness, inadequacy when I pay him. For so long he's carried my parcels, waited patiently while I buy this and that, helped me over difficult places. Once, when I forgot my key, he managed to climb in through a difficult window. Another day we'd crawled along after a flock of sheep for what seemed hours until I began to fidget and say, "Oh my God, can't they turn off somewhere!" when he said reproachfully: "They've as much right on the road as wĕ 'ave." He always knows when it's going to rain; if he puts up a fence, it stays put; if he plants anything, it grows. How can I pay him for all that?

When I first came here, I always left my door open because, after all, I've nothing to steal, and he'd often remark: "You ought to be more careful. There're a lot of strangers about." Though I knew perfectly well that he and his wife call people from the next village strangers, his repeated warnings had an effect. Now I always lock up though thinking sometimes of that very frightening ghost story about the solitary woman who has just turned the key and shot the bolt for the night when she hears a voice behind her saying: "Now we are alone together."

Sir Thomas Browne
From Religio Medici

THERE IS SURELY a nearer apprehension of anything
that delights us in our dreams, than in our waked senses:
without this I were unhappy; for my awaked judgement dis-
contents me, ever whispering unto me, that I am from my
friend; but my friendly dreams in the night requite me, and
make me think I am within his arms. I thank God for my
happy dreams, as I do for my good rest; for there is a satisfaction in them unto reasonable desires, and as such can be
content with a fit of happiness: and surely it is not a melancholy conceit to think we are all asleep in this world, and that
the conceits of this life are as mere dreams to those of the
next, as the phantasms of the night to the conceits of the day.
There is an equal delusion in both, and the one doth but
seem to be the emblem or picture of the other: we are somewhat more than ourselves in our sleeps, and the slumber of
the body seems to be but the waking of the soul. It is the liga-
tion of sense, but the liberty of reason; and our waking
conceptions do not match the fancies of our sleeps. At my
nativity my ascendant was the watery sign of Scorpius; I was
born in the planetary hour of Saturn, and I think I have a
piece of that leaden planet in me. I am no way facetious, not
disposed for the mirth and galliardize of company; yet in one
dream I can compose a whole comedy, behold the action, apprehend the jests, and laugh myself awake at the conceits
thereof. Were my memory as faithful as my reason is then

fruitful, I would never study but in my dreams; and this time also would I choose for my devotions: but our grosser memories have then so little hold of our abstracted understandings, that they forget the story, and can only relate to our awakened souls a confused and broken tale of that that hath passed. Aristotle, who hath written a singular tract Of Sleep, hath not, methinks, thoroughly defined it; nor yet Galen, though he seem to have corrected it; for those *noctambuloes* and nightwalkers, though in their sleep, do yet enjoy the action of their senses. We must therefore say that there is something in us that is not in the jurisdiction of Morpheus; and that those abstracted and ecstatic souls do walk about in their own corpse as spirits with the bodies they assume, wherein they seem to hear, see, and feel, though indeed the organs are destitute of sense, and their natures of those faculties that should inform them. Thus it is observed, that men sometimes, upon the hour of their departure, do speak and reason above themselves; for them the soul, beginning to be freed from the ligaments of the body, begins to reason like herself, and to discourse in a strain above mortality.

We term sleep a death; and yet it is waking that kills us, and destroys those spirits that are the house of life. 'Tis indeed a part of life that best expresseth death; for every man truly lives, so long as he acts his nature, or some way makes good the faculties of himself. Themistocles, therefore, that slew his soldier in his sleep, was a merciful executioner: 'tis a kind of punishment the mildness of no laws hath invented: I wonder the fancy of Lucan and Seneca did not discover it. It is that death by which we may be literally said to die daily; a death which Adam died before his mortality; a death whereby we live a middle and moderating point between life and death: in fine, so like death, I dare not trust it without my prayers, and an half adieu unto the world, and take my farewell in a colloquy with God. . . .

Josephine Jacobsen
On the Island

AFTER DINNER THE DRISCOLLS sat for a while with Mr. Soo, by the big windows looking out and down over the bay. There was nothing to close: they were just great oblong unscreened openings, with all that fantasy of beauty spread straight before them. Mary had not learned to believe in it, any more than she had learned to believe that the shadowy, bamboo-furnished, candlelit room behind them wouldn't be invaded by insects — even perhaps bats, or one of the host of hummingbirds. For storms, there were heavy shutters. But nothing ever seemed to come in; only the air stirred, faintly sweet, against their faces; it grew spicier and more confused with scent as the dark strengthened.

Mr. Soo, in his impassive and formidable way, seemed glad to have them; or perhaps he was only acquiescent, in his momentary solitude. The inn was completely empty except for themselves, Mr. Soo, and the servants. This was rare, she gathered, even in the off-season she and Henry had chosen — and, indeed, their room had been occupied, only the day before yesterday, by another couple. A party of six would arrive after the weekend. Being here alone was part of their extraordinary luck. It had held for the whole trip: in Port of Spain they had got, after all, the room facing the Savanna; on Tobago they had seen the green fish come in, the ones that were bright as fire in the different green of the water; they had even seen, far off, on the trip to Bird of Paradise Island, a pair of birds of paradise, dim and quick through a great many distant leaves, but unmistakable in their sumptuous, trailing plumage.

This still, small place was their final stop before the plane home, and, just as they had planned it, it was beginning as it would end, hot and green, unpeopled, radiantly vacant. "It's the closest we'll get to real jungle," Henry said eagerly. And the jungle was no way away. The inn sheltered in cocoa bushes, shaded by their immortelles: Mr. Soo's plantation was a shallow fringe stretching for acres and acres, with the true jungle less than half a mile behind it. Mr. Soo, she felt sure, had never read one of Henry's books, but obviously was aware of his name, and this perhaps had led him to offer them brandy and sit by them in one of the gleaming, cushioned chairs, as they stared out to the disappearing sea. He did not look to Mary like a man whose pleasure lay in fraternizing with guests. Pleasure? His hair, in short, shining bristles, clasped his head tightly, giving the effect of pulling his eyes nearly shut by its grip. His face was the agreeable color of very pale copper; the mouth straight and thin, the nose fleshy. She and Henry had secretly discussed his age: thirty-eight? forty-four? thirty-seven? In the exhausted light he appeared now almost as though he had been decapitated and then had his head with its impassive face set, very skilfully, back upon his shoulders.

Mr. Soo had been born in Trinidad, but had come here to the island almost fifteen years ago, to raise cocoa. Mary was sure that the friends who had told them about the tiny inn had spoken of a Mrs. Soo, but she was not here and there was no reference to her. Arthur, the major-domo, had said only, "No Mrs. Soo," in response to an inquiry if she were away. Dead? Divorced? A figment of friends' imagination?

"Yes," Henry was saying, " 'like it' is too mild; they can't wait to come again. They're very bird-minded."

Mr. Soo looked at him in astonishment. "Your *friends*?"

"Yes. Very. Why?"

"They seemed to me," said Mr. Soo, obviously shocked, "very nice people. Intelligent. Not bird-minded."

Henry now gaped, baffled.

"Bird-*minded*, Mr. Soo," Mary said nervously. "I think

you're thinking of how we sometimes say bird-*brained*. Bird-*minded*. It means thinking a lot about birds. Anxious to see new ones, you know."

Mr. Soo still had an offended air. "Very intelligent people," he said.

"*Very!*" said Henry and Mary simultaneously.

A rush of wings veered past the window, in the new darkness. "Very few here on the island, intelligent people," said Mr. Soo. "Just natives. Blacks."

There was a short pause. A faint yattering, like the rapid clack of unskilled castanets, came dimly from the upper reaches of an invisible tree.

"Haven't you any Chinese or Indian neighbors?" asked Henry, noncommittally.

"Fifteen miles," said Mr. Soo, "is the nearest. I do not like Indians," he added. "But they are civilized. They come from civilized country. On Trinidad, all the shops, the taxis, all mostly Indians. They have an old civilization. Very few criminals. Except when they are drunk. The criminal classes are the blacks. Every week, choppings."

Oh, God, thought Mary, here goes our jungle holiday. Well, she decided immediately, we don't *have* to talk to him; we can go to our room in a minute. She caught Henry's glance, flicked to his wrist.

"Good heavens, it's after 10:00!" he announced like an amateur actor. "If we're going to get up early for the birds..."

Mr. Soo said quickly, "Lots of birds. Even at night. Pygmy owls. They fool the other birds," he explained. "That honey-creeper, green honey-creeper. The pygmy owl fools him. Like this." He suddenly puckered his lips and gave a tremulant, dying whistle; afterward, he smiled at them for the first time. "And you see cornbirds. Tody-tyrants, too. And mot-mots, with long tails..." He sketched one with a quick hand on which the candlelight caught jade. "They pull out their own tailfeathers. And the kiskadee. That's French, corrupted French. *Qu'est-ce qu'il dit?* Means, what's that he says? Over and over. The kiskadee."

The Driscolls rose, smiling. Are the birds part of the inn,

like the sour-sop drinks and the coconut milk and the arum lilies? — or does he like them? It seemed to Mary that he did.

"There was a bird this morning," she said, "on the piles..."

"A pelican," interrupted Mr. Soo.

"No," said Mary rather shortly. "I know pelicans." (For heaven's sake!) "A little boy told me what it was. But I can't remember. Like 'baby'..."

Henry and Mr. Soo said simultaneously and respectively, "A *booby!* That's what it was, a booby!" and, "A little boy?"

"The *nicest* little boy," said Mary, answering Mr. Soo. "He showed me the fiddler-crab holes and all the live things growing on the big rock, on the sea side."

"What was his name?" asked Mr. Soo unexpectedly. He had risen, too.

"I haven't an idea," Mary replied, surprised. "No, wait a minute..."

"A black boy," said Mr. Soo. "With a pink scar on his cheek."

Mary was not sure why the words she was about to say — "*Victor*, I'm sure he told me" — seemed suddenly inappropriate. In the little silence, Mr. Soo surprisingly bowed. "I am sorry," he said with obvious sincerity. "He is, *of course*, not allowed there. He has been told. This will be the last," he said quickly. "I am *so* sorry."

"Good heavens," said Henry, rather irritably, "he was fine — we enjoyed him. Very much. He was a bright boy, very friendly. He showed us how he would fight a shark — imaginary knife and all, you know."

"He was in the *water*?" said Mr. Soo with a little hiss.

During this contretemps, Arthur had approached; his dark face, lustrous in the candlelight, was turned inquiringly toward them over the brandy decanter.

"No, really, thanks," said Mary. She managed to smile at Mr. Soo as she turned away, hearing Henry say, "We'll be back for breakfast about 8:00," and then his footsteps behind her across the lustrous straw roses of the rug.

Later in the night she woke up. Theirs was the only bedroom in the main building except for Mr. Soo's apartment. Earlier, massed poinsettia, oleander, and exora had blazed just beyond their casement windows in the unnatural brilliance of the raw bulb fastened outside — now, by a round gold moon that was getting on for full, blue and purplish hues had taken over. The bunches of blossom were perfectly still.

She could see Henry's dark head on his pillow; he was spread-eagled with one foot quite out of bed. Very soon, familiar pressure would swallow them. Henry, even here, was immersed in his plots, manipulating shadowy figures, catching echoes of shifting dialogue. It had nothing to do with happiness, or satisfaction, but she knew that increasingly Henry's mind veered from hers, turning in patterns whose skill she admired. Henry believed in his plots. His cause and effect, lovely as graph lines and as clear, operated below all things. This island, which seemed to her full of hints flying like spray, yielded itself to him in information of tensions, feathers, blossoms, crops. More and more, like a god let loose on clay, he shaped and limited. She loved him for this, too: for his earnestness and the perfection of his sincerity; but sometimes now, she knew, her mind seemed to him disorderly and inconsequential, with its stubborn respect for surprises.

A breeze had begun to stir. The blanched crests of blossoms nodded beyond the broad sill and there was a faint rattle of palm fronds. Also, something moved in the thatch.

I will go to sleep if I think of the right things, she said to herself, and she set about remembering the misty horses, galloping easily over the Savanna track in the Trinidad dawn; she'd stood in her nightgown on the balcony to see their lovely, silent sweep. And the fern banks on Grenada: hills of fern higher than towers, deep springing hills of fronded green. And the surf, the terrifying surf, when they'd launched the little boat off Tobago for the trip to Bird of Paradise Island. The turquoise water had broken in a storm of white over the shining dark bodies and laughing faces of the launchers, the boat tipping and rocking, flung crazily upward and then seized again by dripping hands.

She'd felt both frightened and happy; Henry had hauled her in and they'd plunged up and down until finally they reached deep water and saw ahead of them, beginning to shape up in the distance, the trees which perhaps sheltered the marvelous birds. "Nothing is known of the breeding-habits of Birds of Paradise," her *Birds of the Caribbean* said. She repeated this, silently, sleepily. Nothing is known of the breeding habits of Birds of Paradise. How nice.

Suddenly, she heard water, a seeping sound — though, on her elbow, she could see it wasn't raining. She swung her feet over the bed, but not to the floor. Luck had been good here, but in the dark she wouldn't walk barefoot and her slippers she kept under the sheet. She felt her way cautiously to the bathroom door. Inside, she lighted a candle — the generator went off at 11:00. The bathroom was immaculate, but water shone by her feet and seeped toward the depression which served as a shower-floor. The toilet was unobtrusively overflowing in a small trickle. Eventually the floor would be covered and water would ooze under the door. What on earth could they do about it tonight, though? Move in with Mr. Soo? She began to giggle faintly. But it was a bother, too; in remote spots things took forever to get themselves fixed. She put Henry's sandals on the window-ledge, blew out the candle, and closed the door softly behind her. Henry hadn't stirred. She got back in bed, thinking: It's a good thing I saw those sandals — they were *in* the water! The words set off an echo: but, as she remembered what it was, she fell asleep.

By morning, the water was in their room, reaching fingers in several directions; the heavy straw of the rugs was brown and dank. When they came out into the pale, fragrant sunlight of the big room, Arthur was throwing away yesterday's flowers from the two big blue vases on the low tables. Henry, dropping his binocular-strap over his head, stopped long enough to report their problem. Arthur looked at them with an expression of courteous anguish and ritual surprise and said that he would tell Mr. Soo.

When they returned two hours later, hungry and already hot, Mr. Soo had come and gone. His small table, with its yellow porcelain bowl filled each morning with arum lilies, was being cleared by Arthur, who brought them a platter of fruit and told them that after breakfast he would transfer them to Mr. Soo's room. They were astounded and horrified in equal proportions. "That's absolutely impossible," said Henry. "We can't inconvenience him like that. Why can't we go down to one of the beach cottages? Or up on the hill?"

Arthur, who at the moment represented all help except the invisible cook, did not say: Because I can't run back and forth and still do everything here. He said instead, "Mr. Soo did tell me to move you after breakfast."

Henry was anxious to talk to Arthur. Wherever they went, he absorbed gestures, words, inflections, as a lock-keeper received water, with the earnest knowledge of its future use. He was very quick at the most fugitive nuance; later it would be fitted into place, all the more impressive for its subtlety.

Arthur had poured their second cup of coffee. Now he reappeared from behind the red lacquer screen, carrying one of the big blue vases. It was filled high with yellow hibiscus and he set it gently on one of the teakwood stands.

Henry said, in his inviting way, "You do a bit of everything."

Immediately, Arthur came to the table. "Only I am here now," he said. "And the cook. Two boys gone." He held up two fingers. "Chauffeur is gone."

On short acquaintance, Mary did not particularly like Arthur. He had a confidential air which, she noticed, pivoted like a fan. At present it was blowing ingratiatingly on Henry. "Mr. Soo had a lot of trouble with help," said Arthur. Mary saw with a rather malign amusement the guest's breeding struggle with the writer's cupidity. The victory was tentative.

"Now *we're* upsetting things," said Henry, not altogether abandoning the subject. "It's ridiculous for him to move out of his room for us."

"Won't upset Mr. Soo," said Arthur soothingly. "He can shut the apartment off, sitting room, library. Another bath, too, on the other side. Used to be Mrs. Soo."

Mary could see the waves of curiosity emanating from

Henry, but he gallantly maintained silence. "There is a sleep-couch in the sitting room," Arthur went on. "Mr. Soo does want you to be comfortable, and so." He pivoted slightly to include Mary in his range.

His eyeballs had crimson veins and he smelled of a fine toilet water. "Mr. Soo is very angry with that boy," said Arthur. "Mr. Soo does tell he: Stay away from my beach, ever since that boy come here."

In spite of herself, Mary said irascibly, "But that's ridiculous. He wasn't bothering anyone."

"Bother Mr. Soo," said Arthur. "Mr. Soo is so angry he went last night to go to see he grandmother. Told he grandmother, that boy does come here again, he beat him."

"May I have some hot coffee, please?" asked Mary.

Arthur did not move. He swept his veined eyes from one to the other. "Mr. Soo does not own that beach," said Arthur. "Can't no mahn own a beach here. Mr. Soo's beachhouse, Mr. Soo's boat, Mr. Soo's wharf. But not he beach. But he don't let no mahn there, only guests."

"Why does he like this beach so much?" said Mary, for it was small and coarse, with plenty of sharp rocks. "The boy, I mean."

"Only beach for five miles," Arthur told her. "That boy, Vic-tor, come with he brother, come to he grandmother. They live top-side. Just rocks, down their hill. Very bad currents. Sea-pussy, too. Can't no mahn swim there."

"May I have some hot coffee?" Mary said again.

Arthur stood looking at her. At this moment a considerable clamor broke out in the kitchen behind them. Voices, a man's and a woman's, raised in dispute, then in anger. The woman called, "Arthur! You come here, Arthur!"

Arthur continued to look at them for about two seconds; then, without haste, he went away, walking around the screen toward the kitchen.

"All right, all right," said Henry, answering a look. "But you know perfectly well we can't come here for five days and tell Mr. Soo who he must have on his beach."

"It isn't his beach."

"It isn't ours, either."

Something smashed in the kitchen. A door banged viciously. Outside the window went, running easily, a tall, big boy. His dark, furious, handsome face glared past them into the room. He dived down the wooden steps past the glade of arum lilies. His tight, faded bluejeans disappeared among the bushes.

"What was *that* in aid of?" said Henry, fascinated.

Arthur appeared. He carried the faintly steaming enamel pot of coffee, and, coming up to them, poured a rich stream into Mary's cup. Then he said: "The big brother of Vic-tor, he's a bad boy. Daniel. Same name as the man fought the lion." He bowed slightly, thus reminding Mary of Mr. Soo, turned to the other teakwood stand, lifted the empty blue vase, and went off with it behind the screen.

" '*Fought* the lion'?" said Mary, inquiringly, to Henry.

"Well," said Henry, "I suppose Arthur places him in the lion's den, and then improvises."

That was the last of the excitement. They were transferred quickly and easily from their moist quarters; the toilet was now turned off and not functioning at all. Mr. Soo's room lacked all traces of its owner, unless a second bed could be seen as a trace. It had a finer view than their abandoned room, looking all the way down the series of long terraces to the small bright, rocky beach.

Greenness took over; the greenness of the shallows of the bay before it deepened to turquoise, of the wet, thick leaves of the arum lilies, soaked each morning by an indefatigable Arthur, of the glittering high palms, and the hot tangled jungle behind the cocoa bushes shaded by their immortelles. Mary had — unexpectedly to herself — wanted to leave before their time was up. She had even suggested it to Henry right after breakfast on that second morning. But Henry wanted to stay.

"It *isn't* Mr. Soo," she said, trying to explain. "It hasn't anything to do with that. It's something else. There're too many vines. Everything's looped up and tangled. The palms rattle against the tin and give me dreams."

"Don't be fey," said Henry shortly. "We'll be away from palms soon enough."

Mr. Soo continued cordial in his immobile fashion: he talked to them from his small table when, at dinner, their hours coincided. Once, he had Arthur make them each a sour-sop, cold and lovely as nectar, when they came in brown and sweaty from the beach rocks. But by some obscure mutual assent, there were no more brandies. After dinner, the Driscolls sat on their tiny terrace, watching the moon swelling toward fullness, and drank crème de cacao in tiny gourd cups provided by Arthur. They knew they were destined to share their final hours on, and their first off, the island with Mr. Soo. He too would be on the bi-weekly plane to Trinidad. Mr. Soo said he was going to Port of Spain to procure plumbing fixtures. Arthur said Mr. Soo was going to procure a number two boy and a chauffeur. Where on earth did Mr. Soo wish to be driven, over the narrow, pitted, gullied roads that circled the island? Through and through his plantation, perhaps. Arthur took no note of coldness in relation to his comments on Mr. Soo; also, Mary felt, the most ardent questioning would have led him to reveal no more than he had originally determined. His confidences went by some iron and totally mysterious autodecision. She was uncertain how his sentiments stood in regard to his employer.

On their last afternoon, the Driscolls went for a walk. Just before dusk, they decided to go deep along the jungle path. This was the hour for birds; all over the little island they were suddenly in motion. Almost none, except the humming-birds with which the island fairly vibrated, flew in the golden hot midday, but at dusk the air was full of calls and wings.

Mary and Henry went along the middle ledge, above the lilies. Down on the beach, the fiddler crabs would be veering, flattening themselves, then rearing to run sideways, diving down holes into which fell after them a few trembling grains of sand. From here, the Driscolls could only see the white waves, leaping like hounds up at the rocks. They went along slowly, musingly, in the fading heat, up the steep path back of the garden sheds, below the giant saman, the great airy tree with its fringed, unstirring, pendent parasite world. With its colony of toe-hold survivors, it was like the huge rock on the beach, half in the tides, to whose surface clung and grew motionless breathers.

They turned up the small, dusty road toward the solid wave of tree-crests towering ahead. They had been this way twice before; they remembered a goat tethered up the bank at eye-level, a small scrubby cow standing uncertainly in the ditch. They would pass a cabin, half up the slope, with its back to the bay far below, its straw roof smothered under rose-colored masses of coralita. They walked in intimate silence. The road was daubed with the fallen blossoms of immortelles and their winged pods. Once, two laborers passed, stepping quietly on their tough bare feet, the shadows of leaves mottling their bodies and bright blue ripped trousers, machetes swinging gently from their heavy belts.

Around a curve, they came on a dead, long snake, savagely slashed. Just before their path struck off the road, there was a jingle and faint creaking, and around a tangle of scarlet blackthorn rode two native policemen, their caps tilted against the sunset, their holsters jogging their elbows. They pulled their small horses, stained with sweat, into single file; one raised his hand easily in a half-salute and both smiled. These were the first horses the Driscolls had seen on the island, and the first police. Of course, there had to be police, but it was strange how out of place they seemed. When the hushed fall of the hoofs in the dust died away it was as though horses and riders had melted.

Later, sitting on a fallen tree in the bush, Mary thought idly about the snake, the laborers, the policemen. Henry had gone further in, but she had felt suddenly that she couldn't walk another step. She sat on ridged strong bark coursed by ants and thought about the policemen, their faces, their small dusty horses, on that peaceful, hot patrol. Surely there must be almost nothing for them to do. And yet the idea of violence, she realized, had come to the air she breathed. Not violence as she knew it in Henry's books, or in the newspapers at home — riot, rape, murder, burglary. This violence seemed a quality of growth — the grip of the mollusks on the wave-dashed rock, the tentacles of the air plants flowering from the clutched saman. It oppressed her with its silence, its lack of argument. Perhaps she responded in some obscure portion of her feminine heart. An ant ran silently and fast over her hand. She shook it off and stared into the green that had swallowed Henry. His preciousness to her appeared not enhanced but pointed up by her sense of the silent violence of growth around her, as if, among the creepers, windfalls, sagging trees, his face, clear to her love, defined itself as the absolute essential. Of the rest, blind accidents of power, and death, and greenness, she could make nothing. Nothing they might do would surprise her.

There was a wild cocoa bush not ten feet away, dropped into this paroxysm of growth — thin, tall, struggling for light. She could see the pendulous gourds in their mysterious stages of ripeness: cucumber green, yellow, deep rose-bronze, and plum-brown. That plum-brown was on the voluptuous poles of the bamboos, the great, breeze-blown, filmy, green-gold stools of bamboo.

She listened for Henry. There was provisional silence, but no real stillness; hidden streams ran with a deep, secret sound in the throat of distant ravines, and the air was pierced and tremulous with birdcalls, flutings, cries, cheeps, whistles, breaks of song; response and request; somewhere away, lower than all the sounds but that of water, the single, asking, contemplative note of the mourning dove.

All at once, there was Henry. When she saw him, she realized that some portion of her had been afraid, as though, like the police on their little horses, he would melt into the greenness for good.

"Did you realize I'd forgotten my binoculars?" he asked, infuriated with his stupidity. "Of all idiotic times!"

Suddenly, she flung herself at him, winding her arms about his neck, linking their legs, covering his face with quick, light kisses. He held her off to look at her, and then folded her tightly in his arms, as though she too had come back from somewhere. "We haven't a flashlight, *either,* " he said, "and, if we don't look out, we'll be plunging about in the dark, breaking everything."

On the way home, they went more rapidly. The birds were almost completely silent. Now and then one would flash in the tree-crests far above them, settling to some invisible perch. We've left this island, Mary thought. There came a turning point — on a wharf, on a station platform, in the eyes of a friend — when the movement of jointure imperceptibly reversed. Now they were faced outward — to their suitcases, to their plane, to the Port of Spain airport, to Connecticut and typewriters. Mary began to worry about the dead snake, in the thick dusk; she didn't want to brush against its chill with her bare, sandaled feet. But, when they came to the spot, she saw it at once. It seemed somehow flatter and older, as though the earth were drawing it in.

As they rounded the bend to the final decline, a sound came to them, stopping them both, Mary with her hand digging into Henry's arm. They thought at first it was an animal in a trap, mistreated or dying. It was a sound in unhuman, concentrated, self-communing pain, a dull, deep crying with a curious rhythm, as though blood and breath themselves caused pain. "What *is* it?" cried Mary, terrified.

"It's a human being," said Henry.

He was right. Drawn close together, they turned the bend in the road, and saw the group from which the sound came; just up the steep slope to their left, in front of the cabin. Raw light from a kerosene lamp on the porch fell on the heads of the men and women, in an open semicircle. Around this space crawled on her hands and knees a woman. Her head was tied in a red kerchief and the light caught her gold earrings. She pounded the earth with her fist, and round and round she crept in short circles.

Dark faces turned in their direction, but the woman did not stop; on and on went the sound. Alien, shocked, embarrassed by their own presence, the Americans hesitated. Then Henry caught his wife's elbow and steered her, stumbling, down the path.

"Oh, Henry, *Henry...*" she whispered frantically to his

shadowy face. "Oughtn't we to stop? Couldn't we?. . ."

"They don't *want* us!" he hissed back. "Whatever it is, they don't want *us*."

She knew he was right, but an awful desolation made her stumble sharply again. The sound was fainter now; and then, in a minute or two, gone. Below them, they could see the lightbulb lashed to the trunk of the saman tree, like a dubious star.

Later, Mary was not sure why they said nothing to Mr. Soo. Neither, strangely, did they discuss it between themselves in their bedroom, showering, dressing for dinner. It was as though its significance would have to come later. It was too new, still, too strange; their suspended atmosphere of already-begun departure could not sustain it.

This sense of strangeness, and also, perhaps, the sense of its being their last evening, seemed to constrain them to be more civil to Mr. Soo. Arthur, bringing their daiquiris, told them there would be a cold supper; the cook was away. His air was apologetic; this was evidently an unexpected development. On the terrace, he set their drinks down on the thick section of a tree bole that served as a stand, and looked through the open casement window into their room, now transforming itself again into Mr. Soo's room: at the open, filled suitcases, the range of empty hangers, the toilet bottles on the dresser.

"You sorry to go?" asked Arthur. "You like it here, and so?"

"Very, very much," said Henry. "We hope we can come back."

"You know, one thing," said Arthur. A gong was struck imperiously. Arthur took his empty tray back through the room. The door closed behind him.

Perhaps it was too late for a more cordial response; perhaps Mr. Soo, too, felt that they were no longer there. Above his lilies in their yellow bowl, he was unresponsive. After one or two attempts at conversation, the Driscolls ate their cold supper, talking to each other in tones made artificial by several kinds of constraint. Over coffee, Henry said, "I'd better see him about the bill now — it's all going to be so early in the morning."

Mary waited for him by the huge open window-frames, where they had sat on their first evening, discussing with Mr. Soo their bird-minded friends. The moon, which tonight was going to be purely full, had lost its blemishes of misproportion; it was rising, enormous and perfect, in a bare sky. She could hear very faintly the sound of the tide as she stared out over the invisible bay to the invisible sea.

Behind her, Mr. Soo and Henry approached, their footsteps hushed by the straw, their voices by the silence. Turning, she was confronted by Mr. Soo's face, quite close, and it struck her that the moonlight had drawn and sharpened it, as though it were in pain.

"I hope you and your husband have been happy here," said Mr. Soo.

"Very," said Mary. (Now we're in for a drink, she thought.) "The birds have been wonderful..." she began, but Mr. Soo was not listening.

"The driver from the airport will be here at 6:00," he said. He turned and left them, walking slowly over the gleaming rug.

The moon hadn't reached their terrace. Arthur, arriving with the crème de cacao, had to peer at the tree-bole before setting down the little cups. He did not go away, but stood and looked at them. Finally, he said, "Do you remember Vic-tor?"

"Of course," said Henry, and Mary added, "The little boy."

"He's gon," said Arthur.

Henry said with interest, "Gone?"

"Dead, gon." Arthur stood there, holding his tray, and waited for them to speak. When they still did not, he said, "He did go off those high rocks. Back down from he house, those high rocks. He did go to swim in that sea-pussy. Like he grandmother told he not to. He is gon, out to sea; no body. No body a-tall. He was screaming and fighting. Two men fishing, they tried very hard to grab he up, but couldn't never get to he. He go so fast, too fast. They will never have no body — too much current, too many fish. He grand-mother told he, but that boy, he gon to swim. He won't even mind he brother, brother Daniel, brought he up," said Arthur, turning away and continuing to talk as he left, "*or* he grandmother, took he in. The cook is gon," said Arthur, faintly, from the distance. "Now Mr. Soo, Mr. Soo is all alone." The door closed.

Mary got up, uncertainly; then she went into the bedroom and began to cry very hard. She cried harder and harder, flinging herself on the bed and burrowing her head in the pillow. She felt Henry's hands on her shoulder blades and told him, "I can't think *why* I'm crying — I didn't even know the child! Yes, he showed me the crabs, but I didn't *know* him! It's not that. . . " She was obsessed by the mystery of her grief. Suddenly, she sat up, the tears still sliding down over her lips. "That was his grandmother," she said.

"It's a pattern," said Henry miserably. "We saw it happen all the way from the beginning, and now it's ended. It had to end this way."

She touched his face. His living body was here beside her. She slid her hand inside his shirt, feeling his flesh, the bones beneath it. The room was filled like a pool with darkness. She ran her fingers over his chin, across his lips. He kissed her softly, then more deeply. His strong, warm hand drew her dress apart and closed over her breast.

"I love you," he said.

She did not know when Henry left her bed. She did not, in fact, wake until a sound woke her. Her bed was still in darkness, but the window was a pale blaze from the moon, now high and small. It struck light from the palms' fronds, and against it she saw the figure on the ledge, in the open window. Young and dark and clear, and beautiful as shining carved wood, it looked against all that light, which caught and sparked on the machete's blade. It was gone; she heard a faint thud on the earth below the window. She raised herself on her elbow. In Mr. Soo's moonlit room she stared at Mr. Soo's bed and at what she now made out on the darkening sheet. It was Henry's dark head, fallen forward, and quite separate. His eyes were still closed, as if in an innocent and stubborn sleep.

Dana Gioia
Insomnia

Now you hear what the house has to say.
Pipes clanking, water running in the dark,
the mortgaged walls shifting in discomfort,
and voices mounting in an endless drone
of small complaints like the sounds of a family
that year by year you've learned how to ignore.

But now you must listen to the things you own,
all that you've worked for these past years,
the murmur of property, of things in disrepair,
the moving parts about to come undone,
and twisting in the sheets remember all
the faces you could not bring yourself to love.

How many voices have escaped you until now,
the venting furnace, the floorboards underfoot,
the steady accusations of the clock
numbering the minutes no one will mark.
The terrible clarity this moment brings,
the useless insight, the unbroken dark.

Howard Moss
Going to Sleep in the Country

The terraces rise and fall
As the light strides up and rides over
The hill I see from my window.
The spring in the dogwood now,
Enlarging its small preconceptions,
Puts itself away for the night.
The mountains do nothing but sit,
Waiting for something to happen —
Perhaps for the sky to open.

In the distance, a waterfall,
More sound than vision from here,
Is weighing itself again,
A sound you can hardly hear.
The birds of the day disappear,
As if the darkness were final.
The harder it is to see,
The louder the waterfall.

And then the whippoorwill
Begins its tireless, cool,
Calm, and precise lament —

Again and again and again —
Its love replying in kind,
Or blindly sung to itself,
Waiting for something to happen.

In that rain-prickle of song,
The waterfall stays its sound,
Diminishing like a gong
Struck by the weakening hand
Of a walker walking away,
Who is farther away each time,
Until it is finally dumb.
Each star, at a different depth,
Shines down. The moon shines down.
The night comes into its own,
Waiting for nothing to happen.

Albert Goldbarth
In Pain

In pain we populate villages, when it
lessens but lingers, anything
distractive: exactly the color of blue
in a potter's window, a rubbish dump, a pew
the cerulean light breaks into
tenderly, through a saint's symmetrical robe.
It's nearly Christmas; by twlight the lavender,
winter blue in the air, and the Chinese
blue of the potter's glaze, have reached an understanding
like the features of people who sleep together,
face to face, over so many years.
And not much later, they do sleep—Thumb,
the drunk who camps at the rubbish dump, and
the woman the village calls Ducky. In
stillness and chill, they look ceramic. Once,
he scratches his cobalt jaw, that's all. The moon
along her hair could be the moon along the fixed waves
of a porcelain basin, sinuous
but hard. It's another way water can crack
besides ice — an ocean applied in a kiln. And
anyway, there's almost ice; their even breathing
collects in the thinnest blue film. Collects, collects

— no wonder clouds begin to gauze across the moon.
Far off, some carolers. . . Cool,
a cool blue globe, this whole world, made to press
against your own red hurting. Soon you sleep.
It's summer. Your bed hums with summer.
And on your desk, in the glass paperweight,
a village is being blanketed under
snow like the slow fall of aspirin.

D. H. Lawrence
Shadows

And if tonight my soul may find her peace
in sleep, and sink in good oblivion,
and in the morning wake like a new-opened flower
then I have been dipped again in God, and new-created.

And if, as weeks go round, in the dark of the moon
my spirit darkens and goes out, and soft, strange gloom
pervades my movements and my thoughts and words
then I shall know that I am walking still
with God, we are close together now the moon's
    in shadow.

And if, as autumn deepens and darkens
I feel the pain of falling leaves, and stems that break
    in storms
and trouble and dissolution and distress
and then the softness of deep shadows folding, folding
around my soul and spirit, around my lips
so sweet, like a swoon, or more like the drowse of a low,
    sad song
singing darker than the nightingale, on, on to the solstice
and the silence of short days, the silence of the year,

the shadow,
then I shall know that my life is moving still
with the dark earth, and drenched
with the deep oblivion of earth's lapse and renewal.

And if, in the changing phases of man's life
I fall in sickness and in misery
my wrists seem broken and my heart seems dead
and strength is gone, and my life
is only the leavings of a life:

and still, among it all, snatches of lovely oblivion, and
    snatches of renewal
odd, wintry flowers upon the withered stem, yet new,
    strange flowers
such as my life has not brought forth before, new blossoms
    of me —

then I must know that still
I am in the hands [of] the unknown God,
he is breaking me down to his own oblivion
to send me forth on a new morning, a new man.

The Ship of Death

I

Now it is autumn and the falling fruit
and the long journey towards oblivion.

The apples falling like great drops of dew
to bruise themselves an exit from themselves.

And it is time to go, to bid farewell
to one's own self, and find an exit
from the fallen self.

II

Have you built your ship of death, O have you?
O build your ship of death, for you will need it.

The grim frost is at hand, when the apples will fall
thick, almost thundrous, on the hardened earth.

And death is on the air like a smell of ashes!
Ah! can't you smell it?

And in the bruised body, the frightened soul
finds itself shrinking, wincing from the cold
that blows upon it through the orifices.

III

And can a man his own quietus make
with a bare bodkin?

With daggers, bodkins, bullets, man can make
a bruise or break of exit for his life;
but is that a quietus, O tell me, is it quietus?

Surely not so! for how could murder, even self-murder
ever a quietus make?

IV

O let us talk of quiet that we know,
that we can know, the deep and lovely quiet
of a strong heart at peace!

How can we this, our own quietus, make?

V

Build then the ship of death, for you must take
the longest journey, to oblivion.

And die the death, the long and painful death
that lies between the old self and the new.

Already our bodies are fallen, bruised, badly bruised,
already our souls are oozing through the exit
of the cruel bruise.

Already the dark and endless ocean of the end
is washing in through the breaches of our wounds,
already the flood is upon us.

Oh build your ship of death, your little ark
and furnish it with food, with little cakes, and wine
for the dark flight down oblivion.

VI

Piecemeal the body dies, and the timid soul
has her footing washed away, as the dark flood rises.

We are dying, we are dying, we are all of us dying
and nothing will stay the death-flood rising within us
and soon it will rise on the world, on the outside world.

We are dying, we are dying, piecemeal our bodies are dying
and our strength leaves us,
and our soul cowers naked in the dark rain over the flood,
cowering in the last branches of the tree of our life.

VII

We are dying, we are dying, so all we can do
is now to be willing to die, and to build the ship
of death to carry the soul on the longest journey.

A little ship, with oars and food
and little dishes, and all accoutrements
fitting and ready for the departing soul.

Now launch the small ship, now as the body dies
and life departs, launch out, the fragile soul
in the fragile ship of courage, the ark of faith
with its store of food and little cooking pans
and change of clothes,
upon the flood's black waste
upon the waters of the end
upon the sea of death, where still we sail
darkly, for we cannot steer, and have no port.

There is no port, there is nowhere to go
only the deepening black darkening still
blacker upon the soundless, ungurgling flood
darkness at one with darkness, up and down
and sideways utterly dark, so there is no direction
    any more.
And the little ship is there; yet she is gone.
She is not seen, for there is nothing to see her by.
She is gone! gone! and yet
somewhere she is there.
Nowhere!

VIII

And everything is gone, the body is gone
completely under, gone, entirely gone.
The upper darkness is heavy on the lower,
between them the little ship
is gone
she is gone.

It is the end, it is oblivion.

IX

And yet out of eternity, a thread
separates itself on the blackness,
a horizontal thread
that fumes a little with pallor upon the dark.
Is it illusion? or does the pallor fume
A little higher?
Ah wait, wait, for there's the dawn,
the cruel dawn of coming back to life
out of oblivion.

Wait, wait, the little ship
drifting, beneath the deathly ashy grey
of a flood-dawn.

Wait, wait! even so, a flush of yellow
and strangely, O chilled wan soul, a flush of rose.

A flush of rose, and the whole thing starts again.

X

The flood subsides, and the body, like a worn sea-shell
emerges strange and lovely.
And the little ship wings home, faltering and lapsing
on the pink flood,
and the frail soul steps out, into her house again
filling the heart with peace.

Swings the heart renewed with peace
even of oblivion.

Oh build your ship of death, oh build it!
for you will need it.
For the voyage of oblivion awaits you.